Understand Eastern Philosophy

WINNIPEG

OCT O 1 2012

PUBLIC LIBRARY

D0858464

AWN

OCT 0 4 2012

WITHDRAWN

Teach®
Yourself

Understand Eastern Philosophy

Mel Thompson

Hodder Education

338 Euston Road, London NW1 3BH.

Hodder Education is an Hachette UK company

First published in UK 1999 by Hodder Education

First published in US 1999 by The McGraw-Hill Companies, Inc.

This edition published 2012.

Copyright © 1999, 2003, 2012 Mel Thompson

The moral rights of the author have been asserted

Database right Hodder Education (makers)

The *Teach Yourself* name is a registered trademark of Hachette UK.

All rights reserved. No part of this publication may be reproduced, stored in a retrieval system or transmitted in any form or by any means, electronic, mechanical, photocopying, recording or otherwise, without the prior permission in writing of Hodder Education, or as expressly permitted by law, or under terms agreed with the appropriate reprographic rights organization. Enquiries concerning reproduction outside the scope of the above should be sent to the Rights Department, Hodder Education, at the address above.

You must not circulate this book in any other binding or cover and you must impose this same condition on any acquirer.

British Library Cataloguing in Publication Data: a catalogue record for this title is available from the British Library.

Library of Congress Catalog Card Number: on file.

10 9 8 7 6 5 4 3 2 1

The publisher has used its best endeavours to ensure that any website addresses referred to in this book are correct and active at the time of going to press. However, the publisher and the author have no responsibility for the websites and can make no guarantee that a site will remain live or that the content will remain relevant, decent or appropriate.

The publisher has made every effort to mark as such all words which it believes to be trademarks. The publisher should also like to make it clear that the presence of a word in the book, whether marked or unmarked, in no way affects its legal status as a trademark.

Every reasonable effort has been made by the publisher to trace the copyright holders of material in this book. Any errors or omissions should be notified in writing to the publisher, who will endeavour to rectify the situation for any reprints and future editions.

Hachette UK's policy is to use papers that are natural, renewable and recyclable products and made from wood grown in sustainable forests. The logging and manufacturing processes are expected to conform to the environmental regulations of the country of origin.

www.hoddereducation.co.uk

Cover image: © Roman Milert - Fotolia

Typeset by Cenveo Publisher Services.

Printed and bound by CPI Group (UK) Ltd, Croydon CR0 4YY.

Also available in ebook

Contents

Meet the author   vii
In one minute   viii
Introduction   x
    But is it philosophy?   x
    What does this book cover?   xiii
    Eastern and Western terms   xiv
    The geography of ideas   xiv

1 Hindu philosophies   1
    Background   1
    Some key concepts   3
    Literature   7
    Philosophical schools   11
    Life: goals and ethics   31

2 Early Buddhism   37
    Background: The Buddha   37
    Key concepts   40
    The self   48
    The Abhidharma   56
    Meditation   60
    Ethics   63
    Buddhism and philosophical speculation   66

3 Jainism   71
    Background: Mahavira   71
    Basic concepts   74
    The self   78
    Reinterpretations of Hindu concepts   80
    Parallels with the Sankhya school of philosophy 81
    Parallels with Buddhist philosophy   82
    Ethics   83

4 Mahayana Buddhism   91
    Background: Development of Buddhism   91
    The bodhisattva ideal   92
    Madhyamaka philosophy   97
    Yogacara philosophy   104
    The Tathagatagarbha doctrine   109
    The Trikaya doctrine   110

	Cosmology	112
	Further developments of Mahayana Buddhism	114
5	**Confucianism**	**119**
	Background notes on Chinese thought	119
	K'ung Fu-Tsu (551–479 BCE)	122
	Developments of the Ru school	136
	Neo-Confucianism	139
	The self and society	143
	Confucianism and the Chinese Republic	149
6	**Taoism**	**151**
	Background	151
	Lao Tzu	152
	Key concepts in Taoism	153
	Change and the Tao	156
	Chuang Tzu (369–286 BCE)	160
	Living in harmony	161
	Religious Taoism	169
	Taoism and other philosophies	172
7	**Tantra**	**174**
	Background	174
	Rituals and meditation	177
	Shiva and Shakti	179
	Tantric sex	182
	Buddhist Tantra	184
	Conclusion	193
8	**Zen**	**196**
	Introduction	196
	Origins and development	197
	Key features of Zen	198
	Rinzai Zen	201
	Soto Zen	206
	The Buddha nature	209
	Zen practice	210
	East meets West	213
	Beyond concepts	218
Postscript		220
Taking it further		222
Glossary		225
Index		235

Meet the author

'How do I make sense of the world?' and 'How do I make sense of my life?' must be the two most basic and important questions anyone can ask. They have led, in different ways, to the development of philosophy, science, religion and psychology. However, those of us brought up in the West can all too easily slip into the common assumption that philosophy deals only with the validity of arguments, science with matters of fact, religion with personal views and commitments, and psychology with the internal workings of the mind. But such compartmentalization has never been satisfactory; what we understand, how we feel and the commitments and moral views we hold, all influence one another. It is therefore wonderfully refreshing to turn to Eastern philosophy and enter a world where the view of human life and its meaning is more holistic.

When I first encountered Eastern philosophy, I found it liberating to explore answers to the questions of life that were quite different from those with which I had grown up, and a fascination with Eastern thought, particularly Buddhism, has stayed with me. I hope you enjoy reading this book as much as I, in revising it for the present edition, have appreciated the opportunity to be reminded again of the whole range of traditions of wisdom and insight that have come from the East.

Mel Thompson

In one minute

This book on Eastern Philosophy is concerned with the traditions of thought and wisdom that developed in the Indian sub-continent and the Far East:

From India, we shall look at the wealth of ideas, mental disciplines, religious and social practices that are collectively known as Hinduism, along with the Jain and Buddhist philosophies that developed within Hindu culture but were critical of Hindu orthodoxy and therefore emerged as separate traditions.

From the Far East, we shall explore the ancient traditions of Confucianism and Taoism, later blending with Buddhism to form the rich mixture of Chinese thought.

We shall also look at two wisdom traditions that are very different in approach – Tantra and Zen – the one based on ritual action and the creative use of the imagination, the other with an intuition of reality that goes beyond concepts.

Together, these traditions have a history that stretches back 3,000 years, and they have contributed vastly not just to the Eastern cultures within which they developed, but to culture globally. A book such as this can do no more than point to the central themes and issues that Eastern philosophy has addressed, and to outline its main approaches and conclusions.

Philosophy asks fundamental questions: How has the universe come into being? Who am I? Do I have a soul that is separable from my body? Have I lived before, and will I live again? How am I to decide between right and wrong? Do I always have to live with the consequences of my actions? What is worthwhile in life? Is there a God or gods? Questions such as these are universal, and the potential answers to them vary between different cultures and over time. Studying Eastern philosophy is not, for someone brought up in the West, simply a matter of looking with detached interest at ideas that come from other cultures; it also challenges our own ideas and assumptions.

Do not be fooled by mention of sacred texts, authoritative teachers, meditation or ritual into thinking that reason and evidence are neglected in Eastern thought. On the contrary, it is intellectually rigorous. You will find arguments and debates here that are as challenging as any in the history of Western thought. Enjoy the challenge!

Introduction

Philosophy is the quest for knowledge and wisdom. At one level, it is an academic discipline; at another, it is the natural activity of all thinking people. Everyone who has ever asked why the universe is as it is, or how we decide matters of right or wrong, or why we call one thing beautiful and another ugly, or how society should be organized, is engaging in philosophy.

Its questions are universal, but the answers and insights that seek to address them are generally coloured and shaped by the cultures within which they have developed, and over time they may change. Our philosophy is therefore enriched and deepened by looking at ideas that have developed in times and cultures other than our own.

Hence the value of exploring Eastern philosophy; it offers someone who has so far only explored ideas in a Western context a range of alternative approaches to the big questions. The Indian term used for a philosophical system is *darsana*, which means 'view' or 'direct vision'. In a religious context it can mean viewing an image of a god or goddess, but in philosophy it points to an important feature of Eastern thought: to achieve a direct view of something requires more than logical reasoning; it also involves perception and intuition. The aim is to 'see' the truth, rather than simply to understand it.

But is it philosophy?

Those who are accustomed to modern Western philosophy may be in for a shock as they move eastwards. In the West, both the content and the methods used in philosophy have become carefully defined. Some areas of enquiry that were once seen as branches of philosophy have been divided off as separate subjects (e.g. natural philosophy has become 'science'). As a result, philosophy has often been seen as a discipline without a subject matter of its own; its task being limited to a critical examination of the presuppositions, arguments and language used within other disciplines.

During the 20th century, particularly in Britain and the United States, philosophy became less concerned with the nature of reality itself, and more with the possibility and validity of speaking about reality: not, 'What is true?' but, 'What does it mean to say that something is true?' Much Western philosophy stopped playing the game, and merely analysed the rulebook.

In the West, one does not expect someone versed in the philosophy of mind to work in a psychiatric unit, nor a philosopher of science to be undertaking fundamental research, nor a philosopher of religion to be necessarily practising a particular religion or teaching meditation techniques. Philosophers stand back, look and comment – their quest is generally for truth in the sense of clarity, less often for truth in the form of experience or action. But this has not always been the case. For much of its history, Western philosophy has been broadly based, and it was only really with the rise of modern science that philosophy handed over much of what it had previously considered its subject matter to the emerging scientific disciplines. Nor may it always be the case; recently, popular philosophy in the West has broadened its range of interests to explore existential questions about life and its meaning, many aspects of our cultural life and also the therapeutic potential of ideas. The narrow, academic view of Western philosophy is therefore not the whole story, but it does highlight a general contrast between East and West.

Moving east, the situation is very different. Philosophy has not limited itself to rational argument, nor has it separated itself from those areas in life through which fundamental questions are asked. Hinduism, Buddhism, Jainism, Confucianism, Taoism: these are religious and social systems as well as philosophies. Zen and Tantra are explorations of meditation and the power of emotions and sexuality respectively. Such systems have practical and physical consequences: they make a difference to people's lives. But they are also philosophies, in that their religious, social and moral teachings are based on, and give expression to, fundamental views about the nature of reality. So the Wisdom of the East is philosophy and psychology and sociology and religion all rolled into one. Or, to be more accurate, it is a wisdom that does not require its insights to be compartmentalized in the traditional Western way.

Sexuality, meditation, ritual, correct behaviour – all of these things have implications for an understanding of the nature of the world and the self, and the quest for insight into them (and through them) may also be considered 'philosophy'. But is it this curious mixture of disciplines, from a Western standpoint, that can sometimes lead to doubts about how much of it should count as philosophy.

In particular, since the 18th century, there has developed in the West a contrast between religious ideas, to be accepted on the basis of 'faith', and philosophy, which is based exclusively on reason and evidence. Without going into a discussion of why that has happened, or how detrimental it has been to both religion and philosophy, we should simply acknowledge that it does not apply to Eastern thought, where personal insight, intuition and spiritual discipline are all able to contribute, alongside rational argument, to a view or philosophy of life.

Please note

These comments present an oversimplification, and in any case apply mainly to the Anglo-American tradition rather than to European philosophy, which has generally taken a broader approach. They are included here simply to highlight the fact that some Western thinkers may be reluctant to accept the broad range of questions and activities that may be included within Eastern Philosophy.

Eastern Wisdom (*prajna* in Sanskrit) is not simply a matter of logic or speculation, but is also concerned with experience and intuition. Prajna can be applied to all aspects of life. But that does not mean that the skills of analysis and assessment of empirical evidence are absent from Eastern thought – far from it; there are many interesting parallels to Western philosophy. The main difference, generally speaking, is that Eastern philosophy has retained its links with religion, psychology and mysticism, whereas Western thought has concentrated on abstracting from them only those claims that can be examined on the basis of reason and evidence.

What does this book cover?

It has been necessary to set limits to what is considered here as Eastern philosophy, simply because the subject could embrace the entire civilizations of the Far East, South East Asia and the Indian sub-continent. We shall therefore look at the main Hindu philosophies, along with Jainism and Buddhism, and then at the Confucian and Taoist traditions of Chinese thought. The criterion used for deciding whether what we are dealing with is philosophy, rather than a social or religious phenomenon, is that:

▶ The ideas being considered touch on ultimate questions about the nature of reality, or society, or human experience – questions which (even if framed differently in the West) are universal.

Examples

It is debatable whether Shinto should be included as an Eastern Philosophy. Although it has had a significant influence on Japanese culture, it does not appear to have a developed philosophy as such, but is rather more a religious recognition of local spirits (*kami*) in a way that does not lend itself to universal application.

On the other hand, Zen – which, of all the 'philosophies' in this book, has least interest in rational argument – introduces features of reality and our experience of it which can be examined and compared with those of other approaches.

Therefore, Zen has been included but Shinto has not.

The other important thing to note is that this book will examine the fundamental questions addressed by each religious and philosophical tradition, but descriptions of the ritual or lifestyle of its followers will be introduced only in so far as they illustrate some fundamental insight. Hence, although the chapter titles might look the same, this is not really a book about Eastern 'religions' as such. On the other hand, an understanding of the fundamental philosophy of each tradition is invaluable for those who want to understand their religious elements.

Eastern and Western terms

Applying Western terminology to Eastern philosophical positions can lead to distortion. For example, if the Hindu word for absolute reality (*Brahman*) is translated 'God', there is a danger that Western ideas of a personal God will be read into that concept, leading to confusion about how the idea of Brahman relates to Hindu devotion to many different gods and goddesses. Questions like 'Is Brahman really "God", and (if so) why do Hindus also have these other gods?' result from using the Western term for a very different Eastern concept.

As far as is practicable, therefore, Eastern terms will be explained and used in the text.

Western

There are interesting parallels between Eastern and Western ideas and approaches, as well as points of contrast. These are noted in 'Western' boxes, such as this. For example, the ancient Greek philosopher Heraclitus (of 'you can't step into the same river twice' fame) had a view of nature as constantly changing, which is similar to that of the Buddha. This does not imply that Heraclitus was a crypto-Buddhist, nor that there was some literal or esoteric link between the two men, but simply that both sought to explore and explain the same phenomenon.

But please note:

It has not been possible to give an exposition of the Western philosophies referred to in these boxes. Sometimes a particular thinker or argument is mentioned by name only. Those who want to follow up the parallels here might refer to *Understand Philosophy* or *Understand Philosophy of Religion* in this series, or to the many other introductions to Western philosophy.

The geography of ideas

Ideas not only develop, they also move. Carried along by trade or religion, they find themselves applied to different cultures in separate geographical areas, and subsequent developments reflect that geographical separation.

By and large, in studying Eastern thought, we are looking at the products of two very different geographical and cultural areas: India and China. Indian philosophy and religion (usually called 'Hinduism' by Westerners since the 19th century) and its offshoots, of which the major traditions to be considered here are Buddhism and Jainism, reflects the culture, and even the climate of that part of the world. You are unlikely to get naked ascetics in polar regions! Its background is very different from Confucian and Taoist ideas, which arose in China and reflect respectively the social and individualistic aspects of life there. When Buddhism moved from its Indian matrix northwards to China and then on to Japan, its character changed to reflect the different cultures within which it found itself.

In this book, we shall be concerned primarily with the approach taken by each philosophy, and the fundamental ideas that developed within it, but it is important to recognize that – however rationally justified – changes in society, the moving of ideas from one area to another, and the passing of time all have an important part to play in the ever-changing pattern of ideas. All we can hope to do here is explore key features of each philosophy and, where possible, to hint at their geographical, cultural background and developments.

It should also be recognized that this book can offer no more than an outline and an introduction to a vast and complex range of ideas. It does not claim in any way to be comprehensive. Its aim is to give an overview, and to whet the appetite for further study.

1

Hindu philosophies

In this chapter you will:
* *consider the background to the philosophies of India*
* *learn the key concepts in Hindu philosophy*
* *explore the principal schools of Hindu philosophy.*

Background

The life, religion and philosophies of the Indian sub-continent are expressed through an amazingly rich mixture of ideas, practices and social customs that have developed over more than 3,000 years. There is no single Hindu religion or Hindu philosophy, but rather a variety of ways of understanding and relating to the world that are blended from a stock of widely held ideas, some more ancient than others.

Insight
Although the religion of the majority in India is generally referred to in the West as 'Hinduism', we should remember that this is simply a convenient Western term for the whole range of ideas and practices to be found in India.

India has been influenced by the many peoples who have invaded it. The earliest of these – about 1500–1200 BCE – was an invasion of Aryan peoples from Central Asia, some of whose beliefs appear to be close to those of the Ancient Greeks, possibly coming from a common source of ideas in the Middle East.

Prior to the Aryan invasions there was an elaborate civilization in the Indus Valley. By 2000 BCE, the city of Mohenjo Daro had a population of 40,000, paved streets, tiled water systems and substantial buildings. Its craftsmen produced jewellery, and it had a system of weights and measures. Although it is difficult to assess the extent to which the Indus Valley civilization influenced the development of Hindu thought, since we do not have any written accounts of their religious beliefs, archaeology has revealed figurines of gods and goddesses, and some seals show a figure sitting in what appears to be a Yoga posture. So, although the Vedas, produced during the Aryan period, came to define Hindu orthodoxy, older strands of religion and philosophy may also have contributed to it.

Later invasions also left their mark. From about 600–500 BCE there was an influx of Parsi people, with their Zoroastrian religion, native to Persia. Later, 300–100 BCE, the Greeks invaded under Alexander. From 800–1800 CE India was influenced by Muslim culture and, finally, from the beginning of the 19th century until 1946, it was ruled by the British.

It would therefore be unrealistic to look at Indian philosophy and expect it to form a single, coherent system. It is a wonderful array of social philosophy, along with abstract metaphysics and religion.

STAGES OF DEVELOPMENT

One way of getting the wide range of Hindu thought and practice into perspective is to consider it in terms of three different periods, each of which had a particular interest which coloured its philosophy.

▶ In the earliest period for which we have written evidence – the period of the composition of the early Vedas (see the section on 'Literature' below) – the main concern seems to have been *Dharma* – the right ordering of society, and of individuals within it, in order to achieve harmony and happiness.

▶ In the second major period – that of the six classical schools of Hindu philosophy, starting in about the second century BCE and on through the first millennium CE – the concern shifted from correct worldly Dharma to the desire for liberation from the world of endless rebirths. Although all that had been said earlier about Dharma remained relevant, the newer concern for individual spiritual liberation (*moksha*) was superimposed over it.

▶ Then, in a third wave of Hindu thinking, starting around the middle of the first millennium CE, there was an emphasis on devotion (*bhakti*) to one's chosen deity, and here the aim was not so much to escape out of the world as to achieve a unity with the divine in and through one's earthly existence.

The influence of all three of these periods is still to be found in modern Hindu thought and practice.

Some key concepts

BRAHMAN

In Western thought, under the influence of Judaism, Christianity and Islam, the word 'God' is used to denote a reality that is both creative and also personal – described as the uncaused cause of everything, but also as a personal deity to whom one might pray and be heard. Moving to Indian thought, the situation is rather different. At the level of popular religion there are thousands of gods and goddesses – each with a particular sphere of influence, either geographical or in terms of a particular aspect of life. So, for example, the elephant-headed god, Ganesha, is thought to bring good fortune and academic success.

Beyond this multiplicity there are three gods who represent fundamental aspects of the process of change seen in the world: Brahma, the creator; Vishnu, the sustainer; Shiva, the destroyer. And beyond these, there is 'Brahman', a word that denotes ultimate reality – that which includes the whole universe with its multiplicity of gods and goddesses. Brahman is seen as the invisible reality within and around everything. All the other gods and goddesses represent particular aspects of Brahman and make it visible, and the goddesses also represent feminine power (*shakti*). We shall examine the nature and operation of the power of shakti in the chapter on Tantra.

Western

In Western terms, one may be monotheist (believing in only one god), polytheist (believing in many gods) or atheist (believing in no god). Indeed, a major part of the philosophy of religion in the West has been given over to arguments about whether or not God exists. This does not really make sense once we turn to Hindu thought. Individual gods and goddesses exist in terms of their images. They represent aspects of reality – but they are not thought of as having an independent, disembodied existence.

Brahman is sometimes represented by the syllable OM (or AUM). Hindus may chant this slowly, the sound rising through three progressive tones, from the chest, the throat and finally the head. It is believed to be the vibration of the life-giving energies of the whole universe, emanating from Brahman, but it also represents a gathering together the whole of the individual in a single expression. This claim, that the chanted syllable is in fact in touch with the universal, reinforces the basic view in the Upanishads (see the section on 'Literature' below) of the identity of Brahman and the self. It is a religious symbol for that fundamental unified (monistic) view of reality.

ATMAN

Whereas ultimate reality is called Brahman, the individual human self is referred to as the *Atman*. One of the key ideas in the Upanishads and in later Vedanta philosophy, is the identity of Atman and Brahman: whatever your physical limitation within this world, your own true essence, or inner self, is identified with the single absolute reality of the universe. Another way to put this would be to say that there is a single reality; when it manifests universally it is called Brahman, but when it manifests in the self it is called Atman.

> 'He [Atman] is myself within the heart, smaller than a grain of rice or a barley corn, or a grain of millet: this is myself within my heart, greater than the earth, greater than the atmosphere, greater than the sky, greater than all these worlds.'
>
> (*Chandogya Upanishad* Bk III, 14:3–5)

In one vedic story a young man, Svetaketu, is told to take a pomegranate and cut it open, then he takes a seed and cuts it open, then he cuts again. Eventually he recognizes that within the heart of this there is 'nothing'. That invisible, central reality – the nothingness that appears when individual things are divided into their smallest constituent parts – is what a person is. *Tat twan asi*: 'you are that'. In other words, the self is only superficially located and defined by the body. In reality the Atman is eternal and infinite in extent. There is no difference between the Atman and Brahman.

Insight

The concepts of Brahman and Atman are important because the key feature of Hindu thought seems to have been the quest for an understanding of why the world has come to be as it is, what place the individual self has within it, and how the self might overcome those things that cause it suffering. Philosophy is not done in a detached way; it is not purely speculative, but is closely linked to the idea of liberation – the assumption being that, once the true nature of things is understood, one is free from the bondage of illusion.

At one level, the self may be identified with Brahman, but at another, a person is defined largely by his or her position in society. This is a person's class or *varna*. Varna means 'colour' and it is possible that the arrival of the lighter-skinned Aryan invaders, ruling over the native and darker-skinned Dravidian peoples, established social distinctions based on colour, which gradually developed into the Indian system of classes and castes. We shall examine this in the section on 'Life: goals and ethics', below.

Varna is not a superficial social phenomenon, but one that is deeply rooted in Hindu philosophy. In the Rig Veda, one of the earliest Hindu scriptures, there is story about the creation of humankind, in which a single cosmic person (Purusha) is divided up, each part of him producing a particular section of human society. This suggests that, far from being the way that Hindu society just happens to be organized, the class and caste system reflects something fundamental and inherent in the nature of humankind.

There is a fundamental issue to reflect on here: Is equality unnatural? Is the Hindu recognition of fundamental differences within society the logical conclusion from an objective assessment of the natural order? Or is this aspect of Hindu thought simply a later rationalization and justification of what happens when invaders impose their views of a subservient native people?

SANATANA DHARMA

Sanatana Dharma might be translated best as 'the eternal ordering of things'. It is based on the concept that the world has a timeless structure and meaning, and that an understanding of this will allow a person to live in a fundamental harmony with life. Dharma here has the sense of 'reality' or 'truth'. To call Sanatana Dharma 'the eternal truth', might suggest that it can be reduced to a proposition, but that would be wrong – it is not truth in the sense of a verbal summary, but the actual experience of reality as it is.

Most Hindu philosophy makes a clear distinction between what is perceived and the absolute reality beneath those perceptions. It is aware of human sensory fallibility. The world of our perceptions is termed *samsara*. It is believed that the self is in some way trapped within the world of samsara, is determined by the working of the law of karma (see below) and is therefore doomed to be born again and again.

Insight

Dharma is a much used word, both in Hinduism and Buddhism. Its precise meaning is generally given by the context within which it is used. In Hinduism it can mean 'truth' or 'reality' or 'teaching' or 'order'. In Buddhism it is the word used for the teaching of the Buddha, and thus one of the three jewels to which Buddhists go for refuge. It is also used (with a lower case 'd') to mean 'thing', so that a process of analysis can be said to reveal the dharmas out of which all compound things are formed.

KARMA

Karma is a concept found within Hindu thought and also in Jainism and Buddhism, although for Buddhists it is understood rather differently. Karma literally means 'action'. It is the term used for the process by which actions are believed to have consequences for the person who performs them. These consequences are not merely the practical and obvious results of action but are regarded as spiritual, in that they influence the passage of an Atman through the world of samsara. What is more, Hindus believe that actions performed in one lifetime will influence what will happen to that person beyond death, on the grounds that the consequences which have yet to mature from earlier karma must work themselves out in future lives. As popularly conceived, obedience to the Dharma (reality, or the 'Eternal Law') here and now will bring about a better rebirth.

MOKSHA

The result of recognizing the identity of Atman and Brahman is *moksha* (release), which is thought of as release from the suffering and limitations implied by a narrow view of the self, and an awareness of one's eternal destiny. The only thing that stands in the way of a person achieving moksha is *avidya* (ignorance), a failure to distinguish between the limited things we encounter in this world (samsara), and ultimate reality.

Notice that the aim of the Hindu is to be released from the imposition of endless lives. Moving on to another life after death, although one might strive for an improved situation through avoiding bad karma and performing good karma, is not the ultimate goal. The goal is *not* to be reborn – very different from most Western views of life after death.

On the other hand, there are parallels between the Eastern contrast of ultimate reality with mundane experience and Plato's distinction between the eternal realities and the particular things we encounter with the senses. For Plato, most people are like prisoners held deep in a cave, seeing no more than the reflections of objects projected upon a wall – samsara, in Eastern terms – and sceptical about any account of reality beyond what they see before their eyes.

These are the basic concepts: the way in which they are used in different philosophies will be examined later in this chapter.

Literature

VEDAS

The Vedas are the touchstone for Indian philosophy – 'orthodox' is what conforms to them, 'unorthodox' is what does not. They are a collection of over a thousand hymns, comprising some 10,000 verses, many of which were probably brought into India by the Aryans in the middle of the second millennium BCE. The Vedas are set out in four volumes:

1 *Rig Veda* – the most important, giving most of the core teaching. It is the oldest of the four, probably dating from about 1200 BCE.
2 *Sama Veda* – which gives music and chanting.
3 *Yajur Veda* – which gives details required for the performance of sacrifices.
4 *Atharva Veda* – contains incantations and spells, which may have been preserved from pre-Aryan times.

Each of these Vedas has three other forms of literature attached to it: Brahmanas (epic tales, composed probably between 800 and 600 BCE); Aranyakas (ritual formulas, probably dating from 600 BCE) and Upanishads (philosophical texts, dating from 600–300 BCE).

The Vedas introduce the pantheon of Indian gods. Indra appears to have been the most popular, in terms of the number of hymns addressed to him. Agni, the fire god, is also important, as in Soma, the god represented by the intoxicating drink taken during religious rituals.

Thus, in the Vedas, cosmic ideas and the world of the gods are presented mythologically, rather than philosophically. The world's origin is seen as an egg, floating on a sea of chaos, or (in the best-known image) as the sacrifice of the cosmic man (Purusha). Towards the end of the vedic period, in the *Atharva Veda*, there appears to have been a dissatisfaction with the mythological form and a move towards speaking of the *asat* ('non-being' or unreal) and the *sat* ('being' or real), the aim of the spiritual person being to move from the former to the latter. Through a great variety of images, the Vedas probe the fundamental philosophical questions about the self and the world, why the world is as it is, and how to make sense of it.

Comment

In the Vedas, ritual sacrifice is seen as the act that holds the whole universe together and gives it structured form. Acting out a ritual is a way of giving meaning. It expressed the deep human need for a sense direction and purpose, both in the self and in the world.

Gradually we see this ritual expression giving way to more abstract speculation – a more 'philosophical' approach. But perhaps we need to stop and ask a crucial question. Can a sense of meaning and purpose best be grasped through abstract reasoning or through gesture and participation? One of the strengths of ritual is that it enables people to participate emotionally in what is being said or acted out, and it engages the unconscious as well as the conscious mind. Can ultimate truths be grasped by reason alone? We shall need to consider this again in the chapters on Tantra and Zen.

In the Brahmanas, there is a concentration on the details of the sacrifice itself. The ritual starts to be seen as that which embodies and maintains the universe, it represents reality itself – Brahman. This makes the person performing the ritual (the Brahmin) and the details of that ritual, supremely important. The Aranyakas, which came to be attached to the Brahmanas, set about interpreting the significance of the sacrifice so that the physical sacrifice can start to be replaced by a mental one, through meditation. From that point, there is therefore a natural progression towards the Upanishads, which move from a mental representation of sacrifice into the area of abstract metaphysical speculation.

In other words, there is a movement away from the use of sacrifice in order to influence divine forces, through sacrifice as expressing the nature of reality, and the idea that the sacrifice can be performed mentally, towards the idea that the universe can be understood rationally and philosophically.

UPANISHADS

Upanishad probably comes from 'upa – ni – sad' which means 'to sit near', and refers to the teachings given by a guru to those disciples who sit nearest to him. In other words, it is aimed at the initiated, rather than the people at large. They were composed towards the end of the Vedic period (800–500 BCE), and introduce key features of Hinduism such as the unity of Atman and Brahman, the cycle of samsara, and moksha (release) from this cycle. As time went on, the Upanishads reflected the early Vedic literature less and less, and interest shifted from the details of sacrifice to abstract discussion about the nature of reality itself.

But the Upanishads still addressed issues for ordinary life and could explain abstract ideas imaginatively. In the *Chandogya Upanishad* (5:3–10), for example, we have the idea of rebirth depending upon actions (*karma*), and the description of the Atman as the separate individual self, and the *Chandogya Upanishad* also contains the memorable and crucially important story of Svetaketu splitting the seeds (see the section on 'Atman' above).

Insight

The Upanishads present the earlier teaching in the form of monist philosophy – in other words, they argue that there is a single reality to which everything belongs. The appearance of separateness, for example between the individual self (Atman) and the ultimate reality (Brahman) is simply an illusion; the ultimate truth is that they are one and the same. However, our understanding of the Upanishads today is probably influenced by later philosophical expositions of them – especially that by Sankara (see the section on this later in the chapter).

THE EPICS

Hindu thought makes a distinction between what is known as *shruti* ('hearing'), which applies to the Vedas and implies eternal truth, and *smriti* ('remembering'), which may be used of other literature which does not have that status. Among the smriti literature are the great epics, the *Mahabharata* and the *Ramayana*.

The *Mahabharata* contains the *Bhagavad Gita* (6.23–40), dated probably 2nd century BCE or a little later. This is the most popular of all Hindu texts, and it marks an important step in the development of Hindu philosophy. It tells of Prince Arjuna, troubled about going into battle and the slaughter that will ensue, being advised by his charioteer, who is the god Krishna. Krishna explains that the self (Atman) is indestructible and eternal. Therefore Arjuna will not be killing the real self of those he slays in battle, but only the body, which is like an outer garment.

The *Gita* (the commonly used shortened form of *Bhagavad Gita*) offers a synthesis of many existing Hindu teachings. Krishna declares that all action done from selfless motives becomes a sacrifice, that disinterested action is true renunciation and that there is no point in withdrawing from the world in order to follow a spiritual vocation, but rather that one should stay but act in a selfless way. In other words, one's karma depends on right motivation. This becomes the first of three ways of achieving release – the 'way of action', *karmamarga*. This is followed by the way of understanding (*jnanamarga*), and finally the way of devotion (*bhaktimarga*). Here Hinduism has moved beyond the necessity of sacrifice, as in the earliest Vedic literature, through the way of understanding and mystical identity offered in the Upanishads, and has arrived at a point at which release is achieved through devotion to deity.

After the time of the *Gita* we come on to the period of classical Hinduism, represented by the great philosophical systems. But we need to be aware that these schools were not entirely innovative, but attempted to create coherent philosophies out of the implications of earlier teachings.

Philosophical schools

Hindu philosophy may be divided up into various schools, which are either *astika* (orthodox) if they accept the authority of the Vedas, or *nastika* (unorthodox) if they do not. The unorthodox schools include Buddhism and Jainism. There are six orthodox schools, which are generally considered in pairs: Nyaya/Vaisesika, Sankhya/Yoga and Mimamsa/Vedanta.

NYAYA AND VAISESIKA

These two schools started independently in about the 4th century BCE, but gradually came together (their unity generally being attributed to Gangesa, a 12th-century thinker) to form a single system of philosophy. The Nyaya school was concerned with epistemology – in other words, it asked how we know that something is the case. So, for example, it argued that there were four valid sources of knowledge:

1 perception
2 inference
3 testimony
4 comparison

and, based on these, it systematically set out to decide what one could know.

The Vaisesika school was more concerned with metaphysics – in other words, it wanted to know about the underlying structure and reality that lies behind our experience. It undertook a process of analysis, starting with the basic substances of earth, water, fire and air and their particular qualities of taste, colour, touch and smell.

It argued that everything is divisible into smaller and smaller parts, and ultimately you come to that something which is theoretically indivisible, which it called *paramanu*. Everything is therefore composed of paramanu.

This philosophy takes experience as the starting point for knowledge: all that we can know comes through the senses. Whatever is experienced can be analysed into *padartha* (categories). There were seven of these:

1 Substance
2 Quality
3 Action
4 Class character
5 Individual character
6 Inseparability
7 Non existence

All of them were seen as 'real'. Thus, what is experienced has an underlying substance, particular characteristics and relations with other things. But those characteristics and relations are as real as the substance of that which displays them. They are all part of the phenomena of the world as we experience it.

Western

The Nyaya-Vaisesika philosophy has parallels with Western empiricism. It makes the basic assumption that what is real is what can be known and described – with the implication that, if it can't be known, it can't be real. There are parallels here with logical positivist approach, and (more tentatively) with the end of Wittgenstein's *Tractatus*, where we must remain silent about that which we cannot describe empirically.

There are parallels between Vaisesika and Western 'atomism' – from the Greek 'atomists' Leucippus and Democritus in the 5th century BCE.

Nyaya-Vaisesika system sees a quality which inheres in a number of individual things as a reality in itself. Thus there is a quality of 'treeness' that inheres in and makes individual things trees. That quality may be divided and may inhere with other qualities in an individual thing (after all, the tree will also – at an appropriate time of year – have the quality 'green'), but each quality still retains its own distinct reality.

Western

There are parallels here with Plato's idea of Forms – universals, in which individual things participate. Plato thinks of these as more real than the objects of our experience. The opposite approach would be to take a 'nominalist' view that goodness, for example, does not have any independent reality, but is merely the name we give to show that a number of acts have a common quality ascribed to them. The issue for both Eastern and Western thought is the existence or otherwise of these universals. Are they simply part of our language and the way in which our brains organize their experience of the world, or do they exist 'out there'?

If all knowledge comes through experience, what does the Nyaya-Vaisesika approach make of the Atman (self)? The body, mind and senses all depend on the Atman, which is their animating principle. But how can we know about the self, either in terms of our own Atman or that of others? It cannot be identified with either the body (since it remains the same while the body grows older), nor can it be identified with a person's experiences, since they are constantly changing. We therefore come up against a fundamental problem:

▶ Are there things that I can be said to 'know' but which cannot be experienced directly through the senses?

According to Nyaya-Vaisesika philosophy, you know your own self by direct awareness. It is the 'I' of your experience. When it comes to other people, however, they are only known by inference from your experience of them. You see only bodies and their actions (along with their words and writings), and from these you infer that they are 'selves', similar to the self you know yourself to be.

The Hindu view of reincarnation implies that the self can remain constant through a succession of lives. Personal characteristics and habits which cannot be accounted for solely with reference to experiences in this life, can therefore be attributed to experiences in previous lives. Buddhist philosophy comes to a very different conclusion from the same observed phenomena, arguing that there is no fixed Atman.

Since there can be no empirical evidence to decide between these two positions, it comes down to personal intuition and choice. The Nyaya-Vaisesika system points to the experience of an ongoing, permanent 'I' through all the changes of life; the Buddhist sees this is an illusion. For Buddhism, the 'I' is no more than a conventional way to describe oneself. There is no 'you' over and above the things you think, feel, say and do, no hidden, unchanging Atman behind the scenes.

When it comes to the Supreme Self (for which we can use the Western term 'God', since there is more of a parallel here than in other Hindu philosophies) this philosophy has an argument based on effects and agents. In its simplest form it can be presented like this:

- ▶ Every effect has an agent.
- ▶ The world is an effect.
- ▶ The world must, therefore, have been produced by an agent.
- ▶ The name given to such an agent is God.

It then goes on to present such a God as both omnipotent (all-powerful) and omniscient (all-knowing).

Western

This has parallels with Aquinas' cosmological arguments for the existence of God.

There are several problems with such an argument, even from the Nyaya-Vaisesika point of view. One is that the premise (that every effect has an agent) is not empirically provable. The second is that some things (e.g. the Atman) are said to be eternal. Now, that which is eternal is not an effect, since there was no time when it did not exist and therefore did not need to be brought into existence. This would imply that individual selves are not subject to the creative action of the Supreme Self, which would seem to make God rather less than omnipotent and omniscient!

Another argument for the existence of God is put forward by Udayana, a 10th-century philosopher, in his *Nyana Kusamanjali*. It says simply:

- ▶ People use the word 'God', so that word has meaning.
- ▶ That word must refer to something (since meaning is given in terms of that to which a word refers).
- ▶ Therefore, God exists.

This depends on the basic assumption in Nyaya-Vaisesika philosophy that whatever is real both exists, and is knowable and describable: if people use a word, it must refer to something that exists or it would never have come into use. This is a thoroughly empirical approach to the theory of knowledge: everything depends on experience.

Such an approach makes the individual word, rather than the sentence as a whole, the basis of meaning. The meaning of a word is given by that to which it refers. If there is no external reality as a referent, then the word has no meaning. All meanings are, of course, conventional – people simply agree together that a certain word is going to refer to a certain external reality.

Western

There are parallels here with the logical positivists, whose view of language sprang from a similarly radical empiricism. They held that the meaning of a word was its method of verification, and that anything for which no empirical referent could be given was meaningless.

Like most Indian philosophy, it is concerned with moksha – liberation from the sufferings of this world. Effort may be required in order to achieve moksha, but that effort needs to be based on understanding. So there is no distinction between knowledge for its own sake, and knowledge for the sake of liberation; the two are part of one and the same process. Understanding is a necessary step towards freeing yourself.

As with all Indian philosophies, there is a delight in detailed analysis and subtle distinctions. This section has done no more than hint at some of the broad areas of approach. Of all the Eastern philosophies, the Nyaya-Vaisesika is possibly the one with the most parallels with Western philosophy – particularly in its empiricism, its approach to language and also the place it gives 'God' (to use its Western equivalent) within its overall metaphysics.

The other important thing to realize about this philosophy is that it is not the product of a single person or era, rather it describes one broad tradition in philosophy that has developed over more than 2,000 years.

SANKHYA AND YOGA

Sankhya is generally claimed to be the oldest of the Hindu philosophical systems, for there may be references to it in the *Svetasvatara Upanishad* and the *Bhagavad Gita*. On the other hand, the word sankhya means 'knowledge' or 'wisdom', so those early references may simply have that general meaning. Two terms used in Sankhya – *prakriti* and *purusha* (representing matter and consciousness) – are certainly found in the *Mahabharata*, so elements of Sankhya are certainly as old as that epic. Traditionally, the founder of this school is said to be Kapila, who lived sometime between 100 BCE and 200 CE, but we do not have any of his writings. The oldest extant Sankhya text is from the 5th century CE.

Basically, like other philosophical systems, Sankhya seeks to give an account of reality and a means of avoiding suffering and achieving liberation. Yoga, the tradition with which Sankhya is paired, sets out the principles of discipline required for achieving such liberation.

According to Sankhya, there are two ultimate realities: *prakriti* (matter) and *purusha* (consciousness):

Prakriti is the reality out of which the world is formed, the cause of everything we experience. But because our experience is not uniform, Sankhya argues that there are three different tendencies or *gunas* (literally 'strands' or 'ropes') within prakriti, which we find in varying degrees in each individual thing we encounter: *sattva* (reality, illumination – at the psychological level this guna produces happiness); *rajas* (foulness, constant restless activity – leading to pain); *tamas* (darkness – referring to dull inertia, leading to ignorance and apathy).

By contrast, purusha is pure spirit. It is not the same thing as mind, ego or intelligence, since in Sankhya these are thought of as refined forms of matter. Purusha is the knower – eternal, free, beyond time and space. There are various arguments put forward for the existence of purusha, including the fact that there must be a subject to experience the pleasure, pain or apathy that is encountered in prakriti. Also, the longing for liberation from this material world only makes sense if there is a separate spirit that is capable of such liberation.

Notice that purusha is not located outside the self; it is not some external deity (Sankhya philosophy is in itself atheistic). Rather, since it is both universal and eternal, purusha must be found as much within the self as everywhere else, but as a pure spiritual self, not the particular self of the ego or the intelligence.

Sankhya then claims that prakriti, having come into contact with purusha, goes through a cycle of evolution and dissolution, producing the intellect, then the sense of individual egos, then mind, sense organs, the bodily organs and the elements, although it is not clear why this happens under the influence of the eternal purusha, or why it should produce things in that order.

According to Sankhya, an individual person (*jiva*), comprises purusha joined to an ego (*ahankara*), senses and a body. Each person is therefore formed from the two fundamental features of the whole world, purusha and prakriti, but the unenlightened fail to see that their true identity is purusha, for they are engrossed in their ego, entirely motivated by their senses and their bodily needs. So, according to Sankhya, once you recognize that you have a pure spiritual nature that is not the same thing as your ego, your intellect, your senses or your body, then you will be free. However, the method of achieving such liberation is left to Sankhya's sister philosophy – Yoga.

Before leaving Sankhya, however, it is worth noting its epistemology (theory of knowledge), and particularly its views on cause and effect. First of all, it claims that all knowledge of the world comes by way of images in the mind produced by the contact that our senses have with the world. Although Sankhya never doubts that the external world exists, it claims that we cannot know that external world as it is *in itself*, only by way of the sense impressions that it produces *in the mind*.

Notice the difference between the Nyaya and Sankhya philosophies. In Nyaya, the world is what is experienced, simply that. In Sankhya, the world is out there, unknowable in itself and distinct from the sense impressions that it gives rise to in the mind.

Western

Kant also makes this distinction between things-in-themselves, which are unknowable, and things as we perceive them to be.

This is the first of three sources of knowledge; the other two are inference (much as we saw above in the Nyaya school) and shruti, knowledge from scriptures. In practice, however, Sankhya did not appeal to the scriptures, generally using just perception, inference and analogy.

Sankhya has a distinctive way of approaching the idea of cause and effect. It starts with the obvious fact that you cannot just get any old effect from a given cause, but that the effect is related to *qualities* in the cause. For example, that you can produce cheese from milk, but not from water. It suggests that, when something causes something else to happen, it is simply making actual what was previously potential. Cheese is a potential within milk. Milk is the material cause of the cheese, but it also requires the efficient cause of churning, and so on, to make the potential cheese actual. The conclusion that Sankhya reaches on this is that cause and effect are not two separate things at all, but are different states of the same substance.

Insight

If causes lead to effects which themselves become causes for yet further effects, the world is a constant process of evolution and dissolution. Sankhya seems to be inviting us to consider the world not as a collection of separate things that react to one another as causes and effects, but as the outworking of the potential of a single undifferentiated reality – prakriti.

Yoga offers a set of disciplines that lead to liberation. Its origins are ancient, but Patanjali (who may have lived 200 BCE or perhaps as late as 400 CE), wrote the *Yoga Sutra*, the oldest of the Yoga texts.

Although in general Yoga follows Sankhya philosophy, there is one very significant difference; unlike Sankhya, it includes the idea of a personal God – *Isvara*. The argument used within Yoga for the existence of Isvara is based on the different grades we give to qualities. We say that one thing is greater than another, which implies that we have some measure by which we can assess them. This in turn implies that there must be some Being who possesses them to the highest possible degree. In other words, making value judgements implies knowledge of that which is of supreme value – Isvara.

Western

Notice parallels with Anselm's ontological argument for the existence of 'that than which no greater can be conceived'. Also, Aquinas put forward an argument from degrees of quality as the fourth of his Five Ways of proving the existence of God. However, although Isvara is eternal, omniscient and omnipotent, he is *not* regarded as the creator of the world of matter, and so is very different from the Western idea of 'God'.

The aim of Yoga is help a person become free from the limitations and suffering of the world of prakriti and to discover his or her real self as purusha, and this requires spiritual discipline. Yoga sets out an eightfold path:

1 Abstention – from harming life, from lying, from theft, from sexual activity and from greed.
2 Observance – of internal and external purification, of contentment, of asceticism, of the study of philosophical works and of devotion to God. (These first two steps provide the moral basis of Yoga.)
3 Posture – control of the body; 'Hatha yoga'.
4 Regulation of the process of breathing.
5 Withdrawal of the senses. (These get the physical body ready for spiritual experience.)

6 Fixing the mind on an object.

7 Contemplation of that object.

8 Samadhi – a state of deep meditation.

At this last stage, the mind may still be aware of the object of its meditation and have an intuitive awareness of what is happening, or it may have gone beyond the process of thought into a state where it is totally absorbed in the process of meditating. It is in this last state that the purusa is liberated from matter.

Clearly, this process reflects a practical response to the nature of reality (purusa and prakriti) as set out within Sankhya. The function of God (Isvara) within Yoga is to provide a source of inspiration, and devotion to him is seen as preparing the practitioner of Yoga for the physical and mental disciplines that follow.

MIMAMSA AND VEDANTA

Mimamsa is concerned with an understanding of the Vedas, which includes the vedic hymns, the Upanishads and the Brahmanas. There are two traditions within Mimamsa:

▶ Purva (earlier) Mimamsa is concerned with the Dharma; with the principles of right action as they are set out in the Vedas. It is sometimes referred to as the Dharma Mimamsa.

▶ Uttara (later) Mimamsa is concerned with Brahman, the ultimate cause of everything. It is also more commonly known as Vedanta, the last of the six philosophical schools we shall be considering.

It is important to realize that Purva Mimamsa is not 'earlier' in a chronological sense, but only in the sense that the Vedanta pressed beyond it to look at the ultimate principles that lay behind the vedic literature.

Note

The origins of both schools are obscure. Traditionally the Mimamsa goes back to the *Mimamsa Sutra* by Jaimini, written down somewhere between the 2nd century BCE and the 2nd century CE, after a long period of oral tradition. It is known mainly through the interpretation of Bhasya of Sabara, in the 3rd of 4th century BCE.

Mimamsa has as its starting point a basic proposition that only statements that prescribe a course of action are meaningful. The reason it makes this surprising claim is that it regards the Vedas as eternally true. Its reason for this is straightforward. Statements about individual events can only be known to be true or false depending on evidence, but there can be no evidence for something that is eternal, since you cannot localize it, or define it. You cannot get to eternal truths through contingent facts. Therefore, if the Vedas are eternally true, they cannot offer facts about contingent events.

What then do we make of the apparent descriptions of facts in the Vedas? Mimamsa's answer to this is that their eternal meaning is given in so far as they introduce or explain some principle for living, some rule or prescription.

Western

In the West, prescriptivism is the term used for a philosophical view that statements about value are really just recommendations about a course of action. If I say something is good, there are no external facts that correspond to the word 'good', it is simply a way of saying that the action I am describing is one that I prescribe.

Mimamsa comes to a similar position. To say that the Vedas are eternal is to give them ultimate value. But such value cannot be expressed in terms of contingent facts, but only in prescribing values.

If everything meaningful in the Vedas is in some way associated with the rules for living (the Dharma, in other words), then there is no point in asking if the Vedas are true, or in trying to check them against independent facts – that would be quite irrelevant. All that one needs to do is explore how one can most appropriately apply the particular Dharma to one's own life. Mimamsa does not challenge or assess the Vedas; it merely interprets the rules it finds within them.

The overall effect of Mimamsa within the Hindu tradition was to emphasize the role of correct performance of Dharma. The Vedas provided a wealth of detailed rules, eternally valid, which needed to be constantly interpreted and applied, if good karma was to be generated and bad karma avoided.

Vedanta remains influential to the present day. The term itself means 'end (or purpose) of the Vedas' and it is primarily concerned with Brahman – the absolute reality described in the Upanishads. Vedanta is also concerned to produce a philosophically consistent interpretation of the wide variety of vedic material. The earliest existing work of this school is the *Vedantasutra*, although this summarizes debates that took place earlier.

A key feature of this approach is that ultimate truth (Brahman) cannot be known by reason or logic but it can be perceived through devotion and meditation. The reasons for this are straightforward:

▶ Brahman has no attributes (it is not 'this' or 'that'; not part of the world of phenomena).
▶ Reason can only deal in concepts and attributes.
▶ Therefore reason cannot comprehend Brahman.

How then can Brahman be related to the world? The answer given in Vedanta is that Brahman transforms itself into the things that form the world, but does so without itself changing. In one sense, Brahman is therefore seen as the cause of the world. But it cannot be that simple, because cause and effect are separate things and if Brahman is eternal then nothing can be separate from it. Therefore Brahman and the world are actually identical. There is nothing that is not Brahman, but at the same time, there is no 'thing' that is Brahman.

Although Vedanta attempted to create a single consistent philosophy out of the material in the Upanishads, there are inevitably some differences of view. One problem concerns the extent to which Brahman can be said to be an agent. After all, if it transforms itself into the things of the world, then it takes a direct role in their coming into being. On the other hand, Vedanta (like other Indian philosophies) includes the idea of karma: that everything is the result of good or bad actions. Does Brahman's role therefore imply that some things are caused by karma and others by the direct transforming action of Brahman? Vedanta does not seem to be consistent on this point.

Sankara (*c*. 788–820 CE)
Sankara's *Brahmasutrabhasya* is one of the most important works on Indian philosophy. In it he comments of the Upanishads, the *Gita* and the *Brahmasutra*. He claimed that the ordinary world as we

perceive it is in fact illusion (*maya*) and that the only fundamental reality is Brahman. This approach is termed *advaita* which means 'non-dualism' – there are not two realities, only one.

Sankara takes the general Vedanta line that reason cannot comprehend Brahman, since perceptions are only applicable to the empirical world. You cannot get *beyond* the senses to perceive something outside the world. On the other hand, the self or soul is an aspect of Brahman, it is therefore possible to know Brahman directly through the self. In fact, if Brahman and the Atman are one (which is a key feature of Hindu philosophy) Brahman is known in the 'I' that acts – the fundamental reality of the self, something separate from the physical aspects of a person that can be seen and described.

Sankara also distinguished between *Nirguna Brahman* (unqualified reality) and *Saguna Brahman* (qualified reality). Nirguna Brahman could be known only as pure consciousness, whereas Saguna Brahman was seen acting as a vital force in everything and also as Isvara – the general term used for 'God'.

There are therefore two levels of truth: conventionally and pragmatically, Sankara saw the world as an evolving and changing system, produced by a divine person and rolling though its cycles, but ultimately he believed that world to be unreal. As all experience is open to misinterpretation, we may be deceived and the world as we know it may be like a dream through which we are living. The only absolute reality is Brahman, identical with the self, the Atman.

The essential self, the Atman, is trapped within many layers, the outermost of which is the physical body. Release, for Sankara, comes by stripping these layers away to reveal our truth. It comes by knowledge (*jnanamarga*) and the result of being released is described as *satcitananda* (or *saccidananda*), a term made up of three components: *sat* = existence, *cit* = consciousness and *ananda* = bliss).

••

Insight

There would seem to be a basic problem with *satcitananda*. Does that state – as suggested by the term *cit* – imply consciousness? If so, of what could someone in such a state be conscious? If it is a state of being an eternal and infinite Atman, at one with Brahman, what else is there to be aware of? Also, if the Atman is in some way self-conscious (and what else can it mean to be in a state of bliss), that implies that Atman/Brahman has personality. But Sankara claimed that Brahman was above personality.

To a certain extent this can be resolved by making the distinction between Nirguna and Saguna Brahman: the second is known but the first is not. But it seems to me that Sankara always wants to have it both ways:

► to be able to speak about Brahman, but at the same time identifying him absolutely with that about which one cannot speak
► to suggest a state of awareness and bliss without being able to give any content to either the awareness or the bliss.

A number of pots are filled with water. The sun is shining and is reflected on the surface of the water in each pot. It is the same sun, but it is seen in many different reflections. In the same way, Sankara argues, Brahman can appear to each individual as his or her Atman – while still remaining the one Brahman. Similarly, just as light is refracted through a pure colourless crystal giving a whole spectrum of colours, so we tend to assume that the reality we see with our senses is a true reality, but in practice it is limited, part of the world of illusion (maya).

Sankara criticized the Sankhya argument that an effect pre-exists in its cause, on the grounds that this would lead to an infinite regress: if everything depends on an earlier potential, which in turn depends on an earlier potential, and so on, how can anything become actual in the first place? Instead, he argues that, in reality, cause and effect are identical. We merely see them as different because that is the conventional way in which we are able to experience them.

Western

This is another point at which Sankara comes close to Kant. Kant argued that space, time and causality were part of the way in which we perceive things, rather than being features of things as they are in themselves. In the same way, Sankara argues that cause and effect are conventionally seen as separate things, while in reality they are identical.

Sankara also argued that:

► No insentient thing, unless it is an instrument used by a sentient being, can do anything in order to achieve a purpose of goal.

- Yet the world appears to have purpose.
- The world should therefore be seen as the product of an intelligence.
- To use his own analogy – the clay needs a potter before it can become a pot.

Western

This is Sankara's version of what was later to develop in the West as the 'argument from design'. Used by Aquinas and (using the well-known analogy of coming across a watch, examining its parts and concluding that there must be an intelligent watchmaker) by William Paley, this argued for the existence of God on the basis of the perceived purpose and design in the world.

Sankara made a point of criticizing rival philosophies. Among those, we have already mentioned his criticism of Sankhya, but he also criticized Buddhist philosophy on a key issue: Buddhism holds that everything is radically impermanent, and the dharmas, of which everything is made, are momentary events. Thus, in Buddhist philosophy, the self is not permanent, but comprises five *skandhas* which are constantly changing and which come together to make a unique individual at every point in time. Sankara would not accept this. In particular he argued that – if there were nothing that persisted from one moment to the next – it would be very difficult to account for the phenomenon of memory or of recognition. If I remember something, according to Sankara, it implies that there is an 'I' that was there both in the past and in the present. And, of course, for him this 'I' is the Atman, ultimately at one with Brahman, the fundamental reality. This remains constant, even if everything else within the world of experience is merely maya and subject to change.

His system left little scope for religious devotion, which he saw as no more than a starting point. A person needed to move on to develop profound knowledge, gained through meditation, in order to achieve moksha.

Between the 8th and the 15th centuries different schools of Vedanta developed. The three main traditions are:

- ▶ Advaita (non-dualism)
- ▶ Visistadvaita (qualified non-dualism)
- ▶ Dvaita (dualism).

The Advaita tradition developed the approach taken by Sankara. At its simplest it may be summed up as:

- ▶ What is real is permanent and cannot change.
- ▶ The objects we experience in the world are not real because
  - ▷ they change
  - ▷ it is impossible to say at what level they might be real. (In other words: Which is real, the cloth or the threads, the clay or the pot?)
- ▶ The self is not part of the world we experience, rather it is self-evident. It cannot be the same as 'my' body, for it is the 'I' that is implied by 'my'.
- ▶ Therefore what is ultimately real is Brahman/Atman – the 'self' that is within everything. It is Pure Being and Pure Consciousness.
- ▶ Even if, conventionally, things are said to exist, ultimately, everything other than Brahman/Atman is like a dream.

Ramanuja (1017–1137 CE)

The *Visistadvaita* tradition affirmed the objective reality of the material world (*acit*), of individual souls (*cit*) and of God (*Isvara*). It is particularly associated with the work of Ramanuja. He taught the way of devotion, and held a theistic view of reality. Devotion leads a person to see himself or herself as a dependent fragment of God. Whereas for Sankara, the absolute is impersonal, for Ramanuja it is personal – Isvara.

This has implications for the nature of the self. For Sankara, the self (Atman) is in fact the same as Brahman – and the awareness of this brings moksha. But for Ramanuja, although the self becomes at one with God, it is not identical to God; there remains a distinction, without which the self could have no identity of its own. This is why this approach is called 'qualified non-dualism'.

This Visistadvaita approach set out a straightforward test for what could be considered real. If something was perceived in two contradictory ways, then one of those perceptions must be false. Thus, in the much-used example, if I think that a length of rope is in fact a snake, but someone else sees it as rope, then one or other of those perceptions must be false. On the other hand, if there is no dispute about what is perceived, then there is no reason to question the reality of what is seen. In many ways Ramanuja's approach here seems rather more in line with common sense than that of the Advaita.

Madhva

Dvaita Vedanta was an approach associated first with the 13th-century philosopher Madhva. Like the Visistadvaita approach, it accepts:

▶ a personal God (in this case Vishnu)
▶ the real existence of finite selves
▶ the real existence of the objective world
▶ devotion as necessary for liberation.

But Madhva went further, by setting out a basic dualism between God (the only independent reality) and everything else (which is totally dependent upon God). Individual things are therefore distinct (i.e. this is the opposite of the Advaita approach) but they are not totally independent (as was the case with the Nyaya-Vaisesika tradition) because they all equally depend on God.

In effect, Madhva was claiming that God was the efficient cause of everything, but that he was not the material cause; matter was eternal, and so were individual souls, but they only continued to exist because willed to do so by God. For Madhva, God cannot be the material cause of the world, because the sentient and the insentient are totally different from one another, and the one cannot convert into the other.

He introduced a view of the liberation of souls quite different from that of the earlier schools, suggesting that there were three, intrinsically different, categories of souls:

▶ those that would eventually achieve moksha (liberation)
▶ those who would stay for ever within samsara
▶ those who would remain in a state of eternal suffering.

The justification for this is that, although progress towards liberation depends upon karma, each individual has an innate disposition which leads him or her to perform particular actions and therefore to suffer (or benefit from) their consequences.

One crucial difference between the souls that are bound for liberation and those that are doomed is that the latter think that they are independent, whereas the former know that they are totally dependent upon God. But Madhva goes one step further and argues that liberation or otherwise is totally dependent upon the will of God – so presumably God established the inherent dispositions, which led to the karma, which led to liberation.

Western

There are many parallels with Christian thought here, and particularly with the later Calvinist ideas of predestination. It is widely believed that Madhva was influenced in his thinking by contact with Christian communities in southern India.

It will be clear by now that Vedanta is a vast area of Hindu philosophy and includes within itself many differences, both obvious and subtle. In general, however, we need to remember that it represents the philosophical development of the Upanishads and that, alongside the authority of scriptures, it accepted both perception and inference as valid sources of knowledge.

NON-ORTHODOX PHILOSOPHIES

The philosophical schools set out above developed within the main Vedic tradition. Others – including Jainism and Buddhism, which we shall consider in later chapters – developed separately, and are particularly associated with the area of north-eastern India, in what was then known as Magadha and is now West Bengal and Bihar.

But there were other non-orthodox schools as well, and a fascinating outline of these is given by Karel Werner in the Routledge *Encyclopedia* (1997, see 'Further reading'). He describes the area as ruled by the Vratyas – a confederation of Aryan tribes.

Vratya philosophy is found referred to in the *Atharva Veda* and in scattered references elsewhere. It was a mystical philosophy in which the term Vratra is used for a cosmic creative power, individualized in Ekavratya (also called Mahadeva, the great god). From him comes the cosmic wanderer – Brahmacari – who establishes the Earth, impregnates it and thus gives rise to multiplicity of our experienced world. This sexual imagery was mirrored in a fertility rite involving the spiritual master, student and female assistant. In religious terms, the aim was to reverse this natural process and regain a simple transcendence beyond the multiplicity of our experienced world. This led to a renunciation of the world as a celibate 'brahmacari' and, once accomplished, one was known as an *Ekavratya* or *Arhat*.

Insight

What you have here is a ritual re-enactment of the process of creativity, with human sexuality mirroring a fundamental creativity in the universe. Then, in response to this, there is a reversal of the process, rejecting the world and seeking a higher mystical unity.

This sexual imagery, and the use of sexuality as expressing creativity, also appears in Tantric practice (see Chapter 7) although any linkage with Vratya remains speculative.

Lokayata philosophy (also known as *Charvaka*) was materialist – it claimed that only those things that are perceived are known to exist. There is no other world, and no survival of death. Belief in such things is thought to be fantasy. No logical proof for the existence of the unseen is possible, for inference cannot be used as a valid source of new knowledge, since it cannot be proved unconditionally. Inference should only be accepted if its results are, at least in principle, perceivable. But, as Karel Werner points out, the basic materialist assumption (what cannot be seen, does not exist) cannot itself be proved true or false. It is therefore simply a metaphysical postulate, a choice about how experience is to be interpreted.

Consciousness, for Lokayata, is simply the result of the coming together of the elements that form the person, just as the property of intoxication is the result of the process of fermentation within a drink.

Western

This is rather like the weak form of the Verification Theory as developed by the logical positivists. They held that, to say that something exists, one should be able to say what sort of evidence could count for or against its existence.

The Lokayata idea of the self would, in Western terms, be called epiphenomenalism; namely, that the mind is a phenomenon that arises on the basis of the physical body.

There were various Lokayata schools, some identifying the self simply with the material components nourished by food (very much a 'You are what you eat' approach), some with the power of sensory perception, a third school is said to identify the self with vital forces, yet another accepts the distinct existence of the mind, although it too was regarded as perishable.

Lokayata ethics follow from the conviction that, since one cannot survive death, one should enjoy the pleasures of this life to the highest measure possible, and the highest bliss was said to be the embrace of a beautiful woman. Sacrifices and studying the Vedas were said to achieve nothing, and were therefore best left to those who lacked intelligence and manliness. On the other hand, Lokayata teaching held that the pursuit of pleasure should not be such as to cause suffering to others. Animal sacrifices and warfare were therefore opposed.

Western

The most obvious parallel here is with Epicurean philosophy. In its approval of happiness as a valid goal in life, but in limiting its pursuit — e.g. not causing suffering to others in the process — there are parallels with utilitarianism.

When we come to look at Buddhism, we shall see that it refers to itself as 'The Middle Way'. This can be understood in a number of ways (as a balance between luxury and asceticism, or between eternalism and nihilism) but one of them, in the context of its origins, probably refers to its position between orthodox Hindu asceticism and this materialistic hedonism of Lokayata.

No Lokayata texts have been preserved, and we know of it only through the attempts of the orthodox schools to refute it. I have no doubt that it was popular!

Life: goals and ethics

Fundamental to Vedic literature is the idea that there is a natural and intelligent order to the world – *rta* – which can be seen not only in the organization of the physical universe, but also in the world of morality, religion and the intellect. Two of the key concepts in Hindu thought, Brahman and Dharma, naturally follow from the idea of rta, expressing, respectively, the absolute underlying reality of the world and the duty of each individual person and thing to act according to its place in the scheme of things. All the various gods described in the Vedas are there to help maintain this rta, and humans maintain it through the rituals of sacrifice and through performing their duty.

From the Vedas, therefore, we have the basic moral concept: dharma. Dharma (which can be translated as right or appropriate action or duty) is that which sustains society, ensuring that it conforms to the natural order of things. Later, in the *Gita*, this is expressed in the term *svadharma*, which is 'dharma for oneself'. In other words, each person will have particular duty to perform, and your svadharma is the dharma as it applies to you as an individual.

VARNASRAMADHARMA

Clearly, the svadharma will vary between individuals according to their particular circumstances. One's dharma depends on one's class (*varna*) and stage in life (*asrama*).

Within Indian society there are four main classes, or *varnas* (a term meaning 'colour', possibly used as a distinction between the fair-skinned Aryans and the darker-skinned indigenous peoples whom they had conquered and with whom they co-existed). One's dharma within society therefore depended upon one's position within this hierarchical social system.

There are four varnas:

1 *Brahmin* (priestly)
2 *Kshatriya* (ruler/warrior/administrator)
3 *Vaishya* (merchant/craftsman)
4 *Shudra* (worker).

These were set out in the Purusa Sukta of the *Rig Veda*, and their origin was expressed graphically in terms of the division of primal man (Purusa) – with the Brahmin as his head, the Kshatriya as his arms, the Vaisya as his thighs and the Sudra as his feet. The fact that they belong together in a single body suggests mutual dependence and harmony, in spite of radical differences in status and function.

The four varna are not the same as the Indian caste system. The word for caste is *jati*, which means 'birth'. You are born into a particular caste, which will determine the work you do, whom you may marry, where you live and so on. Varna is – or should be – determined by a person's natural ability, rather than their birth, but in practice the varnas act rather like caste groups, in that the social position of your birth is likely to be a major determining factor in how you are able to develop and express your abilities.

Western

In *The Republic*, Plato seeks social justice by having three general classes – philosopher rulers, military executives and the merchant or artisan class. Not so different from the four varnas (if you put Vaishya and Shudra together), and with the same underlying quest for a harmony of different abilities.

Alongside varna, the other major factor for determining an individual's dharma is his or her stage of life, or *asrama*. There are four of these:

1 *Brahmacarya* (student)
2 *Grhasta* (householder)
3 *Vanaprasta* (retired)
4 *Sannyasa* (renunciate).

Taking these two factors together, therefore, one's duty was seen as *varnasramadharma* – duty set according to one's by stage in life and one's 'colour'.

Insight

A key feature of Hindu ethics is this flexibility in recognizing that different people, at different stages of life, will have different norms of behaviour. Such an approach will always have the advantage of not having to constantly adapt generalized laws to the needs of particular groups of people. On the other hand, it is difficult within such a system to distinguish between what is right or wrong in any absolute sense, and what is merely a reflection of the social structure. It is also difficult not to allow society to institutionalize what (in absolutist terms) may be seen as injustice.

THE FOUR AIMS OF LIFE

Within the Vedic literature there is a group of sutras particularly concerned with the exposition of Dharma, the most important of which is the *Manudharma Sastra* (or *Manusmrti*). This sets out four aims of life:

1 *Dharma* (virtue/right conduct)
2 *Artha* (wealth)
3 *Kama* (pleasure)
4 *Moksha* (liberation).

The fourth of these has been considered already, since it is an important feature of the classical philosophical systems. The second and third recognize the role of sexual and other pleasures and the gaining of wealth as a valid part of life, provided that they do not go against Dharma or harm others. Clearly Artha and Kama are particularly appropriate for the householder stage of life, where a person is expected to be economically and sexually active.

WAYS TO LIBERATION

Just as Dharma is the principle that underlies all four of the aims of life, so *moksha* (liberation) is the ultimate goal, and we have seen this in the classical Hindu philosophies. There are three different *marga* (paths) leading to moksha.

Karmamarga (the path of action)
Traditionally there were two different ways of behaving that would lead to liberation. The first was to follow the path of the renunciate

(the *sanyassin*) and withdraw from life as far as possible, living as an ascetic. The other was to remain within society, but to behave with moderation and in a way that reflected one's svadharma. These two come together in the concept of *karmamarga*. This is a path advocated in the *Bhagavad Gita*, and it is to act without attachment to the results of that action. In other words, there is both the sense of renunciation (not looking for personal gain) and yet one can practise this while still involved with worldly activity.

Of course, this reflects the earliest teaching of Dharma, which was to act for the good of society but also in accord with one's inner self. The path of action includes the *yamas* (rules concerning things to avoid) and *niyamas* (qualities to cultivate).

The yamas are:

1 *ahimsa* (not killing)
2 *satya* (speaking the truth)
3 *asteya* (not stealing)
4 *brahmacarya* (continence in matters sensual)
5 *aparigraha* (avoiding avarice).

The niyamas are:

1 cleanliness
2 contentment
3 pure concentration
4 study along with others
5 devotion to God.

Jnana marga (the path of knowledge)

We have already seen that philosophy has played a large part in the Hindu tradition. The path of knowledge (*jnana*) involves recognizing the identity of the Atman with Brahman, perception of which can lead directly to liberation. Notice also that study is one of the qualities to be cultivated on the path of action.

Insight

Remember that knowledge, in the Hindu context, is not just a matter or rational understanding and debate, but getting the right 'view' of life, the achieving of which will involve far more than intellectual training, but a whole way of life. Hence the jnana marga requires the morality and qualities of the karmamarga.

Bhakti marga (the path of devotion)

We saw, in examining the development of Vedanta, how, by the end of the first millennium CE, the Bhakti (devotional) tradition exerted a powerful influence over the whole of Hindu philosophy. This may be traced back to the time of the *Gita*, where devotion is seen as a means of achieving liberation. Of course, the whole Bhakti tradition implies the existence of a personal deity, and it is therefore not an option for those who take a non-theistic philosophy.

The three margas are not mutually exclusive, but represent three different emphases within Hindu thought and practice. They also reflect three stages in the development of Hindu philosophy, and for each individual the appropriateness of one path or another will depend on temperament and circumstances.

AHIMSA

We have already seen that killing is the first thing to be avoided, but *ahimsa* is more than merely abstaining from killing; it involves developing a positive attitude towards all living things. Mahatma Gandhi took the principle of ahimsa as the basis of his whole campaign to free India from British rule. In terms of the overall Hindu view of life, ahimsa is crucial. It relates both to the idea of karma and to the key notion that all beings have a svadharma: to do violence to another is to deny that other's right to live in an appropriate way. Ahimsa is also a recognition of the interconnectedness of all living things.

Insight

Notice that ahimsa it is also the key feature of the two non-orthodox philosophies that we shall be considering separately – Jainism and Buddhism. It is deeply ingrained in the whole of Indian philosophical and social thinking.

Within this chapter, we have been concerned with the basic themes that have shaped Indian thought, and there has been no opportunity to examine particular modern thinkers. Those wishing to follow up on Hindu philosophies might wish to look particularly at the work of Swami Vivekenanda (1863–1902), Mahatma Gandhi (1869–1948), Sri Aurobindo (1870–1950) and Radhakrishnan (1888–1975).

10 THINGS TO REMEMBER

1 Hindu thought sees the universe as having a timeless order (*Dharma*).

2 The aim of much Hindu philosophy is to enable individuals to be released from the world of suffering and live in harmony with the universe (*moksha*).

3 Hindu religion includes a multiplicity of gods and goddesses, each of which is a way of representing a particular aspect of the single ultimate reality, Brahman.

4 Acceptance of the authority of the Vedas is the criterion of orthodoxy in Hindu thought.

5 The Upanishads provide philosophical commentaries on the earlier Vedic literature.

6 There are six philosophical schools, which come together in pairs: Nyaya/Vaisesika, Sankhya/Yoga and Mimamsa/Vedanta.

7 Hindu ethics is based on the class (*varna*) to which a person belongs and their stage in life.

8 There are four aims in life: right conduct, wealth, pleasure and liberation.

9 There are three ways of liberation: by action, by knowledge and by devotion.

10 The key moral principle is *ahimsa*, non-violence and respect for all life.

2

....

Early Buddhism

In this chapter you will:
- *examine the basic teachings of the Buddha*
- *consider the place of philosophy and meditation in the Buddhist tradition*
- *explore some key features of Buddhist ethics.*

Background: The Buddha

Anyone living in northern India in the 6th century BCE would have been familiar with three basic philosophies of life:

▶ There was orthodox Hinduism, dominated increasingly at that time by the authority of the Brahmins, based on the Vedas and the correct performance of rituals.

▶ There were what amounted to freelance spiritual teachers (*shramanas*) who offered ascetic training and meditation. Those shramanas who did not accept the authority of the Vedas were regarded as unorthodox.

▶ Finally there was the materialistic and hedonistic philosophy of the Lokayata school, which fully justified the pursuit of pleasure as a valid aim in life.

It was also a time of increasing commerce and urbanization, weakening the links that individuals had with their family homes and village traditions, and fostering a spirit of questioning and spiritual exploration.

Siddhartha Gautama (566–486 BCE, although today some scholars think that he may have died, aged 80, as late as 404 BCE), later to be called the 'Buddha' (meaning 'the fully awakened or enlightened one'), is described as having lived a life of princely luxury and then given it up to follow the life of an ascetic. His quest was to find the cause of suffering and the means of overcoming it and, in pursuing it, he acknowledged having trained under various Hindu teachers prior to the experience that Buddhists speak of as his 'enlightenment'.

In the earliest sutras (the written records of his teaching), we find ourselves in a world where there is wealth and commerce, alongside the phenomenon of large numbers of people who deliberately retire from such worldly concerns as part of a personal religious quest. Spiritual people, often referred to as 'ascetics and Brahmins', wandered from place to place, teaching, attracting groups of followers and often supported in their efforts by wealthy patrons.

It is against this background that the Buddha taught his 'middle way' between the extremes of hedonism and asceticism, of materialism and a nihilistic rejection of all material values.

RELIGION OR PHILOSOPHY?

It has often been difficult to know how to categorize Buddhism. Today it is generally referred to – with justification – as one of the world religions. At one time it was more common to see it referred to as a philosophy, or an ethical philosophy. Viewed from the perspective of Western religion, Buddhism appeared to be a philosophy rather than a religion, since it required no belief in God, nor in the immortality (or even the existence) of the soul. It also expected its followers to accept its teachings only to the extent that each individual could understand and be personally convinced by them; very different from the common Western assumption that religion should be based on faith rather than reason.

On the other hand, from the standpoint of Western philosophy, Buddhism appears quite religious, especially since the Buddha himself did not encourage abstract speculation on metaphysical matters. What he claimed to offer was a practical path leading to full insight into things as they really are (insight which was thought to render speculative questioning unnecessary), along with a set of precepts and practices.

As we shall see later, the key feature of Buddhist philosophy is the idea that everything arises in dependence upon conditions. This it applied not just to the physical world, but also morally and personally.

Thus, the precepts and practices of Buddhism may be described in terms of creating the conditions under which insight and happiness might arise and suffering might be overcome.

So it should be remembered, as we look at Buddhist philosophy, that it needs to be thought of as a description of insight, rather than simply the conclusion to a logical argument or straight inference from experience. On the other hand, at the core of Buddhism there are a number of concepts, centred on the idea of the 'interconnectedness' of all things, which provide conceptual clues to the whole of its spiritual and moral approach, and it is these concepts that make it radically different from both orthodox Hinduism and the other non-orthodox schools.

Insight

In effect, Buddhism is saying 'Look at life this way. Does it make better sense to you?' In Western terms, that is certainly closer to philosophy than religion, since it asks no initial commitment other than the honest examination of its claims. However, that does not imply that Buddhism requires no subsequent commitment from those who choose to follow its path – that was always the case both for monastic and lay disciples – but such commitment is expected to be based on personal conviction rather than 'faith' in a Western sense.

It is also important to recognize at the outset that Buddhist philosophy is based on the analysis of experience. The goal of the Buddhist path, exemplified by Siddhartha Gautama, is enlightenment, which is a matter of seeing things as they really are.

RELATIONSHIP TO HINDU THOUGHT

Some Hindus regard Buddhism simply as an unorthodox form of Hinduism. On the other hand, Buddhists see the teachings they follow as quite separate from the Hindu tradition. In any case there are two fundamental differences between orthodox Hinduism and Buddhism:

▶ Hinduism accepts the idea of a single reality (Brahman) which may be expressed through many different images of gods and goddesses. It also accepts the idea of an immortal soul which is lodged in the body and will, after death, pass on to other lives. Buddhism rejects both the idea that there is a fixed, eternal reality, whether God or Brahman, and the idea of eternal self (Atman). Nothing is permanent; everything is interconnected and in a state of flux.

▶ Hinduism is based on tradition and on acceptance of the Vedas. Buddhism rejects all external authority, and insists that teachings are accepted on the basis reason and experience.

It is these two fundamental differences, rather than any details of moral teachings or styles of worship, that distinguish Buddhism from Hinduism.

Key concepts

Note

Buddhist terms are found in both Pali and Sanskrit. Pali was the language of the earliest collection of the Buddhist scriptures, and it has continued to be used within the Theravada tradition. The Sanskrit versions are generally given here for convenience, since we are also considering other religions that use Sanskrit, and to save any confusion.

PRATITYA SAMUTPADA

Pratitya samutpada is *the* fundamental concept for all Buddhist philosophy and is a distinctive feature of Buddhism. It may be translated as:

▶ dependent origination
▶ conditioned co-production and
▶ interconnectedness.

In its simplest form it may be expressed as 'This being so, that arises. This no longer being so, that ceases.' In other words, things only come into existence because of certain conditions, and when those conditions change, they will cease to be. Their origins are dependent. Looked at in another way: whatever is about to happen will do so because of a variety of factors that exist now. Those factors themselves will depend on other things being the case, and those will depend upon yet others. Thus, everything is interconnected.

As we look at the world, the temptation (especially for those schooled in Western philosophy) is to divide the world up into 'things', each of which has its own separate existence. That is not the Buddhist perspective.

For Buddhism, the world comprises an infinite network of conditions – and everything that exists is the temporary manifestation, in this particular time and place, of that whole network.

Example

Think of the conditions that enable you to read this book. First of all, you require air to breathe and light to be able to see. Your life depends of food and drink, on a whole network of practical things that maintain you, as well as generations of people who have met and coupled to produce children who in turn have produced children, who have become your parents. Imagine the vast number of chances that have determined your heredity. And it is not simply the sexual attraction between couples stretching back through generations, but all the other factors that led each of them to meet one another.

So much for your own existence, but consider also the book, its materials, its publication, its distribution, the circumstances that led me to write it, and which led to you to read it.

In short, it has taken a theoretically infinite number of chances (conditions) to enable you to be born, and for you to be here reading this book.

In other words, if anything in the universe were different, everything would be different, for everything is interconnected. Equally, you are not separate from the rest of the world, you are part of the world, and are totally dependent on the rest of it. When the conditions which enable you to live are no longer there, you will cease to be.

This view might sound fatalistic or determinist, but it does not deny human freedom, since your present actions contribute to what the future holds. If everything else makes a difference to you, then it is equally the case that you make a difference to everything else! This feature of the Buddhist view can be appreciated by a reflection on all the possible consequences of a present action or choice.

THREE MARKS OF EXISTENCE
Pratitya samutpada gives rise to three universal features of the conditioned world in which we live.

Anicca

Nothing is fixed; everything is in a constant process of change. We may have a concept of that which is eternal, we may long for the eternal, but in reality, everything we experience in this life is subject to change, because everything is dependent upon the conditions that maintain it in existence.

Anatta

Not only is everything changing, but nothing exists in and of itself. At every moment, each existing thing depends on everything else. But interconnectedness implies even more – that there is no such thing as an inherent 'self' (like the Hindu Atman). What appears as 'self' in conventional language is, in absolute terms, an illusion. Buddhism sees each individual as a bundled collection of five *skandhas* (see the section on 'The self' later in this chapter) – body, feelings, perceptions, volitions and consciousness. They come together at birth, and are conventionally given an overall term 'oneself'. At death they cease to operate together, and so this conventional 'self' ceases to exist. Like pratitya samutpada, anatta is absolutely crucial to Buddhist philosophy: nothing has inherent and therefore independent or permanent existence; there is no fixed self. The radical implications of this single idea dominate the Buddhist view of reality.

Western

In Western philosophy there is the problem known as the 'elusive I', the failure to find a definition of self that is not also something else as well – the frustration of 'my' mind and 'my' body, even 'my' thoughts, without finding what this 'my' can be in itself. Clearly, Buddhism has no such problem. Although a conventionally useful term, the 'I' has no absolute, independent reality.

Dukkha

If we do not have a permanent self, and if everything is changing and dependent upon conditions, then life will inevitably involve frustration, suffering and death. It is not that such things are imposed on us from outside, but are the natural consequence of being limited, dependent beings. Dukkha is a broad term used to cover all that is unsatisfactory in life. Not getting what one wants is dukkha; getting what one does not want is dukkha. Even pleasant things can involve dukkha, for we know that they cannot last. To pretend that life does not involve dukkha is seen by Buddhists as deliberate refusal to face the facts.

All that follows on the Buddhist path is the result of a radical recognition of the nature of conditioned existence and the dukkha (often rather narrowly translated as 'suffering') that follows from it. The whole aim of Buddhist philosophy is to overcome dukkha. This does not imply that Buddhism seeks to change the reality of the world – that would be quite impossible – but it argues that an understanding of the mechanism by which dukkha comes about, and the response that people have to it, will in itself help them to overcome it. And since everything happens as a result of conditions, the Buddhist path seeks to create the conditions within which suffering may be overcome.

Insight

Buddhist philosophy is sometimes introduced with a bald statement that all life is suffering. In one sense this is correct, for Buddhism teaches that all conditioned things are eventually liable to decay, and that pretending otherwise is wilful delusion, leading to frustration. Yet it can give entirely the wrong impression of Buddhist philosophy. Buddhism is not negative but realistic; it does not focus on suffering, but on the means of overcoming it.

THE FOUR NOBLE TRUTHS

Using a common form of reasoning (parallel with that of a doctor giving a diagnosis and cure) the Buddha is said to have set out his *Dharma* (teaching) in the form of four propositions, each following from the previous one:

1 All life involves *dukkha* (suffering or unsatisfactoriness).
2 The cause of suffering is *tanha* (craving; longing for things to be other than they are).
3 With *nirodha* (the ceasing of craving), suffering too will cease.
4 The way to eliminate craving is to follow the Noble Eightfold Path – called *magga* ('the middle way').

Let us examine the implications of each of these.

Dukkha

As has been outlined above, this claims to be a realistic assessment of the human condition. It does not imply that life is devoid of happiness. Indeed, the Buddha recognized that the quest for happiness and the avoidance of suffering was fundamental not just to human life but to that of all sentient beings. It is simply what happens when you live in a world where everything is interconnected and constantly changing. Reality can never match our dreams, or if it does so, that ideal state cannot be sustained indefinitely.

Tanha

Tanha is *not* the same thing as the natural desire for those things that sustain us or bring happiness. It denotes craving for something to be fixed and permanently available in a world where that is not possible. In other words, it is a form of wanting that is fundamentally at odds with the way the world is.

Tanha may take three forms:

▶ sensual craving (*kamatanha*): seeking permanent satisfaction through sensory pleasure and avoiding situations of sensory deprivation

▶ craving for existence (*bhavanatanha*): the longing to survive as an individual

▶ the third form of craving (*vibhavatanha*) can mean two very different things. Vibhava can mean 'prosperity', in which case it is craving for success and wealth, but it can also mean 'annihilation', and so would refer to the desire to leave the world altogether, presumably by suicide. Vibhavatanha is therefore an 'all or nothing' approach, attempting to avoid the changing and dependent nature of life by opting for one extreme or the other.

Insight

Remember, Siddhartha had experienced both wealth (which failed to satisfy him) and extreme asceticism (which nearly killed him). As Buddha, he therefore rejected both extremes. This was a radical point of view in a culture that generally saw asceticism as the path to spiritual advancement.

Nirodha

Nirodha means 'cessation': if tanha (craving) ceases, then dukkha (suffering/unsatisfactoriness) will also cease. It is tempting, from a western perspective, to interpret this negatively: 'If you don't expect anything from life, you won't be disappointed.' Within Buddhism it is not seen that way, for two reasons:

▶ Craving for annihilation is just like any other craving and leads to suffering – so nirodha cannot simply mean abandoning everything.

▶ Nirodha is often referred to as *nirvana* (*nibbana* in Pali) which (as we shall see below) is the state of happiness and peace to which Buddhists aspire, marking the point at which the 'triple fires' of hatred, greed and ignorance are burnt out, to be replaced by love, generosity and wisdom. So the point at which tanha ceases is thought of as bliss, not emptiness.

Magga (The Noble Eightfold Path)

Although generally referred to as steps on a path, these eight features of the Buddhist life are not intended to be taken in sequence, but simultaneously. They represent features of attitude, lifestyle and spiritual practice which are helpful in setting up the conditions under which a person may move towards the goal of the Buddhist path, namely, seeing things as they really are and thereby being released from suffering.

1 Right (or perfect) view
This refers back to interconnectedness and the fundamental features of the Buddhist view of life described above. Without such a view, the path does not make sense.

2 Right intention
This step introduces the element of personal, existential commitment. The Buddhist path cannot be a matter of detached academic interest, but requires commitment. This is not to take some moral high ground against intellectual frivolity, but implies that the path can only be followed in engagement, not in detached reflection.

3 Right speech
Various forms of speech are to be avoided: false speech, harsh speech; speech liable to cause dissension; idle chatter. The opposite – truthful, gentle, constructive and purposeful speech – is to be cultivated.

4 Right action
The moral precepts that form this part of the path are discussed in 'The Five Precepts' later in this chapter. In brief, they are: not to take life (but cultivate compassion and goodwill towards all living things); not to steal (but to cultivate generosity); not to indulge the senses harmfully (but to cultivate stillness, simplicity and contentment); not to practise wrong speech (see above); not to cloud the mind with intoxicants (but to practise mindfulness).

5 Right livelihood

Clearly, Buddhists are encouraged to follow a livelihood that is in line with the fundamental Buddhist vision and particularly the five precepts given in step four.

6 Right effort

There are four right efforts:

- ▶ eliminating harmful thoughts/desires that already exist
- ▶ preventing these from arising in the future
- ▶ encouraging the arising of positive thoughts/desires
- ▶ maintaining those positive thoughts that have already arisen.

In other words, it is the process of consciously refining thoughts and wishes in line with Buddhist principles.

7 Right mindfulness

The Buddhist path requires a person to cultivate awareness of the body, feelings, mental processes and the objects of thought. This follows from the basic Buddhist view that lack of awareness leads to suffering, and that the goal of the spiritual path is to be fully awake or aware (in other words, 'Buddha').

8 Right contemplation

As we shall see later, meditation of various kinds plays a crucial role in the Buddhist path. In general one might say that the taming and gentle controlling of the mind, calming it and harmonizing the various conscious and unconscious urges that determine its activity, is the means by which the path can be followed. Without it, the insight and determination will be lacking (or will be forced, rather than natural), and the practical steps of speech, action and livelihood will not spring from a naturally integrated vision and desire.

Note

The 'Middle Way' can be taken to refer to the middle way between the extremes of luxury and asceticism, following the example of Gautama Buddha, but it also has a more philosophical meaning, as the middle way between nihilism and eternalism. A nihilist denies the reality of individual things, including the self; an eternalist, by contrast, claims that God and the soul are eternal, self-existing realities. In contrast to both, interconnectedness and a lack of inherent existence suggests this middle path – things have reality, but it is a changing reality, always dependent upon conditions.

The same applies to concepts of value. To the nihilist, nothing in the world has value; to the eternalist, things have their own intrinsic value. The middle way here shows that things have value exactly in their arising in dependence upon conditions and in their relationships with everything else.

The balance of the middle way, in philosophical terms, is not simply one of compromise, but one which reflects the Buddha's fundamental vision of the nature of conditioned reality. In a world in which everything is interconnected, things have their existence and their life insofar as they connect. *Reality does not inhere in the whole only, nor in the individual only, but in the ever-changing set of relationships that lie between them.*

TRIPLE WAY

The Noble Eightfold Path is only one way of setting out the Buddhist dharma (teaching). Another common division is between:

▶ *Sila* (morality) – particularly the Five Precepts
▶ *Samadhi* (meditation) – including the step of mindfulness
▶ *Prajna* (wisdom) – reflecting the first two steps, but in practical terms the most subtle of the three, since it cannot be forced, but arises either in a moment of spontaneous insight, or as a result of practising both Sila and Samadhi.

Wisdom is regarded as accessible on three levels:

▶ *Shrutamayi prajna* – the wisdom that arises as a result of listening to or reading the sutras. It is accepted wisdom from the tradition in which one stands.
▶ *Cintamayi prajna* – the wisdom that develops as a result of personal reflection and thought.
▶ *Bhavanamayi prajna* – the highest form of wisdom, this comes as a result of an understanding that arises in the course of *bhavana*, spiritual practice.

Clearly, these levels are seen as leading on from one to another. First comes an understanding of the tradition, then a conscious, personal reflection on it, and finally the influence of that personally accepted wisdom into meditation and other practices, at which point the wisdom engages both the unconscious mind and the emotions, leading to spiritual insight.

Western

It is important to appreciate this threefold process of deepening wisdom in Buddhism, because it highlights the difference between Eastern and Western philosophy. In the West, philosophy has generally been regarded as a matter of intellectual and logical debate. Arguments are examined for logical coherence. Even with existentialist philosophy, where we explore the implications of personal choice and meaning, the aim is to relate these in a rational way to an overall view of life.

Buddhism regards all such philosophy as a starting point, not an end product. Its teachings are presented as a basis for meditation, allowing personal and unconscious influences to shed light upon them. As a result, much Buddhist philosophy does not appear to have the honed logic of a good Western argument, and it may often appear less rigorous because it may employ flowery imagery or be conveyed through the medium of story. But this merely reflects this three-layer approach to philosophical truth – the deepest level is not necessarily that which can be most easily set down on paper.

The self

The Buddha's teaching reflects the Hindu spiritual practice and language of his day, either by way of development, or by way of contrast. His views on the self may therefore be seen in contrast to those of the majority of Hindu philosophies, as set out in the previous chapter.

Hinduism generally accepts that there is an eternal self (Atman) which is linked with, but essentially independent of, the physical body. Thus, for example, in the *Gita* there is the famous passage in which the god Krishna, disguised as a charioteer, explained to Prince Arguna that people neither kill nor are killed in battle.

The body is destroyed but the self (Atman) continues and lives again. Equally, in the earlier Upanishadic literature, the goal of the spiritual life is the identification of the self (Atman) with the eternal Brahman.

One implication of this was that people were largely fixed by their unchanging identities, which in turn reinforced caste distinctions and – so it may be argued – led to a fatalism in terms of one's inability to shape one's own destiny.

In teaching *anatta*, the Buddha rejected the Hindu concept of the eternal Atman. The implication of interconnectedness is that each 'self' arises in dependence on conditions, is constantly changing as those conditions change, and will cease to exist in its present form at death.

In Buddhist teaching the self is described as made up of five *skandhas* ('heaps'). These are:

- ▶ *rupa* (form)
- ▶ *vedana* (feelings)
- ▶ *samjna* (perceptions)
- ▶ *samskara* (volitions)
- ▶ *vijnana* (consciousness).

Each of these is a temporary and changing 'bundle' of phenomena that, when put together, I conventionally call 'myself'. There is a wonderful illustration of the 'put togetherness' of the self in a book called *The Questions of King Milinda* from the 2nd century BCE. The monk Nagasena, using the fact that the King has come to visit him in a chariot, questions whether each part of the chariot (wheels, axle, etc.) are the chariot, and then points out that there is no chariot over and above these things. In the same way, the self comprises the five skandhas, but does not exist over and above them.

Western

David Hume famously argued that when he reflected upon himself, all he saw was a succession of mental events.

It is important also to note a 'nominalist' aspect of Buddhist thought here. Just because we conventionally name something 'the self' does not imply that there is a separate physical entity to which the name is given. For example, you would not dream of examining an eye and its optic nerve, along with the source of light that it is detecting, and then ask, 'Where, over and above these things, is sight?' 'Sight' is the name we choose to give to this process of seeing. Mind is the faculty of thinking, and consciousness is the name we give to that process of thinking and being aware.

There are parallels between Nagasena's 'chariot' argument and Gilbert Ryle's book, *The Concept of Mind*, where the traditional Western idea of a separate self or soul is termed 'the ghost in the machine'. The main difference, however, is that Ryle comes at the problem from a linguistic point of view, whereas for Buddhism it is part of the overall view of all life as comprising an interconnecting web of ever-changing phenomena.

It is therefore important, in examining the Buddhist view of the self, to set aside all Western, dualistic notions of mind and body. So, let us ask: What am I?

I am, first of all, a changing physical entity on its way from birth to death, a physical body that requires food, drink and oxygen, a body that is processing food into energy to maintain itself, a body that is totally dependent upon the rest of the physical world for its existence.

I am also aware of a constantly changing sequence of feelings, some good, some bad and some neutral, that arise in response to the things we perceive. As a result of our feelings and perceptions we have volitions, we make decisions, we act.

But arising as a result of these four skandhas is consciousness. There are different forms of consciousness, depending on the organ of the body in which it arises – sight, sound, smell, taste and touch (the usual five senses recognized in the West), along with mind, which Buddhism sees as the faculty of thought (just as the eye gives the faculty of sight). Consciousness is simply the process of seeing, touching, smelling, tasting, hearing, thinking; it is not a separate 'thing' of any sort. It is memory that gives the illusion of an on-going entity, since it is memory that allows awareness of continuity over time.

Western

Descartes, prepared to doubt everything known through the senses, could not doubt the fact of his own thought, and therefore concluded *cogito ergo sum* – 'I think, therefore I am'. He saw the mind, therefore, as something radically different from the experienced world of the senses. In Buddhist terms, the task of separating self from world is futile, because the self is part of the world and it totally integrated with it.

Mind is therefore not a 'thing' at all, it is a process (the Pali term for this is *santanna*). As individuals, we are the sum total of our actions of body, speech and mind. To have a mind that is more harmonious, more integrated, more sensitive (which is what Buddhism seeks to promote) does *not* imply that there is some separate entity that has these qualities. It is simply a way of describing the processes of speech and thought to which these qualities can apply.

What is the real me?

To this question Buddhist philosophy has a simple answer. The real you is what you are – what you feel, see, think and choose to do with your life. There is no elusive 'real' you somewhere else. Buddhism denies the validity of the quest for some definitive self other than the present ever-changing psycho-physical organism.

THE 'MIDDLE WAY' ON THE SELF

In presenting the radical difference between the Hindu and the Buddhist view of the self, notice that Buddhism attempts to avoid what it sees as the errors of eternalism and nihilism.

▶ An eternalist view disengages the self from any interconnectedness, and claims that is has at eternal essence. This may be seen as at attempt to gain some permanence and security in world where the body so obviously changes and decays.
▶ At the other extreme, the nihilist denies that there is any such thing as the self.

Both views attempt to make the self a separate 'thing' and then consider whether or not it exists, and if so what its nature can be. Buddhist teaching denies this as a valid way to approach the 'self'. For Buddhism, it is quite impossible to isolate a self from the conditions and connections within which it is embedded and operates. Without them it is nothing but, arising in dependence upon them, it has an interconnecting and changing reality.

Insight

It is important to keep this last point in mind. The idea of anatta (or the later term *shunyata* – which is generally translated as 'emptiness') seems to imply non-existence. But within Buddhism both terms have a positive role, and Buddhist philosophy and ethics only makes sense in the light of them. It is a philosophy of connections, of consequences, of ever-changing patterns. It is about recognizing the flow of life within which one participates. Even at a physical level, the atoms that make up your body have existed elsewhere and will do so again; you are but the name given to their present, temporary arrangement.

When individuals are defensively separated from their context in an ever-changing, interconnected world and forced to be the bearer of all values, Buddhism considers them a sorry sight, for their future inevitably involves decline and death. From that perspective, nothing seems worthwhile, since all ends in dust.

Once interconnectedness becomes a habitual way of seeing things, however, the existential power of suffering is broken. Sickness, old age and death continue, but as a natural part of a world in which an individual has links throughout time and space. This view is expressed through the ideas of karma and (particularly in later, Mahayana developments) of a 'Buddha nature' within all things. That is why, as a personal philosophy, Buddhism can be positive in its appreciation of life, and at the same time hold that only frustration and suffering can come from what it sees as the illusion of an independently existing self.

KARMA

The opening verse of the *Dhammapada*, an early collection of Buddhist teaching, says:

> **What we are today comes from our thoughts of yesterday, and our present thoughts build our life of tomorrow: our life is the creation of our mind.**

Buddhist philosophy does not take interconnectedness in a fatalistic way. Although everything arises in dependence upon conditions, once it has arisen it forms part of the conditions that allow the next thing to arise. In this sense, everything has a constructive part to play in the process of change.

Within its physical limitations, life is shaped by thoughts and decisions – both one's own and those of others. One's intentional actions have consequences. Karma simply means 'action', but within Buddhist philosophy it refers to actions done as a result of conscious act of volition. It is those things that you *choose* to do that shape who you are. There is therefore a constant process of creating new karma and also experiencing the results of past karma.

In Buddhism, there is no fixed essence, so what you will be in the future is determined by what you do now – by generating good or bad karma. In that sense, existence comes before essence – or, more correctly, essence is simply a conventional name given to certain features of existence.

Western

Buddhism and Existentialism agree that existence precedes essence. You do not play music because you are a musician, nor do good deeds because you are a good person; rather, a person who plays music is called a musician and one who does good deeds is called a good person. There are no unseen, inner qualities, simply descriptions of behaviour. You take responsibility for shaping your own life in the context of the circumstances in which you find yourself.

RE-BECOMING

Although Buddhists are sometimes said to believe in 'reincarnation', that is not strictly accurate. Reincarnation implies that there is a soul that lives in a body and then, at death, moves on to be incarnated again in a different body. Clearly, such a view is quite incompatible with the Buddhist view of anatta and the self as an ever-changing collection of skandhas.

For a Buddhist, what you are today is the result of what you were yesterday, and in turn shapes your tomorrow. You are constantly changing, shaped by your karma throughout life. The correct Buddhist term for this process is not reincarnation, but *punabhava* (re-becoming). At death, however, the whole network of inter-connections, and their karma, do not simply come to an end. They are still there, and what you have chosen to do today will have some impact on tomorrow, even if you die in the night. So the idea is that, in the future, other lives will take on and work though the karma that you have created.

An image used to describe this process is that of the flame of one lamp lighting another. The second flame is distinct from the first, but it is burning as a result of the burning of the first, although nothing physical passes from one to another.

The process whereby sensory experience leads to craving, karma and re-becoming may be expressed as a series of 12 links in a chain. These are called the *nidanas*. They are found on the well-known Buddhist 'Wheel of Life' image, running round the circumference of the wheel. This expresses in graphic form the fundamental Buddhist concept of 'conditioned co-production' or 'dependent origination'.

NIRVANA

There is some debate about exactly what the word *nirvana* (or *nibbana* in Pali) means. The literal interpretation is probably 'blowing out', in the sense of extinguishing a flame. It does *not* mean extinction, however, so nirvana is not the point at which the self ceases to exist. Rather, nirvana is described as the point at which the triple fire (of hatred, greed and ignorance) is extinguished because it has no more fuel to keep it burning. Put in a positive way, it is a point of absolute love, generosity and insight.

Nirvana is generally contrasted with *samsara*. Samsara describes the ordinary world, whose changes are the results of karma generated by hatred, greed and ignorance. The whole process of karma – leading from one action to another, from one state of mind to another, from one life to another – is regarded as inherently unsatisfactory. Fulfilment, in terms of Buddhist philosophy and spirituality, comes in getting beyond samsara. This does not imply removal from the world, but achieving a state in which a person is untouched by those things that bring suffering, and therefore also ceases to cause suffering in others.

Within the earliest Buddhist traditions, nirvana is seen as the ultimate point in the spiritual path, and a natural consequence of enlightenment. One who has achieved this is known as an *Arhat*. The other term used for one who has achieved this state is *tathagata*, which means 'one who has gone beyond', and it is generally used of the Buddha.

Insight

Buddhist philosophy does not include belief in God, so there is no union with an external, transcendent God at the end point of one's spiritual journey. Rather, the transcendence of Buddhism consists in progress towards ever higher levels of human consciousness, leading ultimately to enlightenment.

Buddhist philosophy suggests that, from an ego-centric point of view, life is always, ultimately a failure; the ego does not have inherent existence and is therefore always vulnerable to the conditions in which it finds itself. On the other hand, to become more and more aware of the interconnected nature of reality leads to an ego-less awareness, which, it is claimed, is able to free a person from craving and existential suffering.

The scope of the idea of nirvana in Buddhism is illustrated by the names used for it. These include *amata* (immortal), *asamkhata* (uncompounded) and *mutti* (freedom). What is certain is that nirvana does not mean the annihilation of the self, only the annihilation of the illusion of a self.

Nor should it be thought that the state of nirvana is such that, following it, there could be no more ordinary or painful experience. Rather, Buddhist philosophy suggests that the person who has experienced nirvana still experiences sensations as being pleasant, painful or neutral but, unlike other people, he or she does not become bound by them, recognizing that they are impermanent. The Buddha, following his enlightenment, was believed to be in exactly that state. Thus, although he ended up dying in considerable discomfort from what was probably food poisoning, the Buddha saw that as quite natural, and never suggested that his enlightenment should exempt him from such things.

The Abhidharma

Abhidharma means 'higher dharma' and presents a philosophical analysis of the Dharma and its implications. It is found in the Buddhist scriptures alongside the *sutras* (discourses of the Buddha, often presented in the form of dialogues) and the *Vinaya*, or monastic rules of conduct.

The sutras offer a collection of the Buddha's teachings, each set in a particular context; an individual generally approaches the Buddha and asks a question, which then leads into a discourse on that topic. But alongside individual stories, the Buddhist Sangha gathered together lists as an aid to the understanding and transmission of the teachings. The Abhidharma was developed out of these lists with the aim of providing an overall theoretical framework for the Dharma, so that it could be presented in a way that was both clear and comprehensive. Between about the 3rd century BCE and the 1st century CE, each of the early Buddhist schools (see below) would have developed its own Abhidharma, but much of this material is now lost.

THE ANALYSIS OF DHARMAS

Note

Whereas dharma means 'teaching' and, indeed, 'following the Dharma' is the preferred way of speaking about following the Buddhist path, the word dharma has a second meaning – 'thing' or 'entity'. Since the individual things we see and know do not have their own inherent selfhood (anatta), they are seen as composed of 'dharmas'.

We saw earlier that the basic teaching of 'anatta' was that all compound things lacked inherent existence, and were constantly subject to change. At a conventional level, we see individual people, tables, chairs and all the other objects of experience. Each appears to be a separate 'thing'. At the ultimate level of truth, however, they do not exist separately, they are simply a conventional way of gathering together, in something like a bundle, the various bits and pieces of which they are made. If we analyse complex things into their constituent parts, we eventually reach a bottom level at which they cannot be further divided – the 'dharmas'. The Abhidharma argued that these 'dharmas' were ultimately real in a way that complex entities were not.

Insight

From a modern perspective, there is an interesting dilemma at the heart of the whole process of analysis of dharmas.

First, you cannot be certain that your analysis has reached the very basic building blocks. At one time physicists considered the atom to be basic, then came sub-atomic particles, then the various quarks. What next? Is it possible to say that the quark is indivisible? Clearly, the process of analysis is theoretically limitless.

Second, the Abhidharma generally gives the impression that reality lies with the dharmas, rather than with the compound entities that they make up. Thus, through analysis, one comes to see things as they really are, rather than as they are conventionally perceived. So, if analysis is theoretically limitless, your perception of reality remains no more than a possibility. But enlightenment is seeing things as they really are. Therefore, following the logic of this argument, enlightenment must always be theoretical, never actual. One way out of this dilemma is to say that enlightenment is a matter of the experience of reality, and that is not necessarily the same as the analysis of reality, for you can experience something without being able to give an exhaustive analysis of it.

Third, following pratitya samutpada (interconnectedness) things arise in dependence upon conditions. Their reality is not inherent but is contingent upon those conditions. If each thing only becomes itself in connection with the whole (since everything theoretically influences everything else), then reality lies with the whole and in the process by which the whole causes particular things to arise, rather than with the particulars. If that is the case, then analysing dharmas in order to understand reality is a bit like counting individual bytes of memory on a computer chip in order to understand the software programme!

Perhaps the whole process of Abhidharma analysis can be seen as a Buddhist extension of the Hindu Upanishadic story of Svetaketu dividing the seeds, and arriving at a self that is identified with the invisible essence (see the section on 'Atman' in Chapter 1). The analysis of dharmas is a quest for reality. What is distinctively Buddhist, however, is the conclusion that everything that is 'put together' is devoid of self-existence, simply a compound and therefore liable to change.

THE EARLY BUDDHIST SCHOOLS

Because Buddhism did not have a fixed creed, but rather encouraged individual investigation, it was quite inevitable that there would, given time, develop a wide range of philosophical traditions. What is more, as Buddhism developed, it took into itself new cultural and religious phenomena and interpreted them in the light of its distinctive teachings.

It is usual to divide Buddhism into three *yanas* (or 'vehicles'):

▶ The *Hinayana* (a rather derogatory term, meaning 'small vehicle') is used of those who kept to the early and, arguably, narrow interpretation of the Dharma. There were many early schools which were later to be regarded as Hinayana, and it is with these that we are concerned in this section. Of those early schools, the main tradition extending to the present day is the Theravada (meaning 'Tradition of the Elders').

▶ The *Mahayana* (meaning 'large vehicle') developed alongside the early schools and incorporated many of the devotional approaches that are also found to have been developing within Hinduism in the first millennium CE. It became established in the more northern countries, especially China and Japan. We will examine Mahayana philosophy and Zen in later chapters.

▶ The *Vajrayana* (meaning the 'diamond vehicle' or 'thunderbolt vehicle') incorporated Tantric elements. This is found in particularly in Tibetan Buddhism. Tantra is also found within Hinduism and is discussed in Chapter 7.

Although later traditions also claim to go back to the teaching of Gautama, the historical Buddha, it is widely accepted that the early schools, as they have come down to us through the Pali Canon (the oldest surviving collection of Buddhist scriptures), and preserved today within the Theravada tradition, represent the closest we can get to the original Buddhist Dharma.

The Sthaviravadin School

At the Second Council, a gathering of the leaders of the Buddhist monastic community in about 345 BCE, there was a basic split between the Mahasanghikas (who wanted a broader interpretation of monastic practice) and the Sthaviravadins, (who were traditionalists). Of the Sthaviravadins, the only remaining representative today is the Theravada tradition. The Sthaviravadins held that Buddha was an ordinary mortal, and that his enlightened followers (called Arhats) had equalled his attainment. They promoted traditional analytic meditations involving the systematic analysis of dharmas, and tended to reject whatever seemed to be elaboration or speculation in connection with the Buddha.

They held that what we perceive with the senses *is* the external world, and it is independent of our perceiving it. Our experiences are not *representations* from which we have to deduce externally existing objects, they *are* those external objects, as mediated through our senses. Hence the practice of analysis in meditation – one simply becomes more aware of the subtleties of what exists.

Their opponents, the Mahasanghikas, considered the apparent ordinariness of the Buddha was actually an illusion, and that in reality he was super-mundane, born out of his mother's side and having no mundane impurities. This approach was a forerunner of the Mahayana schools of Buddhism. In particular, they started to speak of the Buddha as having a career spanning many different births, in each of which the *Bodhisattva* (meaning 'Buddha-to-be') developed his spiritual qualities.

The Sarvastavadin School

This school divided off from the Sthaviravadins in the third century BCE. Their distinctive philosophy is summed up in the expression *sarvam asti* (everything exists). They argued that all dharmas exist, but in three different modes – past, present or future. When you remember something that happened in the past, you are actually having knowledge of a present dharma, but one which exists in 'past' mode. They argued that the simultaneous existence of all things in this way provided the basis for the operation of the law of karma, for the cause and the effect existed at the same time, albeit in different modes.

Two other features of the Sarvastavadin School, developed within the Mahayana tradition, will be considered there – one is the popular image of the 'Wheel of Life'. The other is the idea that a Buddha-to-be should practice Six Perfections (*paramitas*).

The Sautrantika School

This branched off from the Sarvastavadin School. It rejected the Abhidharma of the other schools, and argued that dharmas were only momentary, and that they could not exist in three modes. It reasoned that, when you perceive something, all you are actually aware of are mental images. There might indeed have been a dharma that gave rise to the mental image, but you cannot get independent evidence for it – by the time you have the image, the dharma has already vanished. Thus, I do not see some 'thing' that is green, I simply see the qualities of greenness and shape and deduce the existence of a 'thing' from them. Everything is just a bundle of ever-changing sensations.

Western

John Locke held that all knowledge comes in the form of sense perceptions, and Bishop Berkeley had a view quite like that of the Sautrantika school, arguing that it is impossible to know that something exists if there is nobody to perceive it.

The Sautrantika approach also has parallels with Kant's distinction between the noumenal and phenomenal realms, since things-in-themselves remain essentially unknowable.

One of the problems this raises is how it is possible, if dharmas have no continuity, for the law of karma to work. How can something that no longer exists affect your present state? The answer given by this school was that actions 'perfume' one's ongoing mental state, and thus influence what will happen later. This view may have given rise to the later Mahayana teaching that there are 'seeds' planted by present action, waiting to ripen at an appropriate time in the future.

There were many sub-groups within these early schools. Their variety was inevitable, given the freedom from doctrinal orthodoxy within Buddhism, and the requirement that everyone should examine and come to his or her own personal conviction. One of the main thinkers representing this early core of Buddhist thought is Buddhaghosa, who lived in the 5th century CE. His main work *Visuddhimagga* (The Path of Purification) gives a synthesis of the teachings found in the Pali Canon.

Meditation

Buddhism is not based on belief in God, but on becoming progressively more aware of reality and living in accordance with the insights gained in that process. The mental practices associated with Buddhism do not, therefore, take the form of prayer to a deity, but exercises designed to cultivate greater sensitivity and awareness.

There are many forms of Buddhist meditation, but they can be divided into two basic forms: *samatha* (which seeks to develop calm, one-pointedness of mind) and *vipassana* (which seeks to develop insight into the nature of reality). Within the Buddhist tradition, these were later developed and augmented by visualization and other practices, some of which we shall consider in the chapters on Mahayana Buddhism, Tantra and Zen.

SAMATHA

The basic samatha practice is 'mindfulness' – *sati* (in Pali) or *smrti* (in Sanskrit). The literal meaning of this term is 'remembering' or 'recollecting', and it refers to any process in which a person consciously seeks to become immediately aware of their body, feelings, mental processes or the objects of thought. Mindfulness is a matter of being aware of what is happening in the present moment, while still being fully engaged in that moment.

This last point is most important in any understanding of the place of meditation within Buddhism and of the philosophy that lies behind it. It is possible to stand back from immediate experience and gain a detached, almost alienated awareness of one's body, feelings or thoughts. This attempts to separate off the observing self from the process that is being observed. But this does not fit Buddhist philosophy at all, for it implies that the self (which is doing the observing) exists independent of the body and its various sensations, feelings and thoughts, while Buddhism teaches that there is no such fixed self: we are the sum total of the processes through which we are living. It is not that we observe sensations or feelings as though they had a separate existence from ourselves, but that we become aware of ourselves experiencing those things.

The other essential feature of meditation, as it relates to Buddhist philosophy, is that it takes place in the present. The past no longer exists, and the future has not yet come into existence. Reality is only to be encountered in the present moment, and even then it is a present moment that is constantly changing. A basic skill to be learned in Buddhist meditation is catching the fleeting experience as it is happening, rather like a surfer learning to balance on the crest of a wave as it moves forward.

Once a person loses the immediate experience and starts to think about it, he or she moves back from the present moment and mentally starts to describe or categorize what is happening, or to dwell in the past (memory) or future (fantasy based on desires or fears). When that happens, the wave of immediacy is lost and the person meditating has re-entered the more habitual state, in which past, future and self-consciousness dominate. Once such a distraction is recognized, the mind has to be brought back to focus on the present and the process starts over again. The surfer has to paddle back and mount the next wave!

Insight

Samatha meditation is the art of being creatively aware of what is happening in the present moment. This is where Buddhist philosophy and Buddhist meditation practice reinforce one another. The experience of the fleeting moment is an experience of anicca and anatta, and that experience reinforces change and interconnectedness as a habitual way of looking at reality.

The other crucial thing to be aware of in Samatha practice is that it is an end in itself, as well as being a preparation for insight meditation. For those who meditate within this tradition, it brings its own benefits and leads to an intuitive grasp of reality, as well as an experience of integration and calmness.

One of the most basic practices is the mindfulness of breathing. In this, attention is focused on the process of breath entering and leaving the body. The apparent simplicity of this is deceptive, and maintaining the awareness of breath is far form easy for a beginner, but it can lead to calmness and a sense of integrity. Notice that awareness is not focused on a theory, or any external concept, but on an actual process – which is indeed the most basic and essential process for life. This is exactly in line with basic Buddhist philosophy, which rejects speculation in favour of immediate experience.

VIPASSANA

Vipassana mediation aims to go beyond the quest for calmness and receptiveness to include direct insight into the Buddhist view of reality. As a result, within vipassana, one may meditate on one or more of the Buddhist teachings in order to engage with that teaching with the whole of oneself – unconscious as well as conscious. The aim is to get a 'feeling' for the teaching, rather than accepting it intellectually.

Is it appropriate to have even these brief comments on meditation in a book on philosophy? I think it is, and have included them because they highlight a crucial difference between Eastern and Western philosophy; namely that Eastern philosophy is concerned with *experienced* reality as well as *conceptualized* reality. The concepts that appear in Buddhist philosophy are not presented simply as a conclusion reached from reason and evidence (even if reason and evidence can subsequently be used to justify them) but on an intuitive grasp of reality, and that process is underpinned by meditation.

Ethics

Buddhist ethics do not generally speak of thoughts and actions being either good or bad, right or wrong, but:

▶ *kushala* (skilful) – if based on compassion, generosity and wisdom
▶ *akushala* (unskilful) – if based on hatred, craving and delusion.

The reason for this is that an action, if analysed objectively, may have quite different interpretations depending on the circumstances within which it is performed. Skilful actions are those that are able to bring about an increase in happiness and are conducive to following the Buddhist path. Unskilful actions are those that lead to unhappiness and make it more difficult to follow the Buddhist path.

Examples

Taking a knife to someone's chest has very different implications depending on whether one is a surgeon or an assassin.

The act of sexual intercourse has quite different implications depending on whether those involved are friends or strangers, married to one another or to other people, willing or unwilling participants.

Buddhist ethics therefore take into account the context of each action and the motivation of those involved. Notice that this is another implication of the fundamental principle of interconnectedness.

Things are not good or bad in themselves, but are only deemed so because of the way in which they relate to those involved. Actions have consequences (we considered this principle under 'Karma'). Equally, actions take place because of existing conditions. An action cannot exist in isolation from its conditions or consequences.

Once again then, we see that Buddhist philosophy has no fixed building blocks, but only a fluid pattern of connections in assessing anything from a moral point of view. Having said that, there are a substantial number of precepts and moral principles available to guide Buddhists.

THE FIVE PRECEPTS

Precepts are not fixed rules, but principles of training. They illustrate the qualities that would be expected of a person who was enlightened, and are therefore a guide for those seeking enlightenment. They are most commonly set out in their negative form, as things to be avoided:

1 I undertake not to take life.
2 I undertake not to take the not-given.
3 I undertake to abstain from misuse of the senses.
4 I undertake not to speak falsely.
5 I undertake to avoid those things that cloud the mind.

Each of these principles of training gives rise to a positive counterpart:

1 To develop loving-kindness and compassion towards all living things.
2 To develop generosity.
3 To cultivate stillness, simplicity and contentment.
4 To seek to speak truthfully, gently, positively and with purpose.
5 To develop mindfulness.

Buddhism aims to balance morality, meditation and wisdom (*sila, samadhi* and *prajna*) in its spiritual path. Buddhists do not present morality as a means to an end, making it a necessary requirement if one is to achieve enlightenment. Rather, since everything arises in dependence upon conditions, Buddhists claim that basic morality is a condition which enables other features of the Buddhist path to arise. It also reflects the view (anatta) that the self does not have separate or independent existence, whereas the illusion of a separate self leads to a privileging of oneself and one's own needs over those of others.

It is important to note that these are not commandments, given by some external deity, with the threat of punishment if they are broken. They are simply the Buddha's summary of the kind of life that allows wisdom and compassion to arise. Buddhists are free to decide how best to apply these guidelines to individual situations, recognizing that every moment and event is unique.

Of course, Buddhist ethics also reflect the theory of karma. Volitional intentions determine future states, and it is the intention that counts, not just the carrying out of the deed – although the karmic consequences are likely to be more serious if the deed is subsequently carried out.

Western

There is a parallel here with Jesus' moral teachings, for he argues that the attitudes of lust or hatred, not just the subsequent deeds of adultery and murder, deserve punishment. The reason for this would seem to be that both Jesus and the Buddha were approaching the matter of morality primarily from a soteriological point of view. In other words, they were primarily concerned with the effect that the action would have on the spiritual life of those concerned. Neither was considering it solely from the point of view of the right ordering of society, from which perspective it is the action that is crucial and the intention is generally of secondary importance.

MONASTICISM

The majority of Buddhists have followed the Dharma while continuing to live a family life. On the other hand, monasticism has always played an important role in Buddhism, and many accounts of Buddhism as a world religion emphasize it to the point at which lay Buddhism may seem but a preliminary or inferior form of the religion.

Following the Hindu ascetic tradition of his day, the Buddha had left the family home to enter into the life of a wandering seeker after truth (a *shramanera*), and his first followers were drawn from these ascetic circles. It was these 'full-time' members who spread the teaching, and handed on its oral and later written traditions.

Much of the Buddhist literature is concerned with rules for those who are have chosen to be under monastic discipline, and this reflects the centrality of the monastic community for the transmission of the teachings.

On the other hand, in his teaching (as recorded in the sutras) the Buddha regularly taught lay people. Although the monastic life makes it easier to follow the Buddhist path, by providing an ordered structure to life and by avoiding obvious distractions, monasticism is not immediately relevant to the fundamental philosophical concepts of Buddhist Dharma with which we are concerned. The basic Dharma remains the same, whether practised by monk, nun or layperson. Similarly, when it comes to ethics, the rules of the monastic vinaya are presented in addition to the basic Buddhist precepts.

Buddhism and philosophical speculation

It will be clear by now that Buddhism is certainly not against philosophy. At its peak, before being destroyed in the Muslim invasions of northern India, the Buddhist University of Nalanda had some 3,000 scholars drawn from all over India and also from China, Korea, Tibet, Mongolia, Sri Lanka and Sumatra. Systematic study was at the heart of Buddhist training, and Nalanda offered courses in grammar and philology, medicine, logic, the fine arts and metaphysics.

On the other hand, the Buddha was concerned to distinguish between things that could be examined profitably and those metaphysical questions that would never be resolved and which might prove to be no more than a distraction. Questions the Buddha refused to answer include:

▶ whether the world is finite or eternal
▶ whether the enlightened person does or does not exist after death.

Now this might seem a major oversight, especially since we are looking at the Buddhist contribution to Eastern philosophy. On closer inspection, however, the matter becomes clearer. What the Buddha was refusing to do was to take sides in contemporary philosophical debate. One reason for this may well have been that all such debate depends on the acceptance of key terms and concepts, and by refusing to enter into metaphysical debate he was emphasizing the inadequacy of existing concepts. As in many areas, the Buddha sought to take a middle path. To have said that the world was eternal would have been inadequate to the point of being wrong. On the other hand, to say that it was not eternal would have been equally misleading. He therefore affirms a 'neither this, neither that' approach and refuses to give an answer that could subsequently be misunderstood.

More importantly, however, by denying the validity of such questions, and by insisting that his sole aim was to resolve the problem of human suffering, he effectively makes speculation for its own sake a sideline, emphasizing the place of the problem of suffering and the means of overcoming it at the heart of the philosophical quest.

In one of the collections of early sutras (the *Majjhima Nikaya*), the Buddha says that any idea of 'I am this' is a conceiving, or 'I shall be formless' is a conceiving. He wants none of this speculation and declared:

> '... *conceiving is a disease, conceiving is a tumour, conceiving is a dart.*'
>
> (MN 140)

By overcoming all such conceiving one may become 'a sage at peace'.

Those who concentrate on the cultural or religious artefacts of Buddhism – the temples, monks and images – may miss the very radical nature of the Buddhist view of reality. It is a view which cannot be encapsulated in conceptual terms alone. But above all else, it is a view of the world as dynamic, as a process of interconnecting relationships and conditions.

Western

For a Western thinker – schooled since Descartes with the idea that 'I think, therefore I am', and thus the self as an indubitable fixed point, or since Aquinas in the idea of God as an unmoved mover, uncaused cause, source of all values, the intelligent and purposeful designer – these twin certainties of much traditional Western metaphysics are removed by Buddhism. In their place is an ever-changing reality which is only known in its immediacy and through participation, never captured conceptually.

For Western philosophy, which takes this element of change and process seriously, one might look at Heraclitus among the ancients. Among modern philosophers, process has been a major theme of H. Bergson and A. N. Whitehead.

If Buddhism were simply a philosophy, the term used for it would be *darsana* (meaning 'view' or 'direct vision' and used of all the major Indian philosophies). In fact, another term is used – *yana*, 'vehicle'. Buddhism is therefore seen as a spiritual vehicle, a means of making progress. Those things that do not contribute to the liberation of human beings from suffering and ignorance may be ignored as irrelevant.

The *Mahaparinibbana Sutta* contains a list of essential teachings, believed to have been given by the Buddha, shortly before his death, to his cousin and companion Ananda. The list contains seven key features, broken down into what are known as the '37 Aids to Enlightenment'. It is interesting that this summary contains no speculative propositions of any kind. It includes the cultivation of awareness of body, feeling, mental states and objects of thought, moving on to describe the right efforts required, spiritual faculties and powers to be explored, even enlightenment factors including mindfulness, awareness of Dharma, enthusiastic effort, rapture, serenity, concentration and equanimity. It also includes the Eightfold Path, described above.

Such a summary should come as no surprise, since pratitya samutpada (interconnectedness) – which is the key concept at the very heart of the whole of Buddhist philosophy – points out that all things arise in dependence upon conditions. What the Buddha set out in his summary of teachings was the set of spiritual parameters that aimed to help individuals to create the conditions which would allow them to become enlightened.

Western

In scientific research, the observer and method of observation may influence the conclusions reached. So, for example, in psychoanalysis the analyst is trained to recognize and eliminate the influence of his or her own prejudices. In other words, there is a recognition of the connection between conditions, method and conclusions. Only if the former is acknowledged and taken into account can the latter is to be assessed correctly.

> In Postmodernism, the material, the medium and the method of artistic creation are the object of attention. One cannot pretend that there is some abstract 'reality' to be communicated which is external to and independent of the vehicle of its communication.
>
> By emphasizing the conditions required for insight, rather than simply stating its conceptual content, Buddhism acknowledges the interconnection between methods and results.

In a traditional Buddhist formulation, the *Ti Ratana Vandana* (Salutation to the Three Jewels), the Buddha's teaching is described as:

> *Sanditthiko akaliko ehipassiko opanayiko paccatam veditabbo vinnuiti.*

A broad translation of which would be:

> *Immediately obvious; always available; something to be examined by trying it out; progressive; to be understood individually by those who are wise.*

In other words, Buddhist philosophy claims to be an undogmatic, rational and pragmatic approach to understanding reality.

10 THINGS TO REMEMBER

1 The key concept for Buddhist thought is interconnectedness (*pratitya samutpada*).

2 The three marks of existence are: anicca, anatta and dukkha.

3 The four Noble Truths are: dukkha, tanha, nirodha and magga.

4 The Noble Eightfold Path is a way of setting out the Buddhist dharma.

5 The self is a bundle of five skadhas: form, feelings, perceptions, volitions and consciousness.

6 Buddhism teaches 're-becoming' *not* reincarnation.

7 The early Buddhist Schools of philosophy practised analysis of dharmas.

8 Meditation aims to cultivate insight to support Buddhist philosophy.

9 The precepts are principles for training, not externally imposed moral rules.

10 Buddhist thought is undogmatic and pragmatic.

3

....

Jainism

In this chapter you will:
- *explore the background to and teachings of Mahavira*
- *learn some basic features of Jain philosophy*
- *consider how Jain philosophy compares with some other branches of Buddhist and Hindu thought.*

Jainism is a philosophy and a religion in which the principle of *ahimsa* (non-violence) is absolutely central to both theory and practice. Like other Eastern philosophies, its aim is not disinterested speculation, but rather the development of a means of helping people overcome the suffering inherent in ordinary human existence. It seeks to do this by conquering worldly limitations, and the word *jina* (from which the name Jainism comes) means 'conqueror'.

Jain tradition claims that there has been a succession of 24 teachers, known as the 'ford-makers' (*tirthankaras*) since they help their followers to cross over the stream of this world to a place of security and salvation. Of these, only the last is recognized as an historical person. He was known as Mahavira (meaning 'great hero') and lived in the fifth or sixth century BCE.

Although Jainism, as it is known today, stems from the teaching of Mahavira, Jains claim that it is far older and that Mahavira was simply repeating teachings, given by the earlier ford-makers, which have permanent and universal validity.

Background: Mahavira

Vardhamana Mahavira was a heterodox ascetic who lived and taught in the area of India now known as Bihar and Uttar Pradesh, and was probably an older contemporary of the Buddha. His dates are sometimes given as 599–527 BCE although he may have lived rather later – 540 to 468 BCE.

The 6th century BCE was a time of great social change in Northern India. Increasing numbers of people were moving from small rural communities to live in cities, trade was expanding, wealth accumulating, and the kingdoms of Kosala and Magadha were consolidating power and displacing the earlier tribal systems of government. It was also a time of great violence. Whole tribal groups were massacred, including those from which both Mahavira and the Buddha came.

It was also a time when orthodox Hindu philosophy and religion were being challenged. Groups of these freelance spiritual teachers and ascetics wandered about, gaining converts and operating quite outside the orthodox pattern of Hindu rituals and the caste system. Such teachers were generally known as *Shramanas*, and in the case of two of them – Mahavira and the Buddha – their teachings have formed the basis of two philosophies that have continued to this day: Jainism and Buddhism.

In order to be regarded as orthodox, Hindu thought accepts:

▶ the authority of the Vedas (scriptures)
▶ the validity of ceremonies performed by Brahmins (priests).

Both of these were challenged by the Shramanas, who were therefore considered to be unorthodox.

Some unorthodox teachers took a basically materialist view. For example, the Lokayata philosophy of Charvaka (see Chapter 2) claimed that all knowledge is ultimately based on the senses, and therefore only what can be perceived in this way can be real. Charvaka therefore argued that there could be no soul and no life after death. The logical implication of this was that happiness in this life was the only valid pursuit, and he therefore took a position that encouraged hedonism. But there were others who, from a similar philosophical position, came to the opposite conclusion and encouraged ascetic practices as the method of gaining moksha (liberation), among them both Mahavira and the Buddha.

Mahavira is said to have left his home at the age of 30, and to have spent 12 years as a naked ascetic, during which time he became associated with Gosala, the founder of the Ajivikas (another heterodox Hindu sect). At 42 he is believed to have achieved enlightenment, and is therefore known as a *jina* (conqueror).

Hence his followers are known as *Jainas* (usually shortened to Jains) or 'followers of the conqueror'.

After teaching for a period of about 30 years, Mahavira died at Pava, near modern Patna, which has become a place of Jain pilgrimage. By the time of his death he had a very large following of monks and nuns (women outnumbering men), who were supported by lay followers. He is mentioned in Buddhist scriptures, where he is known as Nigantha Nataputta, and the situation described there is one in which there is a generally friendly rivalry between the followers of Mahavira and those of the Buddha. Some Buddhist sutras (e.g. Sutra 56 of the *Majjhima Nikaya*) set out philosophical debates between representatives of the two traditions.

THE TEACHINGS OF MAHAVIRA

Sometimes, where there are different sects within a religion, it is difficult to assess which of competing doctrinal claims is the authentic voice of the founder. This is not a problem for Jainism, for although there are two main sects (the *Svetambaras* and the *Digambaras*), the disagreement was on a matter of practice (whether or not their monks should wear clothes) rather than on their interpretation of basic Jain philosophy. We may therefore be fairly confident that the concepts that have been handed down within the Jain tradition do actually reflect the original teachings of Mahavira.

Insight

Although beyond the scope of this brief introduction, you should keep in mind that there are some scholars (e.g. N. N. Bhattacharyya, see 'Further reading') who argue that the materialism taught by Mahavira was later modified in the light of orthodox Hindu ideas, which now mask the very radical and scientific nature of the earlier thought.

He rejected Brahmin rituals as a method of achieving moksha (release), reinterpreting the Hindu concept of karma, which in orthodox Hinduism had been applied primarily to the results flowing from the correct performance of rituals. He also denied the existence of an eternal, divine realm, believed that the human soul was entrapped within the material world, and he made ahimsa (not taking life) absolutely central to his philosophy and practical ethics.

His teachings were not set down in writing until the 2nd century CE, and not until the 5th century CE was there an overall edition of the major Jain scriptures. For understanding Jain philosophy, the key work (accepted as authoritative by all Jain sects) is the *Tattvartha Sutra* ('A Manual for Understanding All That Is'), written by a philosopher-monk Umasvati in the 2nd century.

Basic concepts

A superbly succinct summary of Jain philosophy is given by Nathmal Tatia in the introduction to his translation of the *Tattvartha Sutra*:

> **The central themes of the Tattvartha Sutra *are non-violence, non-absolutism and non-possession. Non-violence strengthens the autonomy of life of every being. Non-absolutism strengthens the autonomy of thought of every individual. Non-possession strengthens the interdependence of all existence. If you feel that every soul is autonomous you will never trample on its right to live. If you feel every person is a thinking person you will not trample on his or her thoughts. If you feel that you own nothing and no-one, you will not trample on the planet.***

Tattvartha Sutra (p. xvii)

There are three basic features of Jain philosophy that need to be appreciated before we can move on to consider the Jain idea of the self and Jain ethics:

▶ non-absolutism in philosophy
▶ atomism and animism
▶ the atheistic interpretation of the cosmic process.

ANEKANTAVADA (NO ABSOLUTES)

Jainism is radical in challenging the basis of its own teachings. In particular, it makes no claim to absolute truth, but highlights the fact that all truths depend on the perspective from which they are viewed, and therefore that all knowledge is partial. So, for example, in considering the nature of the self, it considers that:

▶ The self may be permanent.
▶ The self may not be permanent.
▶ The self may, from different perspectives, be both permanent and non permanent.
▶ The matter may be ineffable (i.e. we cannot know one way or the other).

But – to make matters rather more complicated – these four options may be combined. So, for example, the soul might be permanent, but the matter might also be ineffable (so that it *may* be so, but we cannot *know* that it is so). In which case there are seven different combinations possible.

We can know things both directly and indirectly, but nothing (given the limitations imposed by this world we encounter with our senses) can be known completely or with absolute certainty. What is more, it is argued that the truth or distortion of our knowledge is not determined by our ability to grasp facts, but rather because of the ethical and spiritual values that form our particular standpoint.

An example

Suppose I look at a tree. I may say:

▶ There's some useful shade or shelter.
▶ That would be good to climb.
▶ There's some useful timber.
▶ It is an oak.
▶ It has grown since I saw it last.
▶ It will have to be felled.

Each of these perspectives is valid, whether it is concerned with past, present or future, and whether the tree is seen in itself (and categorized in terms of species) or simply viewed as a commodity or source of entertainment or comfort. Each has an element of truth, but each is limited by its particular perspective. Of course, I may be mistaken – the tree is a beech rather than an oak – but that may not invalidate the other statements about it.

Because absolute knowledge (even if we possessed it) could not properly be communicated using limited concepts, all claims should be seen as relative and provisional, and apparent contradictions may simply be the result of differences in perspectives. This approach does not prevent Jainism from making definite statements, but it adds a qualification to every part of Jain teaching – a qualification that recognizes the standpoint from which it is made, and therefore its limited validity. Jainism always accepts that others may see things differently.

Insight

It is difficult to overstate the importance of this non-absolutism for an appreciation of the contribution of Jain thought. By recognizing the limitations imposed on knowledge by human perspectives and intentions, it took a leap forward towards modern science, and presented a radical challenge to a world still dominated by speculative metaphysics.

ATOMISM AND ANIMISM

In traditional Jain teaching, the atom is the smallest element of matter, and there are four kinds of atoms: air, fire, water and earth. These atoms gather together to form *skandhas* (compounds), which are the objects we experience within the world. But there are other, non-physical elements that also form part of the world: joy, sorrow and life itself – the last of which, in the form of the living self or soul (*jiva*) is most important in Jain philosophy.

Mahavira taught that everything has a soul within it. Not just humans, animals and plants, but even rocks, earth and wind; and not just permanent entities, but even brief events have a soul that is born within them and lives for as long as that event takes place. Jain philosophy therefore recognizes a constant process of interaction between physical matter and the living self. Whatever capacity a soul has – for example to sense things – it has because of the world of matter (sense organs are physical). On the other hand, those organs are nothing if they are not informing a living soul. Although they are equally real and distinct, soul and matter are inseparable.

As we have seen, Jainism is not afraid to offer very different perspectives alongside one another. So it can also speak of eternal substances, each with specific qualities, the highest of which is jiva. In itself jiva is perfect and eternal, but under the influence of the phenomenal world it can take on a body and be born over and over again within the world, taking the form of celestial beings, humans or any other creature.

Insight

Here Jain thought moves closer to orthodox ideas of the unity of Atman and Brahman. What we cannot know is whether these were part of the original teaching of Mahavira, or were the result of later influences. Given that Jain thought accepts the relativity of all claims, this is less important than it would be for a philosophy that claimed its statements as absolute truth.

Thus you have a universe in which everything is a compound, made up of both physical and non-physical elements. It is materialistic (in that the non-physical elements of life and mind are constituents of the individual things we experience) rather than dualistic. Jiva is a substance, part of every compound thing, a view generally referred to as 'animism'.

Western

Within Western philosophy, atomism was one strand of Pre-Socratic Greek thought, seen in the work of Leucippus and Democritus, and later to become the basis of Epicurean philosophy. It is also, of course, the basis of modern science.

In terms of the relationship between matter and spirit, this is not the same as the dualism of Descartes, for Descartes was making a radical distinction between an unextended, thinking self and an extended physical body. One might look more towards the thought of Henri Bergson or Teilhard de Chardin, for the sense of the spirit animating matter.

The Gnostics held a view of eternal souls, trapped within material bodies, and their goal – like that of Jainism – was release from material limitations and achieving awareness of one's eternal nature. But this only applies to one aspect of Jain thought, in which it comes nearer to an orthodox Hindu approach.

ATHEISM AND THE EVER-CHANGING UNIVERSE

Jainism is atheistic. There are no absolutes, and (unlike Hinduism) there is no final unification of the Atman with an eternal Brahman. Instead, final release is the recognition that one's spirit is actually the absolute reality (the point of recognizing this is a state called *kavala*). The world is without beginning, but it is seen as moving through periods of evolution and dissolution. It requires no external explanation, and the process of change comes about because of the working of the laws of karma, and because everything is inherently unstable and compounded. It is karma that drives the universe, not God.

Jainism appears to hold together two contradictory views of things: that they are permanent, but also that they are in a constant state of flux. It does this by saying that something 'real' continues in existence, although it passes through an innumerable number of 'modes'. At any one time, these modes are changing, and the thing appears, therefore, to be coming into existence and passing out of existence. On the other hand, it remains real – and therefore continues to exist – throughout this process. This is another example of Jainism recognizing that truth depends on perspective. Things both have and do not have permanent existence; it all depends on the way in which you look at them.

The self

Since Jainism is not primarily a speculative attempt to understand the world, but a method of spiritual development and release, its aim is to help people to escape from the limitations of the material world within which it sees their souls as trapped. What is says about the self is therefore of key importance, but we need to keep in mind what has been said above about the *anekantavada* world view – namely, that there is more than one way of looking at things, and therefore that souls both have and do not have permanent existence, depending on how you consider them.

SOULS (JIVA) AND PHYSICAL BODIES (AJIVA)

In Jain philosophy, an individual consists of a soul born in the form of a physical body, and salvation lies in releasing the soul from its material constraints. In order to make progress towards this end, the body needs to be controlled and disciplined. This approach is similar to that of the Hindu Sankhya school of philosophy.

One's path through *samsara* (the every-changing world that we experience) is determined, and one can only reach moksha (release) after a long period during which the soul moves through a very large number of different lives. The existence of the soul is not something that Jains feel the need to prove, because they believe that the soul is acknowledged in every act of cognition; thinking, feeling and being aware of being alive is therefore what being a soul is all about.

It is quite difficult to conceptualize the Jain view of the soul. On the one hand it is present everywhere, but on the other it is, in a sense, material. It is almost an animating physical substance, available everywhere and capable of bringing an appropriate body to life. What is clear, however, is that there is a difference between an individual soul and the 'soul material' of which it is formed. Thus there are innumerable soul units in the soul, just as there are innumerable space units in space (*Tattvartha Sutra* 5.8; 5.9) or atoms in the body. In other words, just as material atoms clump together to form a physical object, so soul units gather together to form the individual self. It is this that makes the Jain view very different from that of the orthodox schools.

Insight

It is interesting to compare this view with the Buddhist one. Buddhism holds that everything is subject to change and therefore that there are no permanent souls, just a series of changing features that make up the self. Jainism is just as radical in terms of analysing the process of change, but is then able to say that, from another perspective, there is an enduring 'self' that continues in spite of the changes. Another example of Jainism taking a relativist view of truth.

KARMA-VADA (ACTION AND CONSEQUENCES)

Jainism takes a radical and literal view of the general Hindu idea of karma. In the round of incarnations within the samsara world, one's lot in life depends on one's previous karma. But unlike Buddhism, which regards karma as being generated by one's volitional (ethically significant actions), Jainism sees karma in a broader context of everything that conditions a person. You are affected by karma even without any conscious choice on your own part. Actions produce karma all the time, but karma is said to stick to individuals because of their desires, hence the only way to escape from the rounds of rebirth is to achieve a state of perfect tranquillity and knowledge (kavala), progressively setting aside all desires. What is more, Jains believe that the soul should be omniscient (i.e. it should know everything that it is possible to know), but in this world it has lost this omniscience and is limited in what it can know by its karma. In this way, the ascetic life avoids the effects of karma and thereby enables a person to gain knowledge.

Insight

What Jainism has done is to accept the mechanism of karma, as it had developed within Hindu philosophy, and take it to its logical conclusion in an atheist context. If the avoidance of the effects of karma is the mechanism for improving the self within a world of change, then nothing more is needed; any intervention by a god or gods only confuses the issue – by claiming, through devotion or sacrifices, to override one's karma in order to improve one's spiritual destiny. Karma cannot be subject to divine interference.

....

LIBERATION (MOKSHA)

Although Jainism teaches that your soul (jiva) is eternal and omniscient, it doesn't appear to be so in this world, because it is limited now by its material form and by its karma. Liberation (moksha) comes about when the self is freed from all the implications of past actions. Therefore one must ultimately disengage from all action, good or bad. Good actions are not enough to enable one to achieve moksha, since they only benefit the soul while within the world of samsara, they do not allow it to rise above it.

The goal of Jains is to become a *siddha* (perfect one) – siddhas are said to have infinite knowledge, vision, strength and bliss. In this state, one realizes that the jiva is the ultimate reality and thereby frees it:

> **When all karmic bondage is eliminated, the soul soars upwards to the border of cosmic space**
>
> (*Tattvartha Sutra* 10.5)

Here we see, once again, an example of the fundamentally materialist Jain philosophy taking on the language of dualistic Hinduism. Even though, in the ordinary course of events, souls inevitably interact with matter, the point of liberation is the point at which matter is left behind. It is, however, difficult to decide whether this is the result of the progressive influence of Vedanta on Jain thinking, or whether it simply reflects the ability of Jain philosophy to hold together contradictory perspectives.

Reinterpretations of Hindu concepts

It is important to recognize that Hindu philosophy is very varied – as we saw in Chapter 1 – and it is therefore difficult to define exactly how Jain philosophy relates to the orthodox traditions. The fact that it is regarded as unorthodox does not relate to its philosophy, but to its rejection of the authority of the Vedas and Brahmin rituals. Although confusing, we have to accept that Jain ideas can sometimes parallel those of other schools of Indian thought.

Two of the features already mentioned can be regarded as distinctive to Jain thinking.

1 ATMAN/JIVA

For orthodox Hindus, the Atman (soul) is fundamentally identified with Brahman (the ultimate reality), although the direct awareness of that identity is the final goal of the spiritual journey, rather than something apparent to everyone. The Atman is therefore Brahman indwelling the physical body.

By contrast, Jains see the jiva as a subtle presence which animates the body and is contained within it. It is composed of innumerable 'soul units' and its identity is given in terms of that composition. It does not need to be identified with any external reality (i.e. there is no place for Brahman).

2 KARMA

Within orthodox Hinduism, karma is related to the correct performance of ritual and duty. These are believed to align one's life with that of the universe as a whole and thereby wipe away the unwelcome results of past actions.

By contrast, Jains see karma as the accumulation of the effect of all actions, good or bad. Release from karma comes from detachment from desire and ascetic discipline.

Parallels with the Sankhya school of philosophy

For both Sankhya and Jain philosophy, the world is eternal; hence they are both atheistic and require no speculation about creation by a god or gods. Equally, they both make an absolute distinction between matter and consciousness, with matter being morally neutral. The same term (jiva) is used in Sankhya and in Jainism for the individual self.

These parallels do not point to a simple conclusion that the one borrowed from the other. We only know Sankhya as a system from the period after about 100 BCE, but its origins might be (and probably are) very much older and Kapila, traditionally regarded as its founder, may have lived as early as the 7th century BCE. When it comes to written commentaries, however, we are looking at 500 CE or 1400 CE, by which time Sankya may have been influenced by Vedanta. Perhaps it is safest to say that there is a common stream of thought found in both Sankhya and Jainism.

One important difference, however, was that Sankhya remained an orthodox Hindu tradition, whereas Jainism was unorthodox. Sankhya achieved this by saying that the scriptures were one of the three sources of knowledge (see Chapter 1). In practice, it used this source rather seldom, but its inclusion allowed it to remain within the Hindu orthodox fold.

Parallels with Buddhist philosophy

We have already noted some of these, which are hardly surprising, since Siddhartha Gautama and Vardhamma Mahavira were contemporaries, and had spiritual lives that resembled one another so closely.

▶ Both are atheistic, and both see the world as in a constant state of flux.
▶ Both place great stress of ahimsa (not taking life) as a key feature of the moral and spiritual life.
▶ Both allow a spiritual progression from the domestic to the monastic life.
▶ Both reject the authority of the Brahmin rituals and the Vedas.
▶ Both reject the Hindu requirement that a person's action should be determined by his or her class or caste.
▶ Both encourage the practice of self-restraint, mindfulness and the development of analytic meditation in order to make progress towards enlightenment/omniscience
▶ Both promote the ascetic life (but whereas Jainism holds that it is necessary to follow the ascetic tradition and become a monk or nun in order to gain salvation, the Buddha regarded the monastic life as desirable but not necessary, and there are accounts in the Buddhist sutras of lay followers gaining enlightenment).

There are, however, some key differences:

▶ Jainism sees both the view that the self is impermanent and the view that it is permanent as different but equally valid perceptions, and claims that both can therefore be true at one and the same time. Buddhism, on the other hand, regards the permanent self as an illusion, and – at best – a conventional (rather than an ultimate) way of describing reality.

▶ Jains hold that there are fundamental substances which take on particular forms. Thus, for example, pots may vary and be temporary, but the clay of which they are made is an on-going reality that they have in common. By contrast, Buddhist philosophy argues that all things – both material and spiritual – arise in dependence upon conditions and cease when they cease. The permanence of the clay of which the pots are made is an illusion; all is impermanent.

▶ Some questions (e.g. whether or not the universe is eternal, and whether an enlightened person lives on after death) are matters that Jainism (and Sankhya Hinduism) are happy to address, but which Buddhism is not. From a Buddhist perspective they are speculation, and therefore a distraction.

Both Buddhism and Jainism have often been portrayed in a negative way as offering salvation through an escape from the material universe. To some extent this is inevitable, given the importance of monasticism within both traditions. On the other hand, through the interconnectedness of things and the operation of the law of karma, both explore the interaction between the self and its material environment – an interaction which both teach should be characterized by an attitude of non-violence and compassion – and thus offer a very positive view of the contribution people can make to their world.

Ethics

Reacting against a society of violence, greed and the struggle for political power, Mahavira (and the Buddha) sought to create a community of followers who would reverse the values of the society around them and live in a way that was based on simplicity and respect for all living things.

In doing this, Jainism sees danger in identifying human life exclusively with either the physical or the spiritual. If the spiritual is not recognized, then people may ignore a basic feature of life, which is that souls are there to help one another and that community is essentially about interdependence. A key verse of the *Tattvartha Sutra* states:

> **Souls render service to one another**
>
> (Tattvartha Sutra, 5.21)

On the other hand, if the physical is ignored, humans are unlikely to take responsibility for their actions *vis-à-vis* the material world, with adverse implications for the environment within which they live and on which they depend.

Jain ethics are expressed in terms of five vows:

▶ non-violence (ahimsa)
▶ truthfulness
▶ not stealing
▶ chastity (or faithfulness within marriage)
▶ non-possessiveness (limitation of goods).

Of these vows the most important by far is ahimsa. Not harming living things is taken in a more literal and extreme way in Jain philosophy than in either Hinduism or Buddhism. It is important to avoid bad karma and particularly the effects of destroying life, therefore Jain monks and nuns take ahimsa as far as is possible, wearing a mask over the mouth to prevent accidentally swallowing some insect, straining the water they drink and even (where possible and appropriate) brushing the road ahead of them as they walk, to avoid destroying small creatures. Naturally, Jains are vegans since they would not want to harm or exploit animals for food. But even fruit and vegetables are living things, and therefore any nourishment is going to involve some harming of life. The logical response to this is for Jains to limit what they take to the minimum necessary to sustain life.

Not all Jains are able to follow the vows in the same way or to the same extent. So, for example, some will practise chastity, while others take that vow to require faithfulness within marriage. Since it is assumed that people go through many incarnations before they can attain release (moksha), those who are still involved in business and family life are likely to have rather more incarnations to go than those who live the ascetic life.

Asceticism takes precedence over ritual. Thus, although lay members of the Jain community may make daily offerings before stone images of the ford-makers, ascetics do not. They are beyond making offerings, and in any case should have nothing to offer! Interestingly, however, for a religion which rejected Brahmin ritual, there is considerable emphasis on paying for rituals to be performed, and this is a matter of pride and self-respect within the Jain lay community.

KEY FEATURES

A key feature of Jain ethics is self-control. This is reflected in the term 'Jain' which refers to a follower of one who has 'conquered', in the sense of having conquered the self and therefore being in control of one's personal needs. It implies chastity for those who have taken monastic vows, and faithfulness in marriage for those who have not. It also requires moderation in consumption, of food and of everything else.

The other major quality is generosity and non-attachment to material goods. These things find expression in the following features of the Jain life:

▶ generosity in supporting monks, nuns and temples
▶ the desire to avoid hurting any living thing
▶ living in the most simple way possible.

Thus, the Jain ethic can be summed up in the fundamental precepts of compassion and self-control, as is seen in asceticism (for those who choose monastic orders) or restraint and generosity for those who remain lay followers.

Although, as with all vows that lead to an ascetic life (or the simplified version of an ascetic's vows taken by a householder), the impression can be negative – that life is dominated by things to be avoided – that is not the intention of Jain ethics. The *Tattvartha Sutra* sums up the positive qualities that the vows are intended to cultivate:

> *The observer of vows should cultivate friendliness towards all living beings, delight in the distinction and honour of others, compassion for miserable, lowly creatures and equanimity towards the vainglorious.*

(Tattvartha Sutra, 7:6)

Apart from particular issues that only really apply to monks and nuns, the discipline accepted within Jainism forms a single graded system that includes both monastic and lay members. Naturally, because of their more extreme asceticism, it is the monks and nuns who are regarded as nearer liberation; lay people have many more lifetimes to go – but that does not mean that their efforts are wasted, indeed, everything they do in this life is thought to contribute to future incarnations and therefore to count towards their final release.

Naturally, being atheistic, Jainism does not have the sense of an external deity who is there to accept devotion and facilitate the spiritual path of followers. In the absence of God, progress requires spiritual self-help, inspired and guided by the teaching of the ford-makers.

TWO ISSUES

There have been two features of Jain ethics which, although they may seem remote from modern philosophical debate, illustrate the fundamental insights of Jain philosophy: monastic nudity and death by voluntary starvation.

Monastic nudity

There is a division within Jainism between the Digambaras ('sky-clad', whose monks are naked) and the Svetambaras ('white clad', who allow each monk to wear three pieces of white cloth), a division that originated in about 300 BCE. Although the division appears to be over monastic nudity, in actual fact there were other important issues involved, particularly the preparation of an edition of sacred texts in Patiliputra (modern Patna) while a considerable body of monks was away in Nepal. Those who stayed in Patna and committed their version of the scriptures to writing, formed the basis of the Svetambara sect, and those who returned from Nepal and disputed the newly written edition of the scriptures, formed the Digambara.

As an ascetic ideal, all opportunities for attachment to worldly things are to be rejected. Therefore, since even simple clothes are potentially objects of attachment, a Jain monk should go naked. Both sects held that complete nakedness was ideal, but the Svetambaras compromised and wore robes, while the Digambaras maintained nakedness – although in modern times Jain monks are clothed in public.

Nudity has always been a feature of Indian asceticism, and Mahavira himself practised as a naked ascetic during the 12 years before he became a jina. Although nudity *per se* is not a philosophical issue that divides Jains (since both groups accept it as the ideal), and it is not a fundamental teaching, it highlights the overall philosophical approach which sees a spiritual person as 'naked' in the broadest sense, living without attachment or material status.

Comment

Within the Judaeo-Christian tradition, a sense of shame at public nakedness is associated (through the story of Adam and Eve) with disobedience and loss of innocence. In the popular mind it is also associated with sexuality, since, naturally enough in the absence of its broader social appreciation and acceptance, the intimacy of shared nakedness is seen as inviting sexual activity. In Indian religious culture, nakedness is seen as a means of overcoming shame and sexuality, not encouraging it, so there is no problem with nudity, and images of naked men and women abound in religious art. Nor does it have a problem with depicting sexuality, but that is another matter.

Nakedness is a spiritual state as well as a physical one. As practising naturists will confirm, the joy of nakedness is not primarily sexual, but is a more general sense of natural well-being and self-acceptance. It is standing on the surface of the Earth, free and entire, feeling the touch of wind or sun, and shedding all that is superficial. It is an expression of reality, in contrast to the artificiality that comes with clothing.

Even though clothed, a Jain should therefore remain emotionally and spiritually naked.

There were two other issues that divided the Digambaras and Svetambaras. The former held that an omniscient being would no longer perform any worldly activities or functions – and thus accumulate no more karma. The latter held that a person could become omniscient and still carry on normal functions for the rest of his or her life. The other issue concerned women. The Digambaras held that women could not directly attain liberation, so a woman would have to be reborn as a man at some point further along the spiritual path, while the Svetambaras accepted spiritual equality between men and women.

Today there are very few who are able to take on the full discipline of a Digambara monk. Far more belong to the Svetambara tradition, and in this there are about three times as many nuns as monks – although it should be noted that nuns of neither tradition have ever been allowed to go 'sky clad'.

Insight

Allowing nuns the benefits of nudity might have caused problems for the male monastic community, since one of the practices aimed at supporting the vow of celibacy is:

To avoid: listening to lewd stories about women, looking at sexually arousing parts of a woman's body, recalling past sexual experience, stimulating or delicious food and drink, decorating one's own body.

(Tattvartha Sutra, 7.7)

Clearly, the unfettered inclinations of the male have not changed much over the millennia! It appears to have been assumed, however, that women would not be similarly afflicted.

Death by voluntary starvation

In general, the Jain guideline is that food should be taken in order to maintain life, rather than for the pleasure of eating. This is because all food involves the destruction of life and should therefore be kept to a minimum. Jainism also promotes fasting as a spiritual exercise.

This is the context in which to understand the Jain idea of *sallekhana*, the practice of preparing for death through meditation and voluntary starvation. It is most important to understand that this does *not* mean that an individual should choose, while in good health, to starve to death. That would be utterly against Jain ethical principles. Rather, as with all Indian religious traditions, it is believed that one's spiritual state as death approaches is most important for preparing oneself for rebirth or for liberation, and for a Jain this may involve the decision that one needs no more food.

Sallekhana aims to help a person to die in full awareness of what is happening, and able to maintain his or her vows right through to the end of life. It is a total fast, and should only be undertaken once death is imminent due to some other cause. It is the point at which a person consciously recognizes and accepts that the time has come to die and therefore ceases to take food.

Understood in this way, voluntary starvation is the ultimate sign of self-control. To die in a state of religious discipline is the mark of a true 'conqueror', a 'Jain'.

JAIN LIFESTYLE TODAY

Although Jainism maintains an ethic of non-attachment, there has been a tradition within the Jain community that lay followers should take up businesses, and should seek to prosper. Within the lay community the element of non-attachment is shown through generosity, for they are encouraged to use their wealth to contribute to the building of temples and the support of the monastic community. Within the lay community, such generosity is a sign of piety.

Originally, Jain teaching emphasized that, in order to achieve salvation, it was necessary to reject society and all the material clutter that comes with it – an understandable emphasis given the society within which Mahavira taught. However, because of this emphasis on renunciation, Jainism has often been portrayed as taking a generally negative view of the world. If all kinds of action, both good and bad, lead to consequences that bind the individual to the material world, the logical way to avoid this is by practising ascetic detachment.

This has led to a certain frustration within the Jain community in that, although Jains can claim to have made a great contribution to art, literature and culture generally, their philosophy is generally perceived as being concerned only with liberation beyond death, whereas in fact followers of the Jain religion interpret ahimsa (non-violence) as encouraging an engagement with social concerns. From its earliest days, the Jain community has sought to promote a community of sharing, equality and simplicity.

A key feature of Jain ethics today is care for the environment. This springs naturally from the desire to show compassion and to avoid the taking of life. It is also prompted by the Jain insistence that jiva (self or soul) is a feature of all things and all situations, and is not simply a human phenomenon. Jains today see themselves as promoting a philosophy based on non-violence, compassion and love. As such they believe that they have an important contribution to make to modern society.

10 THINGS TO REMEMBER

1 Jain philosophy is based on the teachings of Mahavira.

2 It considers all knowledge to be partial and all truth relative.

3 It sees everything as composed of atoms, both physical and mental.

4 It is atheist, seeing the world as eternal and needing no creator.

5 The self is composed of different 'soul units' which are present in everything.

6 All actions produce karma.

7 Release is absolute knowledge and freedom from the effects of karma.

8 Jain ethics are based on five vows: non-violence; truthfulness; not stealing; chastity or faithfulness; non-possessiveness.

9 To cease eating as death approaches is *not* euthanasia or suicide.

10 Jain philosophy promotes concern for all species and the environment.

4

Mahayana Buddhism

In this chapter you will:
- *examine the differences between the principal schools of Buddhism*
- *explore key Mahayana Buddhist teachings*
- *consider two principal Mahayana philosophies.*

Background: development of Buddhism

Over a period of two or three hundred years, starting probably about 100 BCE but tracing its origins back to the Mahasanghikas of the Second Council in the 4th century BCE (see 'The early Buddhist schools' in Chapter 2), there developed within the Buddhist community a strand of thinking that criticized some traditional ways in which Buddhist Dharma (teaching) was presented. This criticism focused on two things:

1 It argued that the goal of individual liberation, as it had been presented in the early schools, was too narrow and selfish. In its place, it sought a new ideal (which became known as the Bodhisattva Path) of working towards Buddhahood not simply for one's own benefit, but for the sake of all sentient beings.

2 It also saw the Abhidharma as promoting a form of wisdom that was too simply analytic – an exercise in breaking down all complex experience into its constituent dharmas (which, in this context means the basic components out of which every compound thing is made). It argued that becoming aware of dharmas was not in itself the end of Buddhist wisdom; there had to be something more, something that came to be called the 'Perfection of Wisdom'.

These criticisms may be summed up in two key terms that describe the thrust of Mahayana philosophy – compassion and wisdom.

In this chapter we shall start by looking at the compassion implied in the Bodhisattva ideal, and the ethical implications of this. We shall then look at the philosophy that developed as a result of the new approach to wisdom.

The Bodhisattva ideal

A *bodhisattva* is literally an 'enlightened being'. It was a term used for a being that was on its way to becoming a Buddha, but who had deferred that final step in order to assist others to make spiritual progress, and thus to show compassion for all suffering creatures.

In early Buddhism, Siddhartha is described as a bodhisattva prior to his enlightenment. Stories of his previous births also provided images of himself as a bodhisattva, and it was believed that at some time in the future, when the present teaching of the Dharma had died out, another teacher would appear, the Bodhisattva Maitreya.

Mahayana Buddhism enlarged the scope of the bodhisattva considerably. It included all beings who aspired to enlightenment – thus all practising Buddhists were regarded as apprentice bodhisattvas. It also included a whole range of archetypal beings who could be visualized in meditation and who represented aspects of the enlightened consciousness (see 'The Trikaya doctrine' below).

The Bodhisattva ideal thus introduced into Buddhism not merely a spiritual goal for the individual, but also a whole range of spiritual beings to whom devotion could be paid. This is what makes Mahayana Buddhism very much richer in terms of its religious practice, when compared with the simplicity of the earlier Theravadin approach.

ETHICAL IMPLICATIONS

There are traditionally six qualities of the enlightened being, termed *paramitas* (perfections):

- ▶ *Dana* (generosity)
- ▶ *Shila* (morality)
- ▶ *Kshanti* (patience)

- *Virya* (energy, expended in pursuit of what is good)
- *Dhyana* (meditation)
- *Prajna* (wisdom).

These are seen as principles of self-transcendence. They do not prescribe any particular course of action, but indicate the qualities that would inform the actions of an enlightened being – and therefore those that an aspiring bodhisattva should seek to adopt.

By emphasizing the paramitas, as the qualities of an enlightened being that all Buddhists may seek to follow, some ethical issues take on a different emphasis, and one that reflects the householder rather than the monastic setting.

In early Buddhism, the ethics of the Buddhist community focused on the five precepts (see Chapter 2) that applied to all Buddhists, monastic and lay, along with the additional precepts that were accepted full-time by the monastic community and might be accepted for limited periods by the laity. There built up, in addition to these precepts, a whole body of rules and traditions which became the monastic Vinaya.

It was always recognized that these were not absolute rules, but principles by which conduct could be assessed. In the absence of any concept of God, and recognizing the fact of constant change, there was no basis for an absolutist approach to ethics. The development of the Bodhisattva ideal did not go against this earlier ethic, but it provided a new way by which one's actions could be assessed – a way based on imaginatively entering into the situation of one who is enlightened.

Insight

In other words, instead of saying 'What, according to the teaching, should I do in order to make spiritual progress?' it asked, 'What would I do in this situation if I were already an enlightened being? How, if I were enlightened, would I display the qualities of generosity, morality, patience, energy in pursuit of the good, meditation and wisdom?'

This places emphasis on the qualities displayed in, and the intention that lies behind, an action, rather than on the action itself, and reflects the general Buddhist view that actions are not so much good or bad as skilful or unskilful. Every action is an expression of a person's awareness (reflecting his or her wisdom) and intention (reflecting his or her compassion). It is the wisdom and compassion behind an action that decides its ethical quality.

There are some distinctive ethical issues that developed within the Mahayana. For example, within Tantric practice (which was developed by some of those within the Mahayana – see Chapter 7) there is a view of sexuality which encourages its use as a vehicle for insight. This is in contrast to the earlier view, where sexuality is voluntarily given up for the sake of the spiritual quest within monasticism, and for the laity is seen as at best neutral and at worst a hindrance to the spiritual life.

There is also a distinctive Mahayana contribution to the issue of vegetarianism. Clearly, the first precept (against the taking of life) would suggest that meat should be avoided, but in the *Lotus Sutra* (one of the most important Mahayana scriptures) there is the suggestion that rebirth can take the form of plant as well as animal life. This has radical implications, since the taking of vegetable life is therefore in principle no different from the taking of animal life.

In practice, the guidelines used for overcoming this dilemma are that although all intentional killing is unskilful, it is less so in the case of animals than of humans, and therefore by implication, less so in the case of vegetable than animal life.

Comment

If everything is linked to everything else in this world, then there is a price to be paid for maintaining one's life – none can be absolutely harmless. The dilemma is that, if you were desperate to harm no other living thing, you would only end up harming yourself – which would also be against the first precept. This dilemma cannot be solved in terms of a moral rule – it has to be a matter of developing sensitivity (which is what the Mahayana emphasis on wisdom and compassion is all about).

Of course, unintentional killing is not considered an offence, since it is the intention that gives rise to an act that determines its karmic implications, and thus whether – for that person at that time – it can be seen as skilful or unskilful.

This last point is important for Buddhist ethics in general. If I am held responsible for all that I could change, but do not, irrespective of where it is happening or my individual involvement, then, for example, I am responsible for starvation in another part of the world even if I did not directly bring it about, simply on the grounds of whatever action I knew I could take to alleviate it but chose not to take. I cannot be held responsible for that which I cannot do, but can be held responsible for anything that I could have done but consciously declined to do.

Notice, however, that ethics in this context are quite different from the assessment if guilt or otherwise. What we have here are the ethical implications of following an ideal – that of the bodhisattva. An enlightened being, displaying all the qualities of wisdom and compassion, would understand what is needed in every situation and would respond accordingly. The paramitas give an outline of just such qualities.

As we have seen, in assessing a situation, this approach asks in effect: 'What would an enlightened being do in these circumstances?' Again, remembering the basic Buddhist view that there is no inherent selfhood, it is no excuse to say 'but I am not enlightened', as though enlightenment were an inherent quality to be possessed. Rather, it is the actions of an enlightened being that demonstrate enlightenment – so one's own actions (or lack of them) demonstrate one's own spiritual state. To be able to see a need and respond accordingly *is* to make progress towards enlightenment.

Comment

This approach may sound selfish – that doing the right thing is precisely for the purposes of helping one's own progress towards enlightenment. But that would be to misunderstand enlightenment, for, from the standpoint of the Bodhisattva ideal, to be enlightened is to behave with selfless generosity and wisdom. To perform an action simply in order to gain merit would be counterproductive, since the *intention* would be selfish, and for Buddhists it is the intention that counts morally.

Once again, the key feature of Buddhist ethics, springing from its fundamental philosophy, is overcoming the illusion of ego-identity. The enlightened being can act with compassion towards all, simply because he or she is free from the selfishness produced by the illusion of a permanent and independent self.

REASON TINGED WITH EMOTION?

All Buddhist philosophy is based on reason and analysis. One is encouraged to examine propositions and test them out in experience; one is also encouraged to become increasingly aware of one's present experience and one's response to it. It is this fundamental orientation that enables us to study Buddhism as a philosophy. On the other hand, reason divorced from emotion turns its back on a significant part of human experience. To have a philosophy of life that does not engage the emotions is a contradiction in terms.

The criticisms made of the earlier schools by the Mahayanists, particularly as reflected in their development of the Bodhisattva ideal, were in part an attempt to engage the emotions in the Buddhist path, and thus prevent the whole philosophical and religious enterprise from becoming excessively analytic and dry.

Part of the process of engaging the emotion took the form of a more imaginative approach to meditation. Whereas all Buddhist practise had involved developing awareness and analysis of states, the Mahayana tradition included the visualization of a range of images of enlightened beings – images with which the meditator could identify and also use as an object of devotion. We shall see later in this chapter how this developed into the *Trikaya* (three bodies) idea. For now we need to recognize that the Bodhisattva ideal gave rise to an imaginative development in which there could be a great variety of bodhisattvas – from the ordinary Buddhist practitioner, who was considered an aspiring bodhisattva, through a range of imagined forms used in visualization.

From the image of early Buddhism as an analytic discipline leading eventually to arhatship and personal enlightenment, there developed a rich variety of forms within which the Buddhist path could be explored, with images to inspire whatever qualities of wisdom or compassion a particular person needed to develop.

The Bodhisattva ideal provided the vehicle for much of this development.

Insight

This does not imply that the Mahayana schools denied the validity of the earlier, more strictly rational approach, but they sought to supplement and enrich it in order to engage the whole person in Buddhist practice.

Madhyamaka philosophy

The two principal schools of philosophy within Mahayana Buddhism developed out of a tradition of interpreting those sutras that had not been accepted as part of the Pali Canon.

The Madhyamaka school interpreted the *Perfection of Wisdom* sutras, and the Yogacara school interpreted a range of other sutras which, in Western terms, we would call 'idealist'. The two schools of philosophy were later divided into various sub-groups, and attempts were also made to synthesize them. For the purposes of this book, however, we shall be concerned only with the basic approaches of the Madhyamaka and Yogacara. It is important to recognize also that those using the Mahayana scriptures did not think that they were innovating. They believed that the traditions embodied in these sutras had been taught by Siddhartha Gautama himself, and had remained part of the oral tradition – albeit (as we shall see later), a part that was reserved for the initiated rather than preached to those who were not yet ready for their more advanced ideas. In this way, the Mahayana schools saw themselves as part of the original stream of Buddhist teaching, not as importing anything new or as setting aside earlier traditions.

THE PRAJNAPARAMITA SUTRAS

The *Prajnaparamita Sutras* are a collection of philosophical works, compiled and reshaped over a considerable period of time, on the theme of 'The Perfection of Wisdom'. The most succinct of these (and one of the latest) is known as *The Heart Sutra*. It is particularly important because, being short, it is easily memorized and recited and has thus been a key way of gathering and propagating this particular philosophy.

The Heart Sutra deals with issues that are key to an understanding of Mahayana Buddhism, and we will be examining these in the course of this chapter. They may be summarized as:

▶ All phenomena lack inherent existence; they cannot exist independent of one another.

▶ Although complex entities (like the body) exist conventionally (i.e. for practical purposes we need to be able to speak about them as single entities), careful analysis shows that they do not exist over and above their constituent parts (i.e. there is no 'body' other than the sum of all the bits and pieces that make up the body).

▶ All phenomena are therefore mere appearance. (I may see a tree in front of me, and conventionally I may call it a tree. In fact, it could be analysed into individual molecules and atoms. The tree is simply an accumulation of all these atoms, it does not exist independently of them – and of course, they do not exist independently of all the rest of the world and the way in which the universe is made up.)

▶ Everything is both form and emptiness. (Where 'form' is the tree, and 'emptiness' the fact that it does not exist in itself but only as an arrangement of constantly changing atoms etc.). Neither exists without the other.

▶ Unless we are enlightened, we cannot see both form and emptiness simultaneously.

▶ The goal is to become enlightened, to see everything as being 'empty' of inherent existence, and therefore accepting it as it is, in its ever-changing reality, without grasping at it or attempting to project our own ideas upon it.

Inevitably, this is an over-simplification of a very complex set of ideas, but it is necessary to grasp the basic concepts of 'form' and 'emptiness' in order to understand the philosophies of the Mahayana.

The Abhidharma of the earlier traditions concentrated in breaking down all compound things into their constituent dharmas. The intention of this process was to make a person aware of the compound and therefore impermanent nature of things. The problem with this, from the standpoint of the Perfection of Wisdom tradition, was that it suggested that the dharmas were themselves permanent. But for those sutras, and for Nagarjuna interpreting them, it was a key feature of the whole Buddhist view of reality that absolutely *nothing* has *svabhava* (own being, inherent existence).

The reason why it is always important for Buddhism to deny svabhava, is that it implies permanence. Once you locate something that is permanent you can attempt to cling to it and rely on it – and that leads to suffering. Buddhism insists that *nothing is permanent*, and thus that seeking permanence is always as illusion.

Insight

Modern science tends to agree. Whereas atoms might originally have been thought to be permanent (as opposed to the molecules and more complex entities that they combine to form), it is clear that matter only comes into existence below a certain temperature and that, above that temperature, it is re-converted into radiation. Some things in the universe are of very long duration, but none has svabhava, for none can exist in complete independence of the conditions that bring it about.

What is the 'perfection of wisdom'? That is a reasonable question to ask, since Perfection of Wisdom (prajna) is the name of this body of literature. The key is in the idea of 'emptiness' (shunyata), but it involves more than an intellectual grasp of that concept. An important feature of Mahayana philosophy is that it is not to be taken exclusively at an intellectual level; it is a view of life into which a person can enter. Seeing things as 'empty' changes a person's attitude to them, which in turn influences moral choices and actions. Emptiness is therefore an attitude of mind in dealing with life, not just a way of highlighting the impermanent nature of things. The Mahayana claim is that such an attitude of mind is, and has always been, fundamental to Buddhism.

NAGARJUNA

The Madhyamaka school of Buddhist philosophy was founded by Nagarjuna, a monk who lived in the 2nd century CE. The name of this school means 'middle position', which reflects its central teaching:

▶ things do not exist absolutely
▶ nor do they not exist at all
▶ therefore they exist relatively.

Nagarjuna claimed that this was simply an explanation of the Buddha's original teaching, in rejecting both eternalism and annihilationism.

In interpreting the *Perfection of Wisdom* sutras, Nagarjuna did not offer any new philosophy, other than to emphasize the absolute centrality of the idea of shunyata in the Buddhist view of reality. Instead, his main thrust was to use reason to show the logical incompatibility of the claims of others, using *reductio ad absurdum* arguments. His arguments are set out in the *Mulamadhyamakarika* (*Verses on the Fundamentals of the Middle Way*).

Western

His approach was like that of Socrates. Look at a commonly held belief; examine its implications; show the logical absurdity of these; then re-evaluate the original assumptions.

SHUNYATA (EMPTINESS)

Shunyata means 'emptiness'; everything is described as being empty of *svabhava* (own being). Although this sounds a rather negative view of reality, that is not its intention. In early Buddhism there was the recognition of two universal features of reality: anicca (everything is constantly changing) and anatta (there is no fixed self). Clinging to a false notion of a permanent self was the cause of suffering. The Buddha's teaching sought to show that everything arises in dependence upon conditions and that those conditions are constantly changing. 'Emptiness', in Mahayana Buddhism, is simply the logical outcome of the basic Buddhist view of conditioned existence.

In the earlier tradition, it was acknowledged that composite things did not exist in their own right, but could be analysed into their dharmas, the smallest units of reality of which everything was composed. The implication of this for the Sarvastivadins was that the dharmas were eternal, whereas the things that were composed of them were not. Nagarjuna challenged this. If everything was dependent upon conditions, then why should dharmas not also be dependent upon conditions? Why should they have self-existence? He therefore considered that dharmas were also shunyata (empty of inherent existence).

Recognizing that something is 'empty' does not mean that it is valueless. For Mahayana Buddhism it is quite the contrary: things are still real, nothing about them has changed, but recognizing them as 'empty' suggests that there is no point in trying to grasp and hold onto them, or expect them to be unchanging.

Comment

On the personal level, Shunyata prevents you from asking, 'What is the real "me"?' You are exactly what you are: your thoughts, words and actions. You are what you are now as a result of what you have been in the past – your karma has produced its results. Equally, what you will be in the future will depend partly on choices you make now, and also on countless other factors over which you have no control.

You are therefore 'empty' – there is no eternal, fixed self that has somehow found itself trapped within this changing world. Like it or not, you are part of the universal process of change, and to pretend otherwise is to grasp at an illusion that will only lead to frustration and suffering.

Shunyata does not imply that nothing exists (which would be annihilationism), but that nothing exists eternally and in its own right. Everything exists only in relation to the conditions that bring it about; once those conditions cease, then it too will cease.

Western

Within the Philosophy of Mind, there has been what is called the problem of the 'elusive I'. The fact that I can speak of 'my body' or 'my mind', for example, suggests that there is an 'I' that exists over and above the body and the mind, but it seems impossible to define or locate it. Buddhism enters this debate by suggesting that the 'I' is elusive because it is an illusion. At most, it may serve as a conventional way of describing oneself. This is not too far from the conclusions of Gilbert Ryle in *The Concept of Mind* (1949), who sees language about the mind as belonging to a different category from descriptions of physical things or actions.

Clearly, there is going to be a problem with language that claims that everything is 'empty', since in ordinary day-to-day speech we need to say of people, animals, physical objects, even events that last only a very short time, that they 'exist'. And in saying that, we are not trying to say that they will exist for all time, nor that they are independent of everything else – merely that they are, rather than that they are not.

The Madhyamaka way out of this dilemma is to speak of two kinds of truth – the conventional and the ultimate:

▶ *Samvrti satya* is conventional truth – the concepts we need to use on a day-to-day basis.
▶ *Paramartha satya* is ultimate truth – the way things really are, shorn of conventional concepts.

Thus, for example, conventional truth requires us to speak of individuals as though they were discrete and permanent entities (otherwise we could not deal with them on a day-by-day basis), but ultimate truth says that there is no such thing as a permanent self.

Insight

On a conventional level, I exist. Other people know me, interact with me, and can (if asked) describe me. But on an absolute level, I do not exist – I am a temporary 'put together' part of the world. My anticipated life span, once deprived of oxygen, is very limited. I am composed of cells that have grown because of the food I eat. I am in a constant state of flux physically, as is every living thing. But equally the 'I' that relates to people is also constantly changing and responding to relationships and environment.

Conventionally, 'I' am all this; in absolute terms, however, I do not exist. By making this distinction between absolute and conventional, Mahayana philosophy was able to continue to make very rigorous analysis of everything, without thereby making normal life and conversation impossible.

Insight

For Mahayana Buddhism, as for all Eastern philosophy, they key thing to appreciate is the personal and religious implications of its view of reality. The conventional world, in which we all appear to exist as individual, permanent selves, is one that can lead to jealousy, pride, competitiveness, love, hatred and all the other passions. Once this is tempered by the awareness that ultimately we are 'empty', there is hope that a less selfish, more balanced view may prevail. Equanimity is not a matter of not caring what happens, or of finding no distinction between one option or another, but of seeing everything in a balanced way, and recognizing that everything is temporary and subject to change.

There are two ways of overcoming the conventional notion of self-existence:

▶ Those things that have been learned – for example, the existence of gods, or that one has a soul – can be refuted by showing logically that everything is dependent upon other things and therefore is not self-existent.
▶ However, when the conventional way of looking at the world does not yield to rational argument, the alternative approach is through the practice of meditation.

Of these, the Madhyamaka generally emphasizes the way of rational argument. Everything is just as it is, but in a temporary and relative way. The Buddhist term for this is *tathata* (suchness). It is not a negative view; it does not deny anything. It is simply a term that seeks to describe things as they really are, letting go of any eternalist fantasy.

Insight

Don't try to say 'this is forever', because you know it is not, and that attitude will only lead to craving, grasping and suffering. Just say 'this is as it is' so that it may be enjoyed for itself, without forcing it to comply with our eternalist fantasy about what it should be for us.

SOME IMPLICATIONS OF SHUNYATA

Nagarjuna came to the conclusion that ultimately there was not the slightest difference between nirvana and samsara. Now this sounds radical, since traditionally Buddhism has been taken to be a method of overcoming the ever-changing world of samsara, with all the suffering that is involved in it, and enabling a person to come to a peaceful state of nirvana. What is the point of all this if they are actually identical?

What Nagarjuna was trying to put over was that if samsara has no inherent existence, it cannot be a separate entity from another one called nirvana. Nirvana is simply the state of seeing the conditioned nature of the constant rushing to and fro that is the world of samsara.

Nirvana is recognizing that *everything* is empty and that nothing may be grasped and held, not even a 'thing' called nirvana.

Insight

An old joke: from the days when there was a simple advert for a headache remedy which claimed, 'Nothing works faster than A*****', to which the quip was, 'Next time, try taking nothing.' The joke works, of course, through the mistaken reification of 'nothing'. Therefore beware of thinking that there is some entity called 'emptiness' – some invisible reality – that is at the base of everything. Not so. The shunyata doctrine says that no such thing exists.

Nagarjuna's philosophy may also be applied to the problem of causation:

▶ Cause and effect cannot be the same (or nothing new could ever be brought about).

▶ Cause and effect cannot be unconnected (or anything could cause just anything, which experience shows not to be the case, for the world is at least partly predictable).

▶ The effect cannot be part of the cause (or nothing new would ever be caused).

▶ Thus, according to conventional thinking, for something to be caused, there has to be continuity but there also has to be something new.

▶ Therefore, conventional reasoning breaks down; it cannot explain the process of change.

▶ The answer lies in 'emptiness'. Neither cause nor effect have separate, permanent existence. Only in a conventional sense are they two separate and distinct entities requiring to be linked in some way.

Thus, shunyata (emptiness) shows that problems about how one thing can be said to cause another are in fact no more than symptoms of our conventional ways of thinking.

Yogacara philosophy

The other main school of Mahayana philosophy was developed by two brothers, Asanga and Vasubandhu, who lived in the 4th/5th centuries CE, and (like the Madhyamaka school) it developed out of a system of interpreting the Mahayana sutras. It is generally referred to as Yogacara (the practice of yoga).

Both Yogacara and Madhyamaka schools agreed that the things that make up the world lack svabhava – in other words, that they do not exist in their own right, but are merely contingent, depending on the conditions that bring them about. This is hardly surprising, since it is basic to the whole Buddhist idea of interconnectedness.

Whereas Madhyamaka emphasized shunyata, claiming that things were 'empty' of inherent existence, Yogacara thought this had moved too far in the nihilist direction and attempted to restore the balance by coming at the issue of the transient nature of experience from a very different angle. It argued that the things we perceive as being in the world are in fact *mental constructs*; that what we experience is an interpretation imposed by our minds.

The Yogacara school of philosophy can be known by three other names, which between them show what it is about:

▶ *Cittamatra* = 'mind only'
▶ *Vijnanavada* = 'consciousness doctrine'
▶ *Vijnaptimatra* = 'perception only'.

In other words, Yogacara is what would be known in the West as an 'idealist' philosophy, since it takes as its starting point our mental interpretation of experience.

The reasoning behind the Yogacara approach can be presented quite simply:

▶ You can be mistaken about what you perceive. (For example, I suffer from tinnitus. It sounds as if there is a waterfall to my left, and someone blowing a rather high-pitched whistle. That is the reality of what I experience, but I do not keep looking over my left shoulder to check if either the waterfall or the whistle exist outside myself.)
▶ You may be dreaming. (Asanga, in his *Mahayanasamgraha*, argued that, when you dream, you are aware of a world of fantastic creatures, but they are merely in your mind. You may see a mirage or hear an echo, mistaking it for the source of the sound. It is therefore possible to have 'real' experiences, but they do not necessarily correspond to anything in the external world.)
▶ You may lack a particular faculty. (For example, you may be colour blind, but that does not mean that the things you see actually lack colour.)

▶ Therefore, all you can know about is what you experience; you cannot get direct knowledge of anything external to that experience.

You might argue that the coherence and involuntariness of our experience suggest an external reality (after all, I have not chosen to see this particular thing, and I know that I have seen it every time I enter this room). But Yogacara counters this by suggesting that in a dream you do not control what you experience, and the people in your dream appear to be consistent.

But what about the regularity of experience? Does that not prove its external origin? Again, Vasubandhu argues that all experience is a sequence of events, and what we call 'true' perceptions are simply those that cohere with that sequence, false ones are those that do not fit with the sequence. He therefore argues that the claim that something is true or false, exists or not, does not depend on the knowledge of any external reality, but only on an assessment of whether it is compatible with the rest of our experience.

Western

There are parallels here with much idealism and empiricism in Western thought, although their main lines of development came just over a millennium after Yogacara. In Locke you have the distinction between primary and secondary qualities, the latter dependent upon our senses. Berkeley argued that to say something exists implies that it is perceived, and Kant effected a 'Copernican Revolution' within philosophy by suggesting that space, time and causality (in addition to the more obvious secondary qualities of colour and so on) were actually the result of the way in which the mind handled its data, rather than structures which we could perceive in the external world. What we see are things as we experience them – governed by our mental faculties – not things as they are in themselves.

THE THREE NATURES

We met the concept of svabhava (own being, or inherent and therefore independent and permanent existence) in looking at Madhyamaka philosophy. Yogacara uses this same term to describe three natures, or ways of understanding reality:

1 It is possible to believe that there are separate and independent objects out there. This it claims to be an illusion. This view is called *parikalpita-svabhava* (imagined own being). It is the conventional way of looking at the world.

2 There is the succession of perceptions and experiences that we have. This is termed *paratantra-svabhava* (interdependent own being). It is what a Buddhist is encouraged to be aware of all the time, and to recognize as arising in dependence on conditions and constantly liable to change.

3 But there is what Yogacara termed the *parinispanna-svabhava* (perfected own being) way of understanding reality. This is the awareness that there are no separately existing objects. Nothing much can be said about this, however, because it is the way in which an enlightened being would view the world, and the direct experience of an enlightened person cannot be put into words – and even if it could, it would not be understood by anyone who was not also enlightened!

Now, according to Yogacara, everyone actually experiences 2 above, but most interpret it mistakenly as 1. Awareness of the conditioned nature of things, however, should ultimately lead to interpretation 3.

Comment

The natural question to ask of Yogacara is this: 'If there are no external objects, what causes the sensations?' We may indeed mistake dreams for some external reality on occasions, but that is only because we habitually experience what we take to be external reality. And what are our senses for, if not to discover something that exists outside ourselves?

The answer given by Buddhism in general is that we are mistaken if we take an 'us and them' view of things – that the world consists of separate entities, each existing in its own right. That may be all right from a conventional point of view (and it is fairly essential in terms of the practicalities of day-to-day living) but actually, reality is interconnected and everything within it dependent upon the conditions that maintain it at every moment.

Perhaps we could summarize what Yogacara is trying to say in this way:

▶ My experience of this person is simply that – an experience.
▶ I cannot get back 'behind' that experience.
▶ I cannot say, 'There is a person out there whom I know quite apart from my experience of them.'
▶ What you experience is what there is. You can either accept it as a constantly changing flow of experience, or you can try to chop it up into separate entities – but to do that is to create an illusion of separateness.

KARMA AND THE STORE CONSCIOUSNESS

If there is only a flow of consciousness, with no continuity in terms of a permanent 'self', how is it that we recognize and remember things, and behave in ways that others find predictable? Also, if everything is mental, how can karma operate? Vasubandu's answer to both of these dilemmas is given in the idea of an *alaya-vignana* (store consciousness).

Insight

You will remember the term *alaya* (meaning 'store place' or 'abode') once you know that the term for snow is hima. The Himalayas are 'the abode of snow.'

The stream of mental events you experience leave *bija* ('seeds') in this 'store consciousness'. These seeds are held in the store until eventually, when conditions are right for them, they mature and can then influence later events. This theory not only explains continuity of experience, but also provides a mechanism for the way in which karma works. You experience the results of past actions now, because those actions have influenced your store consciousness; everything you have done in the past is stored up, influencing the present. Hence there can be a gap between a karmic event and its results, without the need to suggest a permanent on-going self.

Western

Psychoanalysis, and the whole idea of the unconscious mind, can be explored as a parallel with Vasubandu's ideas here. For modern psychology, events leave an imprint in the unconscious mind, remaining undetected until, at a later stage in life, they manifest in terms of psychological problems – exactly the mechanism that Vasubandhu envisaged. His alaya-vijnana is an early attempt to explain the operation of the unconscious mind. The key difference, however, is that karma is primarily concerned with a person's conscious action, whereas for Freud, experiences stored in the unconscious often relate to what others have done to us, rather than what we have chosen to do.

Yogacara has no less that seven forms of consciousness. The first five correspond to each of the five senses. The sixth consciousness synthesizes the first five, producing mental impressions. The seventh and last consciousness is the *klistamanas* ('tainted mind'), which is conventional self-consciousness. It leads to confusion about the self, to a sense of loss or to pride. It is exactly the form of consciousness that Buddhism seeks to overcome, because it sees it as based on a false view of the self and of reality.

Insight

Remember that Yogacara, like all traditions of Buddhist philosophy, aims to free people from suffering rather than engage in metaphysical speculation. By acknowledging the stream of conscious experience as reality, rather than external objects, it seeks to promote a view of the self and the world that helps people to avoid the frustration of grasping and trying to hold onto that which is constantly changing.

The Tathagatagarbha doctrine

Tathagata is a general term for the Buddha, and means 'one who has gone beyond'. *Garbha* means 'womb'. So the *tathagatagarbha* doctrine is the idea that every creature is the womb of a Buddha; that every creature has the potential to grow into Buddhahood. In a sense, this does not actually differ from the teaching of Siddhartha Gautama. After all, he taught the path that would lead to enlightenment, and the early scriptures give many examples of his followers becoming enlightened. Combined with the idea of re-becoming, it is clear that Buddhism sees all creatures as potentially able to become enlightened. Therefore, Buddhism holds that everyone is a potential Buddha. The distinctive feature of the tathagatagarbha doctrine, however, is that we are *already* Buddhas, but we can't see it because of the illusory way in which we understand the world.

This has implications for Buddhist practice. So, for example, a Tibetan Buddhist may visualize himself or herself in the form of one of the Buddhas or bodhisattvas. This is not seen as self-aggrandisement or fantasy. It is an attempt to get beyond the illusion of separateness and see one's true nature: Buddhahood. In the same way, Buddhists of the Soto Zen tradition may argue that for the time during which one sits in meditation one *is* Buddha.

Insight

But – and this is crucial for any interpretation of Mahayana Buddhism – this does not mean that there is a permanent and self-existing inner self called the 'Buddha nature', waiting to be united with some universal Buddha nature, for that would be exactly the same as the Hindu idea of an Atman becoming at one with Brahman. Rather, it suggests that enlightenment is the natural state, and illusion the unnatural. We all have the potential to see things as they really are, rather than living with illusion.

Misinterpreted, the 'Buddha nature' could (like the 'real self' of some New Age thinkers) become something to crave and cling to. And that of course, for a Buddhist, would be self-defeating!

The Trikaya doctrine

Buddha is a title, meaning 'enlightened one', and in its most straightforward use it is applied to Siddhartha Gautama. But Buddhism has enlarged it meaning in three ways.

First, it was believed that there had been and would be other enlightened beings. In the earliest traditions we find the idea of a future Buddha who would come to restore Buddhist teaching when it died out on Earth – the Buddha Maitreya. Within the Mahayana tradition this was extended further to include very many Buddhas, each with particular qualities or displaying a particular form of wisdom. This emphasized the idea that what Siddhartha Gautama achieved had universal significance, and was a potential for all (as we saw in the idea of the 'Buddha nature' in Chapter 2).

Second, the Buddha is also reported as saying that 'he who sees the Dharma (the teaching, or truth) sees me'. Thus, 'Buddha' became a term used not just for someone who is enlightened, but for the truth which their enlightenment reveals.

Third, in the course of meditation and visualization (particularly in the Tibetan tradition) there developed a whole range of images of Buddhas and bodhisattvas (beings who are destined to become Buddhas), with rich iconography and colour, each displaying aspects of enlightenment.

This led to a Mahayana teaching known as the Trikaya (three bodies). It claimed that there were three bodies of the Buddha:

- the *Nirmanakaya*: the Buddha revealed in earthly form (e.g. Siddhartha)
- the *Sambhogakaya*: Buddhas described in the Mahayana scriptures and visualized in devotional practices, and expressing graphically the qualities of enlightenment
- the *Dharmakaya* ('teaching body' or 'truth body'): the enlightened consciousness that is able to see the truth of things.

The first two of these are dependent upon the third. Siddhartha is only called Buddha at the point at which he becomes enlightened. Equally, the various images of the Sambhogakaya only make sense as aspects of the enlightened mind, and they have no reality or power except to the extent that they enable a person to get in touch with that particular quality and thus move in the direction of enlightenment.

Thus, provided it is not mistaken for some literal trinity of Buddhas, the Trikaya doctrine merely makes explicit what was implied originally in calling Siddhartha 'Buddha' – namely, that he was aware of the true nature of things, and that he displayed and taught the qualities implied by such awareness.

Western

It is tempting to seek parallels between the Christian concept of Trinity and the Buddhist Trikaya. However, they are utterly different, since Buddhism is atheistic, and the Trikaya cannot therefore refer to divine beings in any way. From the standpoint of the philosophy of religion, there is a certain parallel in terms of the development of the two concepts.

In the Christian tradition, 'Father' can be taken to refer (via the act of creation) to the fundamental sense of structure and purpose within the universe. 'Son' is a title given to Jesus, as expressing the belief that he is a unique revelation of God in human form, and 'Spirit' would then refer to spiritual qualities experienced within the Christian community.

You could therefore argue that there are parallels between the Nirmanakaya and the Son and between the Sambhogakaya and the Spirit, in terms of their function within an overall religious/philosophical framework. On the other hand, it needs to be clearly recognized that in Buddhism these refer to a process of spiritual development, whereas in Christianity they are taken to be independent spiritual realities, not aspects of human religious experience.

My guess, however, is that this is a discussion that is likely to generate more heat than light, for the two religions have arrived at superficially similar structures from very different philosophical presuppositions.

Cosmology

THE MULTIPLICITY OF WORLD SYSTEMS

At a key point in the *Lotus Sutra* there is the most amazing image of many different world systems, spread out in the ten directions of space, and in each of these world systems there is a Buddha. The cosmology is vast and elaborate. This present world (called the *Saha* world – meaning 'the world in which one endures') is in one sense quite insignificant against this cosmic backdrop, but at the same time, the image suggests that all the other world systems and their Buddhas come together to acknowledge that the Buddha Shakyamuni has preached the true Dharma – the same Dharma that these other Buddhas have preached each in his own world system.

It is tempting to put all this rich imagery down to a tendency to elaborate and develop which we find throughout Buddhist (and other Indian) literature. But it would be wrong to interpret it simply as cosmological speculation. There is a tradition that the Buddha would not discuss whether the world had a beginning or not, since that would be unanswerable and at best a distraction – so cosmological speculation as such is not part of Buddhism. Rather, we should look for the purpose of this material to the effect it is intended to have upon the reader. The thrust of the image is that the present Buddha and world system is placed in a context – that it has a universal and eternal significance, in spite of its appearance within the world of change. In other words, what appears to be cosmological speculation in Mahayana Buddhism may be accounted for by the need to:

▶ show the universal relevance of the Dharma
▶ show the relative insignificance of this present world system.

There is no sense that belief in other world systems is presented as a requirement of faith – that would be quite alien to the Buddhist approach.

HUA-YEN (THE INTERPENETRATION OF ALL THINGS)

Alongside the multiplicity of world systems, there is another important feature of Mahayana cosmology – the concept of *hua-yen*. This is related in some ways to the tathagatagarbha doctrine and partly to the basic Buddhist idea of 'conditioned co-production'. It may be broadly translated as 'the interpenetration of all things', and as such is the basic Buddhist view of reality, but hua-yen has implications for understanding the Buddha nature of each individual, since it claims that each individual has inherent value as a manifestation of the universal Buddha principle.

Notice again here that what might be taken to be cosmic speculation is, in reality, simply a way of presenting the basic Buddhist vision of everything arising in dependence on conditions, and having no independent, inherent or permanent existence.

On the other hand, seeing the universe in terms of the interpenetration of all things has immense implications in terms of one's self-understanding, appreciation of the value of the transient, and one's moral orientation.

Western

Probably the nearest we come to hua-yen in the West is through mysticism, or through the writings of those involved with ecology – since it is within the appreciation of the interconnected nature of life within ecosystems that we touch on the significance of the hua-yen doctrine.

Within the vast arena of Mahayana literature there are other ways we could explore its vision of the nature of reality. One of these, for example, concerns the 'three spheres of reality' – *arupadhatu* (the formless sphere), the *rupadhatu* (the sphere of form) and the *kamadhatu* (the sphere of the senses). Another important approach, especially in terms of religious practice and meditation, is the Mahayana view of the five Buddhas, arranged within a mandala and each related to one of the skandhas. Here there is a graphic expression of a link between the components of the self and the fundamental features of the whole of reality.

Further developments of Mahayana Buddhism

In this chapter, and in Chapter 2, we have been looking at some basic features of Buddhist philosophy. However, Buddhism is a religion as well as a philosophy, and some branches of Buddhism display traits of the former rather than the latter.

TIBETAN BUDDHISM

Between the 7th and 11th centuries, Buddhists of different traditions spread their teachings within Tibet, coming from India, China and Central Asia. As time went on, the Chinese traditions were set aside in favour of the Indian, and there developed a single organized system of teaching called *lam rim*, 'stages of the path'. This approach sees three traditions of Buddhist teaching as three vehicles (*triyana*), which lead on from one to the next in a graded progression:

▶ the Hinayana (the earliest Buddhist teachings, represented in modern times by the Theravada tradition)
▶ the Mahayana, which we are considering in this chapter
▶ the Vajrayana.

The third of these is a Tantric approach to Buddhism, and (since there are elements of Tantra in Hinduism as well as Buddhism) it will be considered separately in Chapter 7. The classics of this approach are Atisha's *Lamp of the Path* and Gampopa's *Jewel Ornament of Liberation*.

BUDDHISM IN JAPAN

Various forms of Buddhism developed in Japan, each with its own particular emphasis. Tendai, for example, was promoted by Saicho (767–822) and accepts the validity of progressive revelations, the highest of which it claims is found in the *Lotus Sutra*. He seems to have promoted the idea that all forms of teaching may lead to enlightenment not because they are the same, but because all that is necessary is commitment to a particular vehicle or path.

Shingon Buddhism, was established by Kukai (774–835), known as Kobo Daishi – 'great teacher Kobo'. This is an esoteric form of Buddhism, in that it holds that the historical Buddha preached a limited dharma, but in reality there is another, hidden tradition, in which everyone can be enlightened and become a living Buddha. You develop spiritually until you achieve a point of seeing the whole universe as a manifestation of the cosmic Vairocana Buddha.

Pure Land Buddhism speaks of the saving power of Amida Buddha, who rules over a pure land into which one may be born after death, depending on one's merits in this life. It arose during the 10th to 14th centuries, is associated particularly with Honen (1133–1212), and is based on the idea that Amida Buddha made a vow to save all beings, recognition of which, rather than any personal effort, is what is needed for salvation.

Honen thought that the world was in decline and, in such a period, it was practically impossible to gain enlightenment. The only answer then was to chant *nembutsu* (Namu Amida Butsu = Hail to Amida Buddha).

Shinran (1173–1262) took this one step further. He was married, and insisted that monasticism was not central to Buddhist life. He also argued that secular life was not an obstacle to spiritual progress, and that insistence on remaining sober and celibate was merely a sign of lack of trust. Gaining the Pure Land did not depend on moral goodness, but merely on trust in the power of Amida Buddha. Shinran took this position because (like Honen) he held that the world was in decline, and that people were fuelled by such blind passion that he could not imagine a way that relied on self-mastery and morality.

This is summed up in Shinran's *Hymn on the Lost Age*, which includes this verse:

> **Because the power of the vow is without limits,**
> **Even our evil karma, so deep and heavy, is not burdensome;**
> **Because the Buddha's wisdom is without bounds,**
> **Even the bewildered and wayward are not abandoned.**
>
> (Kyoto: Ryukoku Translation Centre: 1980)

For Shinran, Buddhism is summed up in the phrase *jinen honi* (*jinen* = 'things as they are'; *honi* = made to become through the dharma). In other words, there is a point of naturalness that is prior to any reflection on human and other nature, or between oneself and others, a point at which one is and acts as part of a universe where everything is exactly as it is – nothing more, nothing less.

Insight

Buddhism becomes, in this view, almost synonymous with naturalness. But notice that you have here a conscious move away from reflection and analysis into what appears to be a 'faith' religion. It is very different from the philosophy of early Buddhism, and it is debatable whether it should be considered a philosophy at all.

Nichiren Buddhism is a particularly influential form of Japanese Buddhism, based on the *Saddharma Pundarika Sutra* (*White Lotus Sutra*) and with an emphasis on chanting as the basic spiritual activity. We shall not examine Nichiren Buddhism further, partly because it is concerned more with 'faith' than with philosophy, and partly because it shares the basic Mahayana philosophy that has already been outlined. There is one concept of Nichiren's that needs to be mentioned, however: the principle of *ichinen-sanzen*. This is the view that every moment of thought contains all world systems. Your mind is not limited to time and place. Just as, at enlightenment one is thought to have immediate knowledge of everything; so, for Nichiren, at the moment at which you chant, you sum up everything that has ever happened in all world systems. The act of chanting '*Namu myo-ho renge-kyo*' (Hail to the Lotus of the Perfect Truth) elevates the individual to a state of Buddhahood and oneness with the whole of cosmic reality.

Insight

Although within a tradition of Buddhist philosophy, it is interesting to see how closely this comes to a traditional Hindu idea of awareness that the Atman is at one with Brahman; the self finds a greater self with which it is identified.

With much of Eastern thought, as was said at the beginning of this book, there is a blending of what in the West would separate into philosophy on the one hand and religion on the other. In this last section it has been important to mention some of the religious developments within the Mahayana tradition, although their exploration in terms of their religious significance is beyond the scope of this book.

On the other hand, there were two very distinctive directions taken within the Mahayana based on very different philosophical principles – Tantra and Zen. These we shall consider in Chapters 7 and 8.

10 THINGS TO REMEMBER

1 Bodhisattva images express qualities to be cultivated on the Buddhist path.

2 There are six 'perfections': generosity, morality, patience, energy, meditation, wisdom.

3 Mahayana Buddhism sought to engage emotion and imagination as a balance to the earlier emphasis on rational analysis.

4 Madhyamaka philosophy emphasizes 'emptiness' (shunyata).

5 There is a distinction between conventional and ultimate truth.

6 Yogacara philosophy argues that what appear as things in the world are actually mental constructs.

7 Personal continuity over time may be accounted for in terms of 'seeds' planted by experience, which come to fruition later.

8 The Tathagatagarbha doctrine claims that we all have a Buddha nature.

9 Elaborate cosmological descriptions may be a way of claiming eternal significance.

10 Some forms of Japanese Buddhism emphasize devotion and chanting rather than morality and discipline.

5

Confucianism

In this chapter you will:
- *look at the background to Chinese philosophy*
- *study the basic teachings of Confucius*
- *examine the nature of society and ethics in Confucian thought.*

Background notes on Chinese thought

Chinese philosophy has a history that stretches back for more than two and a half millennia, and has been shaped by the blending of different traditions. Before the unification of China under the Ch'in Dynasty (from which the name 'China' comes) in 221 BCE, there were many different schools of philosophy, the principal ones being Confucianism and Taoism, both of which originated in the 6th century BCE. Of the others, we will consider the yin/yang school under Taoism in Chapter 6 and we will look briefly at Mohism and Legalism in this chapter.

The thought of a people is shaped by its language and writing. To appreciate Chinese philosophy, it is therefore important to reflect on the nature of Chinese writing. In Chinese, a word gains its meaning largely from the context within which it is used. You can't tell the tense of a verb, for example, except by its context. What is more, Chinese characters are ideograms depicting whole concepts, and those characters change as further ideas are added to them.

It is therefore a good written language in which to set a number of complex ideas next to one another, hinting at their relationship, but not one in which it is easy to weld concepts into a logical argument. One of the first impressions you receive when reading a traditional work of Chinese philosophy, like the *Analects* of Confucius, is that you are presented with nuggets of wisdom, but not long arguments;

you have advice for living well and harmoniously, but little explanation of the rationale behind such advice.

It is also important to recognize the very conservative nature of Chinese writing. A Chinese scholar examines and interprets characters which have remained almost unchanged in meaning since they were originally written. Contrast this with the situation of someone examining Greek philosophical terms, whose English equivalents may themselves have been influenced by earlier Latin translations.

There are two particular features of Chinese thought, which might be summarized by the words 'harmony' and 'tradition':

▶ In both Taoism and Confucianism we find the idea that there is a natural harmony and interconnectedness of everything, and that wisdom comes by recognizing this and living harmoniously in the light of it. Unlike Western religious thought, which has largely been based on a division between the world and God, with events in the former controlled by the will of the latter, the Chinese have tended to look for spiritual inspiration from a sense of harmony within the world of experience. Even when terms like 'heaven' or 'fate' are used, they are more a description of the way the world is, rather than pointing beyond the world to some other reality.

▶ Confucianism promotes a sense of tradition and stability. Filial obedience, and a reluctance to change anything done by the previous generation, is paramount. The cumulative wisdom of the past is taken and appreciated. This encourages social stability in the sense of regulation and class structure, but it has proved a mixed blessing. In Chinese society, from the early 14th right up to the early 20th century, the Civil Service examinations were based on Confucian thought, and thus we find philosophy being endorsed by society as a whole. On the other hand, with the coming of Communism, Confucianism was identified with the old feudal structures, and its influence therefore declined.

It should also be appreciated that in Chinese thought there is a blending of what in the West would be separated into metaphysics, ethics, sociology, religion and politics. Reading the *Analects* of Confucius, you find a great mixture of advice on cultured living, personal qualities and political strategy, as well as a large number of quite inscrutable comments about individuals and situations.

Although from a modern perspective they appear to be religions, both Confucianism and Taoism are referred to simply as *chiao* (teachings). They both developed religious and cultic elements, but it is clear that they originated as philosophical systems, to be followed by 'schools' of teachers and by individuals.

CHRONOLOGY

► Before the unification of China (in 221 BCE) you have what is often referred to as the 'classical' period of Chinese philosophy, with the emergence of a number of schools, including the broad traditions of Confucianism and Taoism.

► From the unification of China through to the 10th century CE, these traditions continue, but are blended with the increasingly popular Buddhism.

► From the 10th century through to 1912, neo-Confucianism (which, as we shall see, was a form of Confucianism which had broadened to include a number ideas and attitudes which may have originated within the Taoist and Buddhist traditions, and had become more religious) became a key feature of Chinese culture, although existing alongside Buddhism and Taoism.

► From 1912 there is an influx of Western ideas, challenging traditional Chinese thought, particularly Marxism as interpreted within the work of Mao Tse-tung.

This book outlines only the main features of traditional Chinese philosophy. It is not practicable to attempt to deal with 20th-century developments, since these reflect a partial acceptance of and reaction to Western thought, and are made more complicated by the great social and political upheavals of the century. However, an appreciation of basic Taoist and Confucian philosophy is essential for those who want to explore modern Chinese thinking and society.

Note on transliteration

There are many different ways of transliterating Chinese characters. Confucius may appear as K'ung Fu-Zi or Kong Fu-Zi. Zhu Xi and Chu Hsi are one and the same. Xun Zi may appear as Hsun Tsu. There may also be confusion between 'j' and 'r'. So, for example, Confucius may be seen as the founder of the 'ju' school or the 'ru' school, and a key concept 'jen' may equally appear as 'ren'.

In practice, the variations should be obvious from the context and an attempt at pronouncing each of them will generally reveal a common Chinese vocalization.

K'ung Fu-Tsu (551–479 BCE)

K'ung Ch'iu is usually known by the honorary title 'Fu-Tsu', which means 'Master'. In the 16th century, Jesuit missionaries in China Latinized this as Confucius, which is why his teachings are now referred to as Confucianism. He is the founder of what is known as the Ru school of philosophy. *Ru* (or *ju*) means 'moralists' or 'scholars'.

Confucius sought the principles upon which a good society should be based, and was concerned with what was involved in being genuinely human – humaneness (*jen* or *ren*). The result of contemplating jen was the formulation of a set of rules of etiquette (*li*). Putting these into practice constituted the moral life (*ch'i*).

A key feature to appreciate here is that, while Confucianism seeks to set out the principles that should govern right action, these are *not* based on a utilitarian assessment of actions and their consequences. The 'gentleman' (and although applicable equally to men and women, the male gender tends to be used in the texts) does what he considers to be right, irrespective of the consequences such action may have for him.

Confucius' work can be summed up thus:

> **The Master took four subjects for his teaching: culture, conduct, loyalty and good faith.**

> (*Analects*, 7.25)

K'ung Fu-Tsu may have been born into an aristocratic family. He sought public office, and became Minister of Justice is the province of Lu. Some accounts say that he was Chief Minister, but these may be the result of later exaggeration. His policies fell out of favour, and in 497 BCE he left Lu and for 13 years he travelled round the neighbouring states, trying to find other governments that would accept his ideas. Failing to do so, he returned to Lu and spent the remainder of his life teaching.

Confucius insisted that he was not expounding new ideas, but was simply handing on existing and established traditions:

> **The Master said: 'I transmit but do not create. Being fond of truth, I am an admirer of antiquity ...'**
>
> (Analects, 7.1)

This saying sets the tone for much Confucian thought, in which the wisdom of the past is revered.

Confucius taught from *The Book of Documents* (which records archives, mainly of Western Chou) and *The Book of Songs*, which he saw as illustrating an ideal age – that of the early Chou (Zhou) Dynasty (1027–266 BCE). In his day, various minor states were at odds with one another, and he looked back to the early Chou as a time of strong leadership, harmony and peace. He therefore he sought to re-establish the moral and social traditions of that time, particularly during the reigns of Kings Wen and Wu.

T'IEN

Confucius spoke of the spiritual goal or purpose of the world as simply *T'ien* (heaven), and a ruler could therefore be called *T'ien Tsu* (Son of Heaven), since he had the responsibility for seeing that everything was correctly ordered.

Confucius regarded his teaching about personal qualities and social issues as also being about T'ien, since they described ways in which the individual could bring his or her life into harmony with the universe as a whole. However, he did not believe that one could speculate about the nature of T'ien; one simply had to acknowledge it and get on with the task of living harmoniously.

The implication of this is that, if we live in a universe that has some sense of order, it makes sense to behave in a way that reflects that order and structure. Once you understand the structure of the universe, then morality follows from living in conformity with it: you follow 'heaven's way'. 'Way' is a translation of the word *Tao* (or *Dao*), which is a key term for both Confucianism and, of course, Taoism.

There are interesting parallels here with the Natural Law approach to ethics set out by Aquinas, and with Aristotle's idea of things having a 'final cause', on which the Natural Law theory was based. For Confucius, 'heaven's way' is not a matter of personal preference, but is a given fact within the universe; it is not something to invent, but something to discover.

Both for Confucians and for those who accept Natural Law, morality is not to be assessed on pragmatic or utilitarian grounds, but is an expression of the fundamental structures and purpose of the whole universe.

One difference worth reflecting on, however, is that the 'final cause' in Aristotle appears to be fixed, in that each object or action has a purpose that is largely independent of its individual circumstances (e.g. the purpose of a knife is 'cutting', irrespective of what kind of cutting the knife is required to do). Within Confucianism, however, the keynote is not fixed purpose, but harmony. Purpose is therefore defined by context. In Taoism this is even more clearly the case, since the Tao is essentially movement, not a fixed essence. Whereas the West has a tendency to dissect experience into particular events and objects, Chinese thought tends to look at movement, direction and interconnectedness.

THE ANALECTS *(LUN-YU)*

The *Analects* is a compilation of moral and social teachings; a complete code of human conduct, with the aim of achieving a harmonious way of living. There is a great variety of styles in the work. Although generally ascribed to Confucius, some of the sayings may pre-date him, while others are later and concern his disciples. Many of them are clearly gathered from oral traditions, and start with the phrase 'The Master said:'.

Some sayings are of general application:

> *1.3 The Master said: 'Clever words and a plausible appearance have seldom turned out to be humane.'*

This introduces the key term jen (humane). In a sense, everything in the *Analects* turns on this fundamental question: What is it to be truly humane? What is true human nature, and how should it be expressed?

Insight

Jen (or ren), as it is used here, is very much a practical and external expression of qualities. Confucius divides people into three categories:

Sheng-ren – a sage, who embodies and transmits wisdom;

Junzi – a noble or 'gentleman' who strives to do what is right;

Xiao-ren – a 'small man' who acts without reference to morality.

Jen enables a person to overcome the selfishness that is fundamental to the behaviour of the 'small man' and to practise etiquette – the right or appropriate behaviour for each occasion – in order to be a 'gentleman'.

In seeking to become humane, tradition and social awareness are important:

> **1.2. filial piety and fraternal duty – surely they are the roots of humaneness.**

Confucius was concerned with the well-being of society, and he therefore promotes a general attitude of benevolence, but such benevolence is not offered universally, but based on what is of most value and on family loyalty (a point that was to be criticized later by Mohist thinkers – see 'Critics of Confucius' below).

> **1.6 The Master said: 'Young men should be filial when at home and respectful to elders when away from home. They should be earnest and trustworthy. Although they should love the multitude far and wide, they should be intimate only with the humane. If they have any energy to spare after so doing, they should use it to study "culture".'**

Insight

Notice how this verse introduces another key element in Confucian thought: culture. Education (which for Confucius meant the study of the classics, which included the collection of poetry used in royal rituals of the early Chou dynasty – *The Book of Songs* – along with *The Book of Rites* and *The Spring and Autumn Annals*, a collection of brief entries about the concerns of that time) was essentially a matter of exploring and assimilating traditional wisdom. For Confucius, the process of thinking was never to be separated from the cultural and historical matrix within which it took place.

For Confucius, it was never enough simply to think, one should also study. Indeed, he saw learning as necessary to prevent almost every other human quality from being spoiled by being taken to extremes:

> **17.7** *If one loves humaneness but does not love learning, the consequence of this is folly; if one loves understanding but does not love learning, the consequence of this is unorthodoxy; if one loves good faith but does not love learning, the consequence of this is damaging behaviour; if one loves straightforwardness but does not love learning, the consequence of this is rudeness; if one loves courage but does not love learning, the consequence of this is rebelliousness; if one loves strength but does not love learning, the consequence of this is violence.*

In other words, an appreciation of tradition and culture helps avoid the harm that can come from the exercise of otherwise positive qualities. Individual thought, assertiveness or courage are not good or bad in themselves, but they are dangerous without a sense of the culture within which they are exercised.

Of course, Confucius recognized that at each stage of life certain things are particularly likely to hinder the development of humaneness:

> **16.7** *Master Kong said: 'There are three things which the gentleman guards against: in the time of his youth, when his vital powers have not yet settled down, he is on his guard in matters of sex; when he reaches the prime of life and his vital powers have just attained consistency, he is on his guard in matters of contention; and when he becomes old and his vital powers have declined, he is on his guard in matters of acquisition.'*

In this verse, he uses the contrast between the 'gentleman' and the 'small man'. This is widely used as a way of highlighting the qualities that make for humaneness. For example:

> **2.14** *The Master said: 'The gentleman has universal sympathies and is not partisan. The small man is partisan and does not have universal sympathies.'*

> **7.37** *The Master said: 'The gentleman is calm and peaceful; the small man is always emotional.'*

> **13.26** *The Master said: 'The gentleman is dignified but not arrogant. The small man is arrogant but not dignified.'*

Generally speaking, his criterion for assessing individual action seems to be whether or not it benefits society as a whole. But this is not simply utilitarian, rather, it is based on the view of the qualities that make a good ruler, and thus the qualities that should be encouraged within society. He seeks to promote a balanced and open-minded view of oneself. For example:

> **4.14** One is not worried about not holding position; one is worried about how one may fit oneself for appointment. One is not worried that nobody knows one; one seeks to become fit to be known.

> **6.18** The Master said: 'When substance prevails over refinement there is churlishness, and when refinement prevails over substance there is pedantry. Only if refinement and substance are properly balanced, does one become a gentleman.'

In dealing with society, a person should be even handed, and should act for the benefit of society as a whole, not for personal profit:

> **4.10** The Master said: 'In his attitude to the world the gentleman has no antagonisms and no favouritisms. What is right he sides with.'

> **4.12** If one acts with a view to profit, there will be much resentment.

There are two key terms used in the *Analects* that need to be appreciated li (rites, correct behaviour or etiquette) and jen (humaneness):

Jen (or ren)
Many passages in the *Analects* give definitions of jen, for example:

> **12.22** The Master said: 'It is to love others.'

> **13.19** The Master said: 'Courtesy in private life, reverence in handling business, loyalty in relationships with others. They should not be set aside, even if one visits barbarian tribes.'

> **17.5** Zizhang asked Master Kong about humaneness. Master Kong said: 'One who can bring about the practice of five things everywhere under Heaven has achieved humaneness.' When he begged to ask about them, he said: 'Courtesy, tolerance, good faith, diligence, and kindness.'

Li
Confucius considered that it was only by following a code of social etiquette that one could achieve humaneness. In this, he was

following the tradition of the literature of the Chou Dynasty that he took as the basis of his teaching. He considered that ritual was able to establish a proper balance in life:

> **8.2** **The Master said: 'If one is courteous but does without ritual, then one dissipates one's energies; if one is cautious but does without ritual, then one becomes timid; if one is bold but does without ritual, then one becomes reckless; if one is forthright but does without ritual, then one becomes rude.'**

Knowing the correct thing to do in any situation (for example, in dealing with those who are in mourning), although it may appear formal and therefore devoid of spontaneity, aims to help shape a person's awareness, and therefore to increase their humaneness.

But one can only follow li if one knows one's proper place in the universal scheme of things. That involves what is called 'the rectification of names.' This is both an argument about the place of philosophy in society, and a warning about misunderstanding concepts. In the *Analects*, it is put like this:

> **13.3** **If names are not rectified, then words are not appropriate. If words are not appropriate, then deeds are not accomplished. If deeds are not accomplished, then the rites and music do not flourish. If the rites and music do not flourish, then punishments do not hit the mark. If punishments do not hit the mark, then the people have nowhere to put hand or foot. So when a gentleman names something, the name can definitely be used in speech; and when he says something, it can definitely be put into practice. In his utterances the gentleman is definitely not casual about anything.**

In other words, one should think and speak precisely, in order not to be confused about what one (and others) should do.

Note

The 'Rectification of Names' issue was taken up later, especially by Han Fei (280–233 BCE) of the Legalist tradition. He was concerned that concepts should relate to actualities, and that there should be logical consistency in all claims. He gave the example of a man who wanted to sell a lance and shield, but who argued that the shield could not be pierced by anything, but also that the lance was capable of piercing anything. Han Fei points out that the two claims cannot both be true. This example gave rise to the term *maodun* (contradiction) in Chinese, being made up of *mao* (lance) and *dun* (shield).

Confucius was concerned to promote hard work, courtesy between people and education. The teaching is practical and secular. So, for example, where there are religious rituals connected with those who have died, they are considered in terms of the effects they have on the living, rather than on any otherworldly beliefs. Notice also that, for Confucius, li allows for a social hierarchy. Each person's li is appropriate for his or her social position.

Much of the teaching offers advice about what is worthwhile and what should be avoided:

> **16.4** *Master Kong said: 'There are three kinds of friendship which are beneficial and three kinds of friendship which are harmful. It is beneficial to make friends with the upright, to make friends with the sincere, and to make friends with those who have heard many things. It is harmful to make friends with the ingratiating, to make friends with those who are good at seeming pliant, and to make friends with those who have a ready tongue.'*

> **16.5** *Master Kong said: 'There are three kinds of pleasure which are beneficial and three kinds of pleasure which are harmful. It is beneficial to take pleasure in the proper arrangement of rites and music, to take pleasure in talking about the good points of other men, to take pleasure in having a large number of friends who are men of quality. It is harmful to take pleasure in the delights of showing off, to take pleasure in a self-indulgent life-style, and to take pleasure in the delights of feasting.'*

His ethics are presented in terms of the qualities that make someone a 'gentleman', but however objectively the duties and rites appear to be set out, it is important to realize that for Confucius (and later thinkers within this tradition) the essential thing is right motivation. You should not do what it right in order to gain respect or acclaim, but only because it follows li or is a natural expression of your cultivation of jen. His ethical position is therefore closely linked with his basic view of the nature of humanity. Asked to sum up his teaching, Confucius gave what is known in the West as a form of the 'Golden Rule':

> **15.24 Zigong asked: 'Is there a single word such that one could practise it throughout life?' The Master said: 'Reciprocity, perhaps? Do not inflict on others what you yourself would not wish done to you.'**

Two verses from the *Analects* sum up this early phase of Confucianism:

> **7.6 The Master said: 'Set your heart on the Way, base yourself on virtue, rely on humaneness, and take your relaxation in the arts.'**

Underlying everything is the idea of *ming* (fate). There is a fundamental ordering of the cosmos, and one cannot escape from what it presents. On the other hand, appreciating a sense of what is inevitable enables one to see also what can be changed and cultivated. The last verse of the *Analects* sums up what is involved in following the Way:

> **20.3 The Master said: 'If one does not understand fate, one has no means of becoming a gentleman; if one does not understand the rites, one has no means of taking one's stand; if one does not understand words, one has no means of understanding people.'**

Note on divination

Clearly, divination plays a significant part in Chinese thought, as we can see from the importance of the *I Ching* (*Book of Changes*). Divination is the prediction of the future on the basis of an awareness of the process of change here and now. But it is recognized that human beings have a part to play in shaping the future – indeed, knowing what one should do (and thus how one should influence the future) is the reason for seeking divination in the first place. Divination is therefore not the same thing as fate. The future is not fixed, but may be the object of wise forecasting.

Insight

Confucius saw a natural harmony between heaven and earth. This does not imply that there is a separate world of 'heaven' which things on earth are advised to emulate, nor a separate world of God or the gods. Rather, 'heaven' refers to an ideal or spiritual order, and 'earth' to the way things are in the here and now. That is why Chinese philosophy integrates metaphysical ideas and moral and social concepts so easily. Heaven and earth may be very different in quality, but they are not two separate realms.

AUTHORITY?

Since there are more statements than arguments in Confucius' work, one may be tempted to ask about the authority on the basis of which he made them. Well, by his own admission, his teachings were not original. He saw himself as one who expounded traditional teachings, especially as they were reflected in the early Chou dynasty. His authority, therefore, is the authority of tradition, and the appeal to it is backed up by the idea of a golden age in the past, contrasted with present chaos.

Insight

It seems that there is a fundamental contrast between the Confucian and Taoist views on the source of valid knowledge.

The Taoist sage Lao Tsu said: 'Without going out of doors, one can know all that happens in the world; without looking out of one's window, one can grasp the law of heaven.' In other words, you start with a concept, either apprehended intuitively or accepted as a result of logical argument, and on that basis you can observe and comment on actual societies, whether past or present. Authority lies with intuition and rational thought.

By contrast, Confucianism is based on the observation of actual societies and the acceptance of traditions that are passed down within them. Its truth may be validated pragmatically; in other words, if you follow this teaching, you will live in harmony and therefore know that it is right.

CRITICS OF CONFUCIUS

Mo Tzu (479–380 BCE or 468–376 BCE)

Mo Tzu criticized the social and moral implications of Confucian thought, on the grounds that it encouraged particular concern for one's own family at the expense of a more universal feeling of goodwill. Mo Tzu claimed that such exclusive loyalty was the root of all evil, and sought to replace it with a view of society based on *jianai* (respect) in which all were to be treated equally.

Whereas Confucius expected people to conform to the hierarchy, Mo Tzu wanted them simply to avoid those things that adversely affected others. Mo Tzu argued for a positive form of the golden rule, namely that one should love others as oneself. He thought that one should act to benefit society as a whole, and that this implied helping one another without distinction based on kinship or rank. He also believed that one should appoint as rulers only those who know and understand the common people. On a practical level Mo Tzu sought greater frugality, and he was particularly critical of the resources that were lavished on funeral rites.

The Confucian response to this complaint was to claim that to have no sovereign and no father was to revert to being like birds and beasts, and that one must love those to whom one is nearest before one can develop love for those far off.

Mo Tzu also criticized Confucius for not believing in gods and spirits, for wasting money on ceremonies and for supporting the hierarchy. He wanted to set aside tradition and authority and examine society on the basis of reason. He seems to have had some idea of a deity – with a purpose and a will – expressed in the perceived sense of order in the universe, and argued that all are equal in the eyes of heaven and therefore that one should love all equally. Mencius (see below) was later to say that this outraged all human feelings.

Mo Tzu argued that people understand what is to their benefit and what to their harm. Therefore the right thing to do is that which is required by the common good, agreement on which should be the ruling principle of society. Consequently, he held that people should rise in society depending on their merits, not on their ancestry.

Insight

In terms of political philosophy, Mo Tzu introduced some important principles, aimed at a practical balance between the extremes of Confucian traditionalism and Taoist individualism. He established a basis for democracy, for a free market economy and for utilitarianism. The essential feature of his thinking is the conviction that individuals do actually know what is in their own best interests, and do not have to discover what is right through publicly accepted traditions.

For Mohists (the term used for those who follow Mo Tzu's philosophy) the highest good was to give of oneself for the benefit of all. They argued for simplicity in living, and were totally opposed to war or aggression of any kind. They were prepared to defend a city against attackers, and if necessary they were prepared to give their lives in doing so, but would not approve of any offensive action.

Of course, Confucius (and later Mencius) would have said that such an approach was naive, and it did not fit the obvious fact that people do not treat everyone equally, but have special concern for their family, their friends and those of like disposition and social status.

Mo Tzu seems to have anticipated the utilitarianism of Bentham and Mill, that one should seek the greatest good for the greatest number, treating all equally, but also Mill's 'harm principle', namely that one should be free to do whatever does not harm others. Mo Tzu's ethical ideal also parallels the ethical teachings of Jesus, in that self-giving love is the highest principle by which to live.

His argument that people know what is in their own best interests, and should be free to pursue them, finds parallels with the economic liberalism of Adam Smith, or even of Milton Friedman.

As well as making these important moral and political points, Mo Tzu also had some very clear views on epistemology (the theory of knowledge). In order to be confidant in accepting the truth of a belief, Mo Tzu recommended that one should do three things:

- ▶ check the source of that belief
- ▶ examine the situation in which that belief applies
- ▶ test out to see if the belief is practical.

One could almost imagine David Hume taking this approach; indeed, it is not far removed from his own examination of evidence. For example, in the case of the claim that a miracle has taken place, Hume wants any evidence to be assessed in terms of its conformity with the rest of experience and also in terms of the reliability of the person who makes a particular claim – in case it is more likely that a person was mistaken than that an event took place. But there is also a hint of pragmatism in Mo Tzu's approach.

Confucius had approved of the idea of destiny or fate. He believed that one should recognize what cannot be changed, in order to enable one to channel one's energies more effectively into what can be changed. In this sense, fate was a guide to action. But Mo Tzu opposed the idea of fate. He thought that any belief in fate would encourage people to be lazy, for they would see no point in making an effort to improve something that was inevitable. Also, he argued that morality should be encouraged by the use of rewards and punishments, and people should be made aware that they have both the possibility and duty to behave morally. This approach contrasted with both Confucius and later Mencius, for whom morality should be its own reward.

Insight
Notice in general how Mo Tzu reflects the Eastern approach to philosophy, which tends to blend epistemology, metaphysics and morals. What you understand to be true depends on the nature of reality, and that is assessed by testing out a belief in practical situations. In Eastern thought, belief is a very practical and social matter.

Yang Chu
Yang Chu was a later critic of Confucian thought (in this case, as expounded by Mencius). We only know of him through the comments of his opponents, since none of his writings have survived, but apparently he argued that the age of the city state was past, and that people needed now to look to themselves and the cultivation of their own integrity. One should therefore refuse to become involved in material things, and should not take one's social position or the wishes of other people as a basis for action. Rather, one should pursue one's own interests and pleasure and assume that others will do likewise. In other words, in Western terms, he was an individualistic hedonist.

The Legalist school
For Confucius, the li of the early Zhou dynasty was basic to his view of morality and society. Moral education was possible, and comprised cultivating a person's ren, and the consequent establishment of *yi* (virtue). Although critical of this in many respects (see above) Mo Tzu also held that is was possible to educate people morally, with the help of rewards and punishments. By contrast (as we shall see in the next chapter) Taoism did not attempt to teach social ethics, but rather encouraged individual self-expression and naturalness.

In contrast to all these positions, the Legalists (e.g. Han Fei 280–233 BCE) gave up any attempt to cultivate moral sensitivity. They argued that the only basis of a good society was the rule of law, and that people did not need to develop their own morality, merely the ability to obey the laws that were established.

They argued that each individual acts basically for himself or herself. In order for society to work, this self-interest has to be curbed, recognizing that everyone has some weaknesses and is therefore unlikely to work for the benefit of society as a whole without the imposition of rules. Such rules should be based on *fa*, the principle of justice.

In other words, they argued that morality should be taken out of the sphere of personal development and ideal human nature, and be placed squarely in terms of the needs of society and the structures that will enable it to work. Legalists looked at society and then examined how individuals could fit into it.

Looking at these critics of Confucius, the key philosophical issue here is the extent to which society can be said to exist over and above the individuals that make it up, and therefore whether you can use an idea of society to provide the basis for ethical action. Confucianism and Legalism see social structures and inequalities as a given fact, and allow them to determine what each individual should do. Social harmony comes at the price of social conformity.

By contrast, Mohism sees a universal principle (in this case equal treatment for all) as providing the norm, and therefore determining how society should be organized. Mo Tzu promotes that norm even if it seems to go against natural inclinations and observed facts of human behaviour.

Yang Chu, faced with the dilemmas of either applying norms to transform society, or accepting society's inequalities, opts out completely and takes an individualistic and hedonist approach.

We shall see also how different this is from the Taoist approach, in which everything is based initially on the individual and his or her living at one with the Tao.

The fundamental question here is, 'Is society natural?' If it is, then its inequalities and structures are an inevitable development of human nature and should be accepted as such. If it is not, then we can expect individuals to criticize the norms of society and provide individual or global principles of action by which existing societies can be judged.

The Legalists would certainly have approved of Thomas Hobbes' call for strong leadership and the rule of law in order to prevent lawlessness from allowing life to become 'nasty, brutish and short'.

As to the question of whether it is possible for people to get together and set aside their own particular needs and views in order to decide on a set of rules that will benefit the whole of society, this is exactly the issue addressed by John Rawls' important work *A Theory of Justice*.

Developments of the Ru school

Confucius had combined jen (humanity) with li (etiquette or propriety). A person should cultivate the inner passions and energies (*de*) in a way that was appropriate for his of her social position, thereby maintaining social stability and harmony. His ideas of jen were elaborated by Mencius, who further developed a system of moral self-cultivation, and the idea of li was expounded by Hsun Tsu into a set of objective social norms.

MENCIUS (MENG K'O OR MENG TZU) 390B CE–305 BCE

Whereas the teachings of Confucius, as they have come down to us, take the form of strings of aphorisms and images, each giving particular insights into his understanding of the nature of reality and the appropriate human response to it, Mencius offers a rather more coherent interpretation, although *The Book of Mencius*, which is an important text for Confucianism, also contains many anecdotes.

Mencius was concerned with social justice, and that the *min* (the common people) get what they deserve from the *jen* (the aristocracy). He considered the well-being of the common people to be the criterion by which a ruler should be judged, and was concerned above all with establishing political and social stability. In his view, the world needed to be unified, and such unity could only come about with the aid of clear principles.

Much of his teaching places emphasis on the practical. On work, he says:

A constant mind without a constant livelihood is impossible.

(Mencius, 3a:5)

and on government, its task is:

. . . to produce the necessities of life in sufficient quantity.

(Mencius, 7b:12)

Jen brings about *te* (power), which has the sense of authority rather than physical force. A ruler should govern by *wang* (true kingship) rather than *pa* (physical force); in other words, one should govern through superior virtue.

Mencius believed that everyone is born good and only subsequently learns to do what is evil. His example to illustrate this is the natural response that everyone would have to save a child who is in immediate danger of falling into a well. In fact, he thought that there were four things that pointed to innate goodness:

- ▶ a natural feeling of compassion
- ▶ a sense of shame
- ▶ courtesy
- ▶ a sense of right and wrong.

Mencius held that, although human nature (*hsing*) was essentially good, it needed to be nurtured:

To preserve one's mind and nourish one's nature is the way to serve heaven.

(Mencius, 7a:1)

Western

Jean-Jaques Rousseau's theory, here, rather than that of Hobbes!

But, although a person's character is shaped by human nature and by *hsin* (mind), these in themselves cannot determine exactly what will happen to that person in life – that is down to *ming* (fate), which is in the hands of heaven.

He held that the basic substance (or energy) of the universe was *ch'i*, and that some ch'i was heavy and some more refined and subtle. Human beings were a mixture of the heavy and the subtle ch'i and the recognition of this gives the possibility of self-development in line with the natural harmony of the universe. We shall see later how these ideas came to be further developed within neo-Confucian philosophy.

HSUN TZU (XUN ZI) 312 (OR 325 OR 289)–238 BCE

By contrast with Mencius, the other main philosopher of the Ru school, Hsun Tzu, was an atheist and rationalist. For Hsun Tzu, heaven was impersonal; he identified it with nature and the natural process.

Insight

In a way, this identification of 'heaven' with the natural process brings the Confucianism of Hsun Tsu nearer to Taoism, since (unlike Confucius who sees 'the will of heaven' as an external, ideal structure to which individual people and events should conform) Hsun Tsu finds his guidelines exclusively within the natural process.

Unlike Mencius, he held that humans were actually born with a naturally selfish hsing (nature) and had to be educated to become good; human nature needed to be tamed and guarded by li (conventional etiquette).

So li – the rites of early religion which had become a code of conduct for Confucius – was seen by Hsun Tsu as a way of controlling the lives of those who had not yet been fully tutored into goodness, a training device for social control. His key theme was self-improvement through study, and consequently he considered that the proper function of an educated man was to govern.

For Hsun Tzu, the human mind is central. He held a totally rationalist and humanistic view, and was against superstition of any sort. If humans are born selfish, that is the way life is, and he does not seek to explain it away, rather he tries, through education, to enable individuals and society to rise above their natural state.

These three early philosophers – Confucius, Mencius and Hsun Tzu – form the basis of what was later to be known generally as 'Confucianism', although – as we shall see – there were later developments.

During the last couple of centuries BCE, Confucianism accepted ceremonies, and in this sense started in the direction of becoming more like a religion than a moral and social philosophy, which it had certainly been under its founder.

At the same time, Confucian thought became more influenced by the Chinese view of balance within nature in the form of the Yin and the Yang. The Yin represents darkness, passivity and the feminine principle. The Yang represents light, activity and the masculine principle. Life requires both, and they should balance one another. This balance of Yin and Yang is particularly important within the Taoist tradition, and a description of it is given in Chapter 6. But it should be noted that yin/yang is a view of nature that really constitutes a separate school of philosophy, and it certainly influenced Confucianism as well as Taoism.

Neo-Confucianism

Although during the Han dynasty (202 BCE–220 CE) Confucianism had briefly been accepted as the state cult, the major change took place with the Sun dynasty (960–1279) during which it became the official cult. By this time it had been influenced by Taoism, Buddhism and yin/yang philosophy, and the result is generally referred to as neo-Confucianism.

CHU HSI (ZHU XI) 1130–1200

Chu Hsi started out as a student of Buddhism, but he could not accept the Buddhist idea of anatta (no fixed self), he therefore turned to the Confucian tradition and became the main exponent of what is called neo-Confucianism. His teachings were accepted as orthodox, during the long period of the Ming and Quing dynasties (14th–20th centuries), and this form of Confucianism was influential in shaping China's social fabric right up until the Communist takeover in 1949.

Four books form the canon of neo-Confucianism: *Lun Yu* (the *Analects* of Confucius); *Meng Tzu* (the book of *Mencius*); *Ta Hsuch* (*The Great Learning*); *Chung Yung* (*The Doctrine of the Mean*).

Ultimate principles

The Confucianism of Chu Hsi is far more metaphysical than the earlier tradition. He linked human conduct and tradition with a set of ultimate principles, and in doing so gave new meaning to some basic Confucian terms. In early Confucianism, li was the term used for the principle of moral behaviour, which can perhaps best be translated as 'doing what is right and appropriate'. For Chu Hsi, however, the term li is used for the ultimate principle behind everything; eternal, unchanging and good. The li of something is its true nature, it is the reason it is as it is. It therefore includes the earlier meaning of 'right order or behaviour' but now involves much more. But nothing can be pure li – it needs a physical basis, the actual stuff out of which is it made. That physical element Chu Hsi called ch'i. Thus the ultimate principle (li) is expressed within everything through the ever-changing material force (ch'i), which is the energy and matter of the cosmos.

The hsing (nature) of human beings is the expression of the li within them. Individuals do not always understand their li, however, because their minds are clouded through the dulling effect of impure ch'i, and as a result their natures, although basically good, may be distorted. The process of self-cultivation is one of shedding the distorting effects of ch'i to reveal the underlying li.

Western

There appears to be a basic dualism here, with the ultimate principle on the one hand and matter on the other, but it is not the same as the Western mind/matter dualism. Ch'i produces both mind and matter. It is safer to keep away from Western dualistic notions in looking at neo-Confucianism, and simply to think of li and ch'i as, respectively, the 'principle of reality' and 'actual expression of reality'.

Ch'i, as the material force of the universe, integrates to produce life and disintegrates to produce death. Since ch'i produces the mind and consciousness as well as the body, these too arise as a result of the integration of force, and cease to be once disintegration takes place. All of life and death is therefore a direct expression of ch'i.

Yin/yang philosophy is integrated into this general metaphysical scheme, since yin/yang is the vehicle for change. Both these passive and active aspects of life are expressions of li (the ultimate principle) and come about through ch'i (material force)

As always in Eastern philosophy, metaphysics leads on to matters of morality. But there is a basic problem for Chu Hsi:

▶ If all is ruled by li, and if li is good, where does evil come from?

His answer was to hold that, although human nature is fundamentally good, it can be influenced by the dulling effect of material forces. There is no positive force of evil, but rather a range of impurities within material form. Another way of expounding the same thing is in terms of balance and imbalance. When there is natural balance and harmony, the li of the cosmos is reflected and all is well. When there is imbalance, brought about by the density of material forces, then the li is obscured and the result is evil.

Chu Hsi, following the original terminology of Confucius, went on to say that the unhindered operation of li through an individual was shown as ren – right and noble conduct. He gives a positive role to individuals in generating ren. Evil is overcome by knowledge, in that a person needs to investigate things and see the ways in which material forces are obscuring the basic li, in order to overcome them. By cultivating an awareness of the fundamental principle within things (li), one will naturally develop noble conduct.

TAI CH'I (THE SUPREME ULTIMATE)

In neo-Confucianism li does not just refer to external behaviour, but is a principle of reason that exists eternally in everything. This gives rise to a further term – *Tai Ch'i* – which is the li of heaven and earth. There is therefore a Confucian cosmology: at its starting point is Tai Ch'i, from which there arises ch'i, which is the material basis of things. The ch'i gives rise to the *yang* (movement) and the *yin* (quiescence), representing the ongoing process of change and balance, and these in turn give rise to the five elements – metal, wood, water, fire and earth – of which everything is composed.

In one sense, however, these elements are not merely physical, they refer to dispositions within everything. Thus the 'five powers' theory of nature expounds the five natural processes in a way that enables them to be related to human activity and dispositions:

- ▶ water – has the quality of flowing down
- ▶ fire – has the quality of flaming up
- ▶ wood – has the quality of growing either bent or straight
- ▶ metal – has the quality of alteration
- ▶ earth – has the quality of allowing itself to be cultivated.

This is all part of the natural integration of the Chinese view of life – the five powers are symbols of processes which bind human beings to the rest of the natural order.

Neo-Confucianism developed many different schools, each with particular emphases. One thinker who deserves special mention is Wang Yang-Ming (1472–1529). Self-cultivation is at the heart of Confucianism, and the way in which one is to set about this is therefore of great importance. Chu Hsi – as one might imagine from the way in which he set out the normative canon of scriptures – considered that one ought to study the classics as a means of self-cultivation. This became the standard view, and the norm for entry into the Civil Service was just such knowledge. Wang Yang-Ming, however, emphasized the importance of reflecting on one's own actions and thoughts, becoming vigilant for signs of selfishness and other distorting factors.

Insight

Watching the mind at work as a method of self-cultivation has many parallels within the Buddhist tradition, where 'mindfulness' has always been a key feature, and it was the Ch'an tradition of Buddhism that had a particularly important impact in China. It is clear that much neo-Confucianism was influenced by Taoist and Buddhist thought, but from time to time there were attempts on the part of Confucians to distance themselves from the resulting metaphysics and get back to a study of the classic texts.

For neo-Confucianism, morality reflects a natural balance within the cosmos. There are interesting Western parallels to this, particularly in the pre-Socratic philosophies of ancient Greece. One might explore the ideas of Heraclitus, who – in a world where everything is in a constant state of change – sought the 'logos' or principle behind everything, and the natural equilibrium of things. Equally, Pythagoras spoke of moral qualities in terms of finding an expression of heavenly harmony within the human soul.

Relating morality to essential human nature is a feature of the Natural Law approach to ethics.

To sum up:

▶ Neo-Confucianism is about becoming harmoniously integrated with the whole cosmos.
▶ Some parts (e.g. Yin/Yang) sound Taoist.
▶ Some parts (e.g. investigation of conditions) sound Buddhist.
▶ But they were integrated into a single overall philosophy which has been immensely influential within Chinese thought and culture.

The self and society

PRINCIPLES OF CONDUCT

For Confucius, li (correct behaviour) found its expression in the five different kinds of personal relationships (sovereign/subject; father/son; husband/wife; elder/younger brother; friend/friend) but, in considering behaviour, he also distinguished between two different categories of people – *junzi* (prince, or ruler) and *xiao ren* (common person). This distinction was not simply one of social position, but between those who lived by superior or inferior moral standards, the moral requirements placed upon the ruler being superior to those expected of the common man. But what is remarkable about this is that Confucius sees the 'gentleman' as being distinguished by his or her behaviour, not by social status. In a hierarchical society, that was radical and gave a moral edge to the whole social order.

Western

One could explore interesting parallels between what Plato demands by way of personal and moral qualities of the guardian rulers in *The Republic* and the moral standing of Confucius' junzi.

But li is an outward expression of an inner quality (jen), which is expressed in good-heartedness, humaneness or love. So, although one's *yi* (duty) lies in performing li, that does not imply that it is a matter of formally or mechanically following rules; at its best, it reflects the cultivation of inner quality and a natural integrity of action. Li is the natural expression of jen.

Confucius thought that a ruler should not govern by threats or force:

> *If you govern them by regulations and keep them in order by punishments, the people will avoid trouble but have no sense of shame. If you govern them by moral influence, and keep them in order by a code of manners, they will have a sense of shame and will come to you of their own accord.*

(*Analects*, ii:3).

However, Mencius argued that people had a right to rebel against a ruler if he behaved unjustly. This could be done on the basis of the 'rectification of names'; if the ruler was not behaving as a ruler, he should no longer be considered to be a ruler and therefore removed.

Western

John Locke insisted that a ruler should not be above the law, and might therefore be removed if he or she acted against the interests of the people – a fundamental feature of democracy. Mencius worked on the same principle, but without the democratic structures to put it into effect.

It is important to see the place of destiny or fate (ming) within the Confucian moral system. Unlike Buddhism, which saw events as the working out of an individual's karma, Confucianism sees events as decided by destiny, not as a result of moral goodness or lack of it. Therefore Confucian thought encourages a person to choose what to do single-mindedly, without taking consequences into account, since the future is already decided. (This had been opposed as unrealistic by Mo Tzu, see 'Critics of Confucius' above.)

In assessing conduct, and what individuals might or might not be expected to do, a basic question remains: 'Is human nature fundamentally good or bad?' Confucius refused to give an answer to this. Mencius held that we are all naturally good. Although both the negative assessment of Hsun Tzu and the positive one of Mencius existed for a long time within Confucianism, in the end it was the positive view that became Confucian orthodoxy.

Thus the movement from nature to social training can be summed up in the opening of the chapter on 'The Doctrine of the Mean' from the *Book of Rites*:

> **That which is decreed by heaven is what is meant by 'nature'; to follow his nature is what is meant by the 'Way'; cultivation of the Way is what is meant by 'education'.**

RITUALS

Rites, or the norms of social etiquette (li) aim to set down a framework for society and define civilized human behaviour. For example, there are rites in connection with paying respect to one's ancestors, thereby strengthening family ties. Confucius generally believed that a state would prosper if everyone performed the appropriate rites correctly. As we have seen, the concept of li was later broadened and it became a term for the nature of things in themselves.

The six arts

These are: ceremonies, music, chariot driving, archery, writing and arithmetic. They come from a period before Confucius, and are found in the Classic texts that formed the basis of Chinese culture.

Music had a particularly important role in Confucian thought:

> **Education begins with the Odes, is confirmed by practice of the rites, and is completed by music'**

> *(Analects, viii:8)*

Music was thought to influence a person from within, unlike the rites, which operated externally. Music was therefore seen as a force for harmonizing and levelling the emotions. Hsun Tzu said that those who listened to music are filled with a sense of harmonious reverence. When rulers and ministers, members of a family, or the young and old together listen to music, the result is social harmony and the leading of people into a single Way (Tao). In other words, he endorses the idea of music as an instrument of social control and civilization.

Insight

Notice here the balance between internal attitude and external performance. External rites both influence and give expression to inner attitudes. Equally, music, which operates on the emotions, can be used in order to achieve external social cohesion. This would seem to be typical of Chinese thought generally – that the goal of wisdom is to harmonize the inner and outer aspects of reality.

The five cardinal virtues

These have been described already, but we review them here to show the balance of qualities that is sought within Confucian philosophy:

▶ *Jen (ren)*: sympathy towards others; noble, civilized – it is a very general quality of goodness. It finds expression in five qualities: Politeness, liberality, good faith, diligence, generosity (*Analects* xvii:6). Jen is wanting for others also what one wants for oneself, plus coming to appreciate the needs of others. Mencius insisted that such altruism must be completely disinterested: you should do what is right for its own sake, not for the sake of your reputation, or to be praised.

▶ *Yi*: duty – putting jen into practice.

▶ *Li*: the rites that determine good manners; the *Book of Rites* has 300 major and 3,000 minor rules of behaviour. Notice how this concept has broadened out, first to include all correct activity, and later – in neo-Confucianism – to be a metaphysical principle underlying the universe.

▶ *Chih*: wisdom; the sense of right and wrong.

▶ *Hsin*: trustworthiness.

Sexuality in Confucian thought

Generally speaking, the only valid use of sex according to Confucian thought is the conception of children, and particularly of sons who will be able to honour and make sacrifices to their father after his death. There is a sense that male energy is dissipated through sexual union (there are parallels here with Taoism), and that men may be worn out both physically and morally by too much sex. Indeed, sexual excess on the part of a ruler is given as a valid reason to take from him the right to rule.

Insight

In general, sexuality is seen very much from a male perspective in Confucian writings. This is perhaps understandable, given the social situation at the time of early Confucian philosophy. On the other hand, one might have expected the neo-Confucian ideas of cosmic balance and harmony to have been reflected in a similar male/female balance within sexuality.

Ancestors

The family is central to Confucian ethics, and there is great respect for those who are old. Beyond death, respect is paid to ancestors, and one should act as thought they were still alive, doing nothing which would offend them. Like many features of Confucianism, what appears to be a metaphysical belief (that the ancestors are still alive in some way, watching over the family), is actually justified in terms of social cohesion; paying respect to dead ancestors reinforces the sense of identity and the coherence of the family group. It should not be assumed that the object of that respect continues to exist after death, for Confucius himself was dismissive of questions about death:

> **Until you understand life, how can you understand death?**
>
> (*Analects*, xi:11)

In the neo-Confucian period, Chu Hsi believed that consciousness ended with death. On the other hand, there was also the belief that, when sacrifices are made to an ancestor, that person's spirit reassembles during the time of the offering, and then disperses again afterwards.

Essential goodness of the self

We have already noted the conflicting views of Mencius and Hsun Tzu on this. Mencius held that people were naturally good, while Hsun Tzu held that they were naturally evil, needed to be trained to be good, and that society needed laws and guidance to restrict what people might otherwise be inclined to do. Hsun Tzu saw good conduct as conventional rather than innate.

This has implications for education. In Mencius' view, education is a matter of drawing out what is already in people. In terms of morality, they already know what it right and need only the opportunity to reflect and act on it. By contrast, Hsun Tzu's view is that morality needs to be instilled in people for the good of society. And, of course, Taoism would take a view closer to that of Mencius.

Insight

There is a key philosophical problem raised here. Is there (as Confucius implied in calling his moral system 'heaven's way'), a fundamentally moral structure to the universe? If there is, then morality needs to conform to it in order for people to live according to their natures. It would imply that morality is fixed, since fundamental reality does not change with circumstances. Or is morality socially constructed, an attempt to apply reason to potentially unreasonable and destructive human desires, and therefore changeable to suit different social circumstances?

Social change and the natural order

Neo-Confucianism developed alongside Taoism and Buddhism, but its attitude to society was fundamentally different from those other traditions. There was an important sense in which Confucianism wanted to develop and improve society, and whether morality was to be revealed or instilled, there was no doubt that the good of the individual was to be seen in terms of his or her contribution to the overall good of society.

By contrast, both Taoism and Buddhism tended to start with the individual and his or her desire for spiritual progress. Indeed, both traditions tend to revel in the most eccentric of behaviour at times, in order to break down conventional thinking. At risk of over-simplification, one may say that neo-Confucianism saw its task as improving society, thereby helping individuals, while Buddhism and Taoism aimed to improve individuals and thereby help society.

There was another side to Confucianism, however. If the li of relationships is fixed, then changes in the social order violate natural law. Therefore, although Confucianism was always concerned with social well-being, it was a well-being that arose simply as a result of conforming to already established norms of behaviour. As time went on, therefore, Confucianism became increasingly seen as an obstacle to social change.

For a Taoist or Buddhist, the justification for social change would seem to be the degree to which it allows individuals within that society to develop and express themselves. For a Confucian, social relationships are already defined and established. Any change which does not conform to those relationships, even if it allows individuals to express their own personalities, is seen as being, in the long run, a threat to a properly ordered and harmonious society.

Confucianism and the Chinese Republic

Confucianism is not 'other worldly', but is concerned with traditional norms of behaviour. For this reason, it has been closely associated with the culture within which it developed, reinforced by the fact that neo-Confucian texts were at the heart of the Chinese civil service.

After the end of the last (Ch'ing) dynasty and the formation of the Chinese Republic in 1912, Confucianism lost the social and political basis that had supported it, and its influence diminished rapidly. It quickly became identified with Chinese feudalism, particularly in the way that its concepts of filial piety and loyalty had reinforced regimes, and a whole way of life, that was then being seen as repressive. Nevertheless, many of the moral qualities instilled by centuries of Confucianism continued to be followed by individuals.

On the other hand, Mencius had insisted that the people's welfare should take precedence over that of the ruler, and that they had the right to replace a ruler if he did not prove to be just. This feature of Confucian teaching was used to justify social change in the early 20th century. Overall, however, the arrival of communism and the rejection of social hierarchy put an end to Confucianism as a working basis for society.

Confucian ethics, particularly in connection with hard work and family loyalty, may have aided the rise of the commercial and industrial economies of the Far East, but for many, the potential of Confucianism in modern times is mainly in terms of the benefits for individuals of a philosophy that encourages times of quiet, moral reflection.

There has been renewed interest in Confucianism, but mainly in terms of the preservation of Chinese culture and a rejection of Westernization. In particular, it has been emphasized that although Confucianism is a philosophy of life which includes political views, it does not want a return to the old social order.

10 THINGS TO REMEMBER

1 This philosophy is rooted in the *Analects* of Confucius.

2 It is based on *jen* (humaneness, personal goodness) and *li* (correct behaviour).

3 It is a this-worldly philosophy, not one that seeks its justification in an external or eternal realm.

4 Mo Tzu criticized Confucius for the priority he gave to family and friends, seeking a more general and equal concern for all.

5 Mencius thought that everyone was naturally good.

6 Hsun Tzu, by contrast, thought people were naturally selfish and needed to be educated and controlled for the benefit of themselves and society.

7 Neo-Confucianism blended Confucian philosophy with ideas from Taoism and Buddhism and became established as the state cult.

8 Confucian philosophy promotes the use of rites and social etiquette in order to benefit both society and individuals.

9 Confucian ethics tend to start with the need for social harmony, to which individuals are expected to conform.

10 Being associated with social conservatism, the influence of Confucianism waned in China after the establishment of the Chinese Republic in 1912.

6

Taoism

In this chapter you will:
- *explore the teachings of Lao Tzu*
- *explore developments within Taoism*
- *consider the Taoist view of living in harmony.*

Background

Before examining Taoism, it is important to remember its context, in terms of the various Chinese philosophies, recapitulating what was said at the opening of the chapter on Confucianism. Prior to the unification of China in the 3rd century BCE there were a number of different philosophical schools, including:

▶ Taoism
▶ Confucianism
▶ the Ying/Yang school
▶ Mohism
▶ the Legalist School (Pa Chia)
▶ the School of Names (Ming Chia).

Although they did not all survive as independent schools of thought, they influenced one another. Confucianism and Taoism, the two principal traditions, were by no means fixed. As we saw with Confucianism, and will see again in Taoism, there were quite radical changes brought about by subsequent interpretations of their basic ideas.

With the introduction of Buddhism into China there was a further blending of thought. Buddhism adapted itself to fit into the Chinese culture and, in turn, it influenced the existing philosophies. What emerged from this was a triple tradition, comprising Confucianism (in the form that is generally referred to as Neo-Confucianism), Taoism (in both its religious and philosophical forms) and Buddhism.

As we shall see, Taoism is very different from Confucianism, in that it is based on the individual, and tends to reject the impositions of organized society. Within China both traditions have embedded themselves into the general consciousness in such a way that people may accept both but apply them to different aspects of their lives. In terms of the personal balance of one's life, Taoist teachings may be followed; in terms of social etiquette, one becomes a Confucian. And, indeed, in the face of suffering, one may respond as a Mahayana Buddhist. In the Chinese consciousness, boundaries between these are largely unnecessary, for each contributes to the overall wisdom with which life may be encountered and interpreted.

In general, it would be true to say that these traditions did not demand exclusive loyalty. The Chinese were happy to accept a blend of all three, taking from each tradition what was most appropriate for their particular social or personal circumstances.

Lao Tzu

If Taoism can be said to have a founder, it is Lao Tzu. But that means 'old master', and it is therefore an honorary title rather than a name. There is a tradition that he was an older contemporary of Confucius in the 6th century BCE, but in fact he may have been a considerably more ancient figure. It is also clear that the *Tao Te Ching*, the work that contains his teachings, is in fact a compilation of sayings that have been gathered, perhaps over a considerable period of time, some being ascribed to Lao Tsu, others to his disciples. In any case, what matters is not the individual, but the tradition of teaching that his name stands for.

The *Tao Te Ching* is essentially a collection of aphorisms, arranged by subject. Three words make up the title:

► *Tao* means 'way'.
► *Te* means power.
► *Ching* can mean 'essence', but here it means a work of authority; perhaps 'authoritative handbook' or 'classic' is the best translation – something which deals with the essence of the subject.

So one might translate the title as 'Authoritative Handbook on the Way and its Power'.

Key concepts in Taoism

THE TAO

Tao (or *Dao*) means 'path' or 'way', and it refers to the natural way things are. The aim of Taoism is to help individuals to be aware of, and live in unity with, the Tao, characterized by behaviour that is natural, spontaneous and in harmonious balance.

But before examining the individual's response to the Tao, let us first of all look at the way in which Taoists view the world, for the Tao is seen as the principle of creation and the source from which everything arises. The Tao is thought of as so fundamental that it is beyond description. In the famous opening statement of the *Tao Te Ching*:

> **The Tao that can be talked about is not the true Tao.**

And Chapter 42 gives what amounts to the Taoist sequence of creation:

> **The Tao**
> **gives birth to the One;**
> **The One**
> **gives birth to the two;**
> **The Two**
> **give birth to the three;**
> **The Three give birth to every living thing.**
> **All things are held in yin, and carry yang:**
> **And they are held together in the Ch'i**
> **of teeming energy.**

(translation: Element Books, 1993)

We shall look at individual aspects of this a little later.

....

Insight

Although the Tao is thought of as the creative source of everything, it should not be identified with the Western idea of a creator God, a being who is in some way independent of or external to his creation. The creativity of the Tao is a creativity within everything.

....

The Tao is described as the 'origin and mother of the Ten Thousand Things', a standard phrase to indicate everything that exists. It is said to achieve everything without force; it gives life without thereby possessing the things it has created. It is the very essence of naturalness. It is that by which all things become what they are. It is boundless, and it produces the constant flow of ordinary, limited things.

One popular simile used to describe the Tao is water. Water is soft and pliable, but it can exert great force, and will eventually wear away even the hardest rock. To follow the Tao is to find a natural way of achieving one's end, and that may require similar qualities. Another image used by Lao Tzu to describe the Tao is that of a pair of bellows. Once they are being pumped, bellows can provide a constant supply of air, and yet they themselves are empty. They are not diminished by the air coming from them, nor is the air part of them – but there would be no air pumped without them.

The Tao should not be thought of as a separate being or entity of any sort. It is not something that 'exists' in the sense that individual things exist. If anything, it would be more accurate to describe it as 'non-being'. It is that out of which beings emerge. In this respect it is like the Buddhist concept of shunyata (nothingness). Tao is universal and all-pervading; it is also indestructible. In terms of metaphysics, the Tao represents a silent background out of which things emerge and into which they move again. It is not a separately existing thing, but the ground of the coming and going of all existence.

According to Taoist philosophy, rest is prior to motion, and stillness prior to action; therefore the Tao is prior to everything. The Tao, although motionless in itself, offers the basis for all movement. It is that which is absolutely natural. But having said these things about the Tao, we have not thereby defined it in any way, for it is important to recognize that Tao is not something that can be grasped with the intellect (that was the essential thing to recognize in that opening sentence of the *Tao Te Ching*). One may become aware of it, but not define it.

Western

Here we have a parallel with the unmoved mover and uncaused cause of Aristotle and Aquinas. The Tao acts as exactly the unmoved and uncaused basis of everything. The crucial difference, however, is that whereas Western thinkers went on to say that this uncaused cause was 'God' and therefore set over against created things, within Taoism (and other Eastern philosophies) the source of life is not distinct from individual beings, but is their true nature. Becoming aware of the Tao is therefore also to become aware of oneself, just as for Mahayana Buddhists there is awareness of one's own Buddha nature. This is not pantheism, which simply identifies the physical world with God. Probably the closest Western equivalent is panentheism, which argues that everything is within God, and also, therefore, that God is within everything.

TE

Tao is essentially unknowable, and yet is said to bring about everything. What can be seen, however, is *te*, which means 'power'. This represents the presence of Tao within individual things; the energy of Tao in the world.

For Taoism this is not merely a statement about metaphysics (general concepts about how the world is), it is also practical. If a person or thing is following its Tao (in other words, if it is acting naturally) then it will be filled with power (te). This is not thought of as a coercive power, seeking to force change in the world, for that would be contrary to the fundamental insights of Taoism, but a natural power by which something acts to its full potential.

CH'I AND MING

The word ch'i literally means 'breath', and refers to the spirit, energy or life-force within everything. Traditional Chinese medicine speaks of the ch'i as the vital energy flowing through the body at different levels of refinement – physical, sexual, psychological, mental.

The ideal state is one in which a person is at one with the Tao, a state of total satisfaction and naturalness in which there is no need for any struggle or artificial goals. This ideal state is termed *ming* (enlightenment); it is the state in which one sees the eternal law (*ch'ang*) which causes the constant flow and change of everything.

Insight

In many ways, the Taoist idea of ming is like that of Buddhist enlightenment. Both describe the point at which a person becomes aware of the natural process of change.

Change and the Tao

Taoism holds that everything is in a constant state of flux, but that flux is balanced by the Tao. Chinese thought has always recognized that the ultimate is not something fixed but a process of flow and change. An ancient classic text exploring this is the *I Ching*. 'I' means 'change' and 'Ching' means either 'authoritative text' or 'handbook', so the *I Ching* can perhaps best be described as a handbook for divination, a way of interpreting and predicting events and assessing the appropriateness of courses of action on the basis of those predictions. It engages with the individual using it, so that (rather like astrology) the individual must contribute an element of interpretation if its predictions are to be used wisely.

Like Buddhism, Taoism sees everything as changing and impermanent. The only thing that is permanent is ch'ang – the eternal principle or law which governs that process. However, there is always a temptation to interpret the present entirely in terms of the past (the reason why things have worked out like this) or the future (this is what I want to happen eventually) – seeking some justification or explanation for the present. However, Taoism (like Buddhism) insists that one should focus on the reality of the present moment. Chuang Tzu (in Chapter 14 of his book of the same name) commented:

> *If people could follow the ancient way, then they would be masters of the moment.*

Here there is another important feature of Taoist thought. The world is as it is, and if there is any perfection, it is the perfection of what is, not what we imagine it should be. But if that is the case, then any attempt to change the world is only going to result in making it less perfect. To find perfection, we have simply to rest in that which is natural. In other words, the enemy of human perfection is the unnatural, which includes the forced, the premeditated and the socially prescribed.

Western

Within a Western Judaeo-Christian tradition, the world is fallen; it is a place where being natural is to be in a state of sin and separation from God. The best hope of redemption is to be restored to the state that

Adam found himself in before the Fall. From a Western religious perspective, perfection is never possible, because it is a quality that can only really be applied to God. From a secular Western perspective, perfection often seems to be located in the future, as a hope rather than a reality to be experienced in the present. Thus, to be natural is to be fallen, and some of the most powerful aspects of naturalness, like sexuality and aggression, therefore need to be restrained and allowed to operate only within narrowly prescribed parameters.

Taoism is quite the reverse. It seeks to be rid of that which is rational, socially prescribed or restrictive, in order to return to the Tao, the natural balance of nature.

YIN AND YANG

In the creative process by which the Tao is said to bring forth the multiplicity of things (as described in the quotation from the *Tao Te Ching* given above), there is reference to 'The Two', a first differentiation in the movement from the one to the many. This is a reference to *yin* and *yang*, a pair of concepts that are found in both Taoist and Confucian thought, and (as we saw earlier) may actually be considered to constitute a school of philosophy in its own right.

The idea of yin and yang is probably very ancient, but its first systematic formulation was set out by Tsou Yen in the fourth century BCE. It is also set out in the *Shih-I*, a commentary on the *I Ching*, written in the third century BCE.

Yin (dark/female) and yang (light/male) were regarded as the two universal energies, which combine with the five elements to form the basis of everything. Just as the Tao restores balance, so yin and yang, the male and female, need to be balanced. In fact, like the sunny and shady sides of a mountain (from which image we get the terms 'yin' and 'yang') they are quite inseparable and imply one another. Life cannot be all sunshine, nor will it be all shadow; to think otherwise is to be immature.

The T'ai-chi-t'u is 'the symbol of the supreme ultimate':

The dark area represents the yin and the light the yang. Notice that each defines the other. You cannot have yin without yang or vice versa. Notice also how one flows into the other in perfect balance. There is also a small seed of each of them within the heart of the other. This represents the continual flow of male/female, light/dark within everything, recognizing that in the heart of the female there is a male side, and a female side in the heart of the male.

Notice also that there is constant movement in the symbol. There is no point of static balance, only of balanced flow. This balance of the yin and yang aspects of life is influential in all aspects of Chinese thought and culture, but it is not an exclusive philosophy, and it is compatible with other religions.

In examining Buddhism, with its acceptance of the universal phenomenon of dukkha (suffering or unsatisfactoriness), we saw that the philosophy was not negative or pessimistic, but merely sought to be realistic. Similarly, the yin/yang balance is not imposed in some fatalistic way, but is simply offered as a realistic assessment of the way things are. To pretend that you can always live in light without shadow, or that the shadow is some accident that has happened in a world designed to be all light, is fundamentally alien to Eastern thought as a whole. The balance of growth and diminishment, happiness and sadness, gain and loss is an essential feature of life. From this perspective, wisdom consists in seeing it, living in harmony with it, and thereby finding a happiness that is not dependent upon permanent sunshine.

In the West, there has been a tendency to define how life should be, and then struggle with the fact that life does not conform to such a definition. Typical of this is the 'problem of evil', where belief in a good and loving creator is challenged by the fact of suffering and death.

In the East, as exemplified by the blending of yin and yang, there is a recognition that in reality life is always a balance between opposing energies.

See also, for example, the Hindu concept of the god Shiva as both creator and destroyer, or the Buddhist 'Wheel of Life', where the craving for life is depicted as a process held within the jaws of death. Yin and yang, distinct but inseparable, express the natural flow of the Tao.

There is another important feature of the yin/yang balance in life: yin represents inactivity, rest and reflection; yang represents activity and creativity. The ideal is to balance these two features of life. Taoist philosophy suggests that you cannot act effectively without periods of quiet reflection, but equally such periods of inactive reflection lead naturally into taking skilful action. This balance is not merely a feature of lifestyle, but reflects the very basic feature of the Tao, that it restores balance. When anything reaches one extreme, it starts to swing back to the opposite; there is a constant movement from activity to inactivity and back again.

A person's identity is also related to yin and yang. Whether male or female, we have both yin and yang aspects, and this produces a process of change and apparent contradiction which cannot be resolved. But it is important to realize that for Taoism it would be wrong to attempt to resolve this particular struggle, for it is simply our particular manifestation of the yin/yang movement within everything.

We do not have a fixed identity – that is the central feature of philosophical Taoism's approach to the self (as in Buddhism). We are what we are through a natural process of change. At no point do we arrive at a true or authentic self. As with the universe, the only thing that is fixed is the process of change itself.

Notice how radically different this is from some Western thought. For Plato, there are ideal forms of which individual things are but imperfect copies, and the within the Philosophy of Mind, the dualist tradition has separated off the true self or mind from the physical body. Religious groups have suggested that your true self will one day be revealed, either because you are essentially eternal, merely trapped within the material world (as was held by many Western Gnostic groups), or because God will eventually raise you to a new life in heaven, where your true nature will be displayed through a process of judgement, with eternal rewards or punishments to follow.

Taoism is so different from all this. Like Buddhism, there is no fixed self; there is no single essence that is you. Rather, you are the dynamic process by which different elements, both yin and yang, are blending and flowing on, the one never displacing the other. The only Taoist equivalent of the 'eternal' judgement of Western thought is the recognition that beneath the duality of yin and yang there is the basic life force, the ch'i, and that beyond that there is the Tao, the creative origin of everything. Mystical awareness of the Tao puts the whole process of change into perspective, but it does not stop it.

Chuang Tzu (369–286 BCE)

At about the same time that the ideas of Confucius were being set down in a systematic and logical form by his disciple Mencius, the work of Lao Tzu was being given a similar treatment by Chuang Tzu. In the book which bears his name, he gave a careful exposition of what we now refer to as 'philosophical' Taoism. Of the 33 chapters in that book, the first seven are by Chuang Tzu himself and the others by his disciples.

Much of what has already been said about acting naturally was expounded most clearly by Chuang Tzu. In particular we see him using the term li (principle) to explain the operation of the Tao in continually transforming things.

Notice that Chuang Tzu uses the term li for principle. This is not the same as the Confucius' use of the word li, which referred to the ordering of society, but is closer to the use of li by Chu Hsi in neo-Confucianism – an example of where neo-Confucianism reflects Taoist thought.

Whereas Lao Tzu had expressed ideas of the Tao using images, Chuang Tzu tried to express it through philosophy. He was well aware of the limitations of language, however:

> *The fish trap exists because of the fish; once you've caught the fish, you can forget the trap... Words exist because of meaning; once you've gotten the meaning, you can forget the words. Where can I find a man who has forgotten words so that I can have a word with him?*

> (*Chuang Tzu*, trans. Watson, 1968)

Western

Ludwig Wittgenstein comes to a similar conclusion at the end of his *Tractatus*; once you've climbed up using the philosophical ladder, you can discard it.

One particularly important concept expounded by Chuang Tzu was an approach to life and ethics called *wu wei* (no action). This lies behind both Taoist spirituality, and also the practical and material expressions of the Taoist vision of what constitutes the natural balance of activity, and will be considered in the next section.

Living in Harmony

According to Taoism, both the universe as a whole and each individual share three life-forces: *shen* (spirit), *qi* (breath) and *jing* (vital essence). In meditation a person tries to align the microcosm (self) to the macrocosm (world). In order to do this, it is necessary to get rid of all dualistic concepts like subject and object, so that one may sense oneself as being at one with everything. This spiritual identification with the whole is generally termed mysticism. The mystical unity of all things is not something that can be rationally explained, it is to be directly experienced. And that, of course, is very much in line with the basic position of Taoism, where the Tao that can be spoken about is not the true Tao. What is known through meditation is not the same as the attempt to describe it.

In Taoist thought, the whole universe is found within each individual. Meditation is the method by which Taoists become aware of this. Living in a way that follows the Tao is therefore not something alien to the individual, nor does it involve a loss of the self. Rather, by allowing the self to live consciously in harmony with the universe, Taoists believe that, by doing this, one is also being true to one's own nature.

Western

The great divide between the thinking self and the external material world, so widespread in Western thought (a dualism particularly associated with Descartes), does not feature in the same way in Eastern philosophy. In Western thought, with the constant temptation to define the self over against the world, mysticism might be seen as a way of 'losing' the self in some undifferentiated other. In the East it is seen differently. Whether we are considering Taoism or Buddhism, the self arises out of and finds its natural expression within the 'all'. It does not have an inherently separate existence.

If everything is in a state of constant change, then to hold to a fixed self is a painful illusion, and one that is doomed to failure. Sooner or later the reality of change prevails. Central to Taoism, therefore, is the acceptance of change, and an individual is encouraged to strive to allow the natural process of change to take place, so that he or she can consciously become part of the flow of the Tao.

Insight
In Taoism, meditation does not aim to bring a person to a place of peace, free from further change. Rather, it develops an attitude that allows a person to change in a natural way.

FENG SHUI

If meditation is the internal means of living in harmony, then the most obvious external one is Feng Shui. The literal translation of this term is 'wind and water', the natural elements that shape the landscape. Feng Shui is a theory that recognizes the movement of the ch'i (life force) throughout nature and seeks to design the human environment in a way that takes account of that natural flow of energy so as to be able to benefit from it.

The design and orientation of a building, even its furnishings, can affect the flow of ch'i. A building reflects and influences the lives of the people who live in it, and a Feng Shui consultant can advise on how to make the living space positive and life-enhancing. The result of good Feng Shui is that a place can feel homely, or offer a natural sense of welcome.

In terms of the basic philosophy behind it, what Feng Shui is doing is bringing those artificially constructed aspects of life into a natural balance. A house that is balanced and correctly arranged, it is claimed, will give out positive energy and become more naturally attractive to those who enter it.

Insight

Feng Shui is a good example of the way in which traditional Eastern philosophy is not divorced from other aspects of life, or restricted to the area of academic enquiry. Here we have a very practical technique, claiming to improve the quality and energy available in one's life, which is directly the result of applying fundamental metaphysical concepts.

WU WEI: NON-ACTION AND NON-ETHICS

Wu wei means 'non-action', but it does not mean total inactivity; it is action that is undertaken on two principles:

▶ no effort should be wasted
▶ nothing should be done that is against nature.

Wu wei might be translated as 'spontaneous' or 'natural' action. It is the sort of action that is done intuitively, not as a result of premeditation. It displays the skills of a child, who will see and act quite naturally, without giving thought to the appropriateness or consequences of what he or she is doing. It is action based on reality, not on fantasy.

We often act against our nature in order to promote an idea or principle to which we feel we ought to conform. In this, we may be inwardly torn, our emotions wanting one thing, our rational mind demanding another, our conscience prompting yet another course of action. Our action is neither effective nor natural, but is the result of a compromise between warring priorities. By contrast, wu wei is spontaneous and natural. It is what happens when we don't stop and ask how we should do something, we just find ourselves doing it.

Chuang Tzu argued that one should only act when that action can be effective; if nothing *can* be done, nothing *should* be done. He saw wu wei as the key to successful living. In Chapter 3 of the *Chuang Tzu*, he gives the example of a butcher whose knife remains sharp for a long time although he is constantly carving up animals. The reason for this is that he is so skilled that he never cuts into bone or ligament, but allows the knife to slice through natural cavities with maximum efficiency.

Examples

For vegetarians and others who might not welcome Chuang Tzu's example, let us consider two others:

1 Watch a learner drive a car. He or she is constantly thinking about when to change gear, how to be positioned on the road, where the indicator switch is located, how slowly to take the foot off the clutch, where the brake is. While the learning process is in its infancy, each action is made as a result of remembering a rule and applying it, having first located the required instrument. Then watch an experienced driver. He or she does not consciously monitor all the various controls, but acts instinctively. Faced with a sharp bend or an accident ahead, there is no time to think, 'I need to slow down, and to do that I must press this middle peddle with my foot' – the driver slams on the brakes instinctively.

2 Ballroom dancing. Need I say more?

Wu wei is the skill that makes everything look easy. It is the art of completely unselfconscious action, confident and spontaneous. Wu wei happens when your unconscious mind is working so quickly and effectively that your conscious mind does not have time to catch up, and so learns to trust what happens.

That is why the heading of this section includes 'non-ethics'. Ethics implies the rational consideration of right and wrong. Sometimes the considering is done after an action has taken place – assessing whether (and on what grounds) it might be judged right or wrong; other times it is part of the decision-making process that goes on before we act. Legal, social and religious rules come to bear on a person's conscience as he or she struggles to know what would be the right thing to do. Where the matter is not obvious to the person concerned, they find themselves in a moral dilemma. Ethics as a subject thrives on moral dilemmas, since if everything were obvious there would be nothing to discuss. Taoists don't favour ethics in this sense. If one acts spontaneously, one does not stop to weigh the consequences or take account of the rules.

Insight

Ethics is the study of what happens when one is out of touch with the Tao, and therefore needs to reason out what is likely to be the best course of action. But Ethics may also refer to the process of retrospectively considering whether an action was right or wrong, which is another matter..

It is worth noting the fundamental difference in approach between Confucianism and Taoism on the matter of ethics. Confucianism is always ready to intervene in life, to prescribe certain courses of action, to define how one should behave. In other words, there are actions that should be performed for the good of society, even if they are totally contrary to the natural or spontaneous behaviour of the people concerned. By contrast, Taoism will have none of this, since artificial intervention is a failure to perceive the natural ordering of the Tao.

Life throws up similar problems for everyone, but Taoist philosophy suggests that, by being natural, one can minimize the damage they cause. Chuang Tzu, in an example that illustrates his wit, comments on the fact that a drunk can fall from a carriage without hurting himself, whereas someone who is sober would be injured by the same fall. The reason he gives is that the drunk is 'united', his body is reacting naturally, whereas the sober man, perceiving danger, tenses himself and thus makes himself vulnerable.

INDIVIDUALISM

The self, for Taoism, is a direct expression of a person's te (power), which is the energy of the Tao in him or her. The aim of a Taoist is to achieve a unification of everything within the self, and this is to be done by returning to the source of oneself – the Tao.

Notice that this is focused on the individual, not on society. In looking at Confucianism, we saw that the correct way to behave was to accept the li, the etiquette accepted by society and given by tradition. By contrast, Taoism starts with each individual. The great debate between Taoist and Confucian approaches to life is between the natural and the artificial, the spontaneous and the imposed.

Thus, Chuang Tzu insisted that one should not introduce any external motive into action – whether in the form of social approval or the anticipation of praise or blame. That does not imply that one's action will necessarily be to the detriment of others, or that it should not take them into account, simply that the effect on others should not be the primary reason for taking that action.

Chuang Tzu takes the position that nothing is inherently good or bad, but that it depends on the circumstances and the people concerned. This does not mean that moral rules have absolutely no place within Taoism, but rather that there comes a point at which one has to be prepared to go beyond all moral rules.

He points out (in Chapter 2 of the *Chuang Tzu*) that, where two people disagree, it is quite impossible to get fair and absolute arbitration, for whoever is brought in to arbitrate is bound to take one side or the other, and will have a view of his or her own. In other words, in matters of moral choice, there is no absolute that can be brought to bear on the process of decision making or evaluation – everything and everyone has a particular viewpoint.

Insight

Mo-tzu, a critic of the Confucian philosopher Mencius, promoted universal love, and criticized Confucian thinkers for accepting a natural scale by which one paid greater respect and love for one's own relatives and friends than to those who were deemed worthy of that love. At the opposite extreme, Yang Chu, an older Taoist thinker, claimed that it would be wrong for him to take any action that would harm himself, even if the whole of the world would benefit as a result, since the two basic aims of life were to be keep oneself away from harm and to live for as long as possible. To what extent that can be taken as the only logical conclusion to be drawn from applying Taoist principles is a matter of debate.

Relativism in the West has come to the same conclusion, that each perspective provides its own self-contained scheme of reference. In the *Philosophy of Science*, Thomas Kuhn argued that there is no way to get independent adjudication between competing paradigms for exactly Chuang Tzu's reason.

NATURAL SPONTANEITY AND SIMPLICITY

Like flowing water, one should take the line of least resistance. The Taoist ideal is therefore to live in simplicity, free from all desires and ambitions. But freedom from desire may seem to be threatened by education, for increased knowledge tends to lead to an increase in desires and ambitions. For this reason, there developed a strand of Taoist thinking that resisted intellectual progress and education.

One's natural simplicity is called *p'u*, and it is characterized by wu wei, spontaneous action. This reflects a natural harmony. The naturalness of wu wei produces both simplicity and integrity – it is action in which the whole, undivided self is engaged. Chuang Tzu's work had a great impact on Buddhism when it arrived in China, since it shared Buddhism's quest for an immediate awareness of 'no-self', losing what we conventionally call ourselves within a larger perspective.

It was also influential in terms of Chinese landscape painting and poetry. Knowing exactly the right and natural place for something within a landscape, or giving a very simple poetic evocation of an experience – these come from a sensitivity towards the natural that Chuang Tzu encouraged. Within Chinese art there are many aspects of balance. In landscape painting, for example, there needs to be a balance between mountains (yang) and water (yin). Sometimes the artist will deliberately give the impression of the constant changes within the landscape, for example, rocks are seen to crack from the pressure of tree roots. In particular, people and dwellings are generally small within the overall landscape, and placed with care. They are placed (as in Feng Shui) to reflect the right balance, a harmonious flow of energy.

Taoism extends into all aspects of life. Just as Feng Shui considers the artificial environment and attempts to bring it into line with the natural energies of the Ch'i, so a consideration of yin and yang influences Chinese cooking. Some foods (e.g. meats) are considered to be yang and others (e.g. vegetables) are yin. Within a dish, or certainly within a meal, there needs to be a natural balance of yin and yang. Hence one would serve beef (yang) with nuts (yin), and with a meal including meat, one would choose a yin drink (e.g. tea) rather than a yang (e.g. alcohol).

In the West, probably the best known of all Taoist practices is T'ai Ch'i. This uses a sequence of carefully balanced movements, performed in order to balance the yin and the yang, leading to an enhanced sense of poise, balance and harmony. It is a most visible expression of what Taoism is about, for the person who has learned the sequence of movements can be absorbed in their performance without conscious thought, but allowing a natural flow of physical and emotional energy. It originated in the 14th century, and is still practised by many people who experience its benefits without knowing anything of the Taoist theory that underlies it.

Insight

Here we have culture that deliberately strives to reflect its underlying philosophy. Beyond social convention, it seeks to reflect metaphysics (in the sense of the underlying structure and meaning of reality) in everyday life, thereby making naturalness and integrity possible.

MINIMALIST POLITICS

A major theme of the *Tao Te Ching* is its critique of the artificiality of human culture and social life. It argues that government should not interfere with the natural process. Lao Tzu sought something that was deeper and more natural than the social and political reality he encountered around him.

Since it takes the individual as its starting point, Taoism sees the organizations and imposed rules of society as frustrating people's natural desires and abilities. As an ideal, the state should therefore interfere as little as possible in people's lives. The principle that a ruler should do as little as possible was probably adopted largely in response to the observation that rulers tend to act in their own interests, rather than in those of their subjects.

The most obvious Western parallel here is with anarchism (see, for example, the 19th-century anarchist Proudhon, or even Leo Tolstoy), but it finds echoes in many conservative views about the value of having a minimalist state and maximum individual freedom.

Religious Taoism

There are two very different forms of Taoism: philosophical and religious. Religious Taoism developed from about the 2nd century CE and included rituals, temples and priests. Unlike the earlier philosophical Taoism, it became fundamentally a quest for healing and immortality, so that the principal concern of Taoists become the retaining and enhancing the vital forces within the self in order to prolong life.

Here we shall examine just two features of religious Taoism – its views on immortality and on sexuality. Both serve to illustrate the very different philosophical basis being used.

IMMORTALITY

There are two very different attitudes to death within Taoism. In the earlier philosophical Taoism, death is seen as natural, and the fear of it misguided. Chuang Tzu (in Chapter 2 of his work) said:

> *How do I know that loving life is not a delusion? How do I know that, in hating death, I am not like a man who, having left home in his youth, has forgotten the way back?*

(trans: A. C. Graham *Chuang-Tzu: the Inner Chapters*, Mandala, 1986)

By contrast, the main pre-occupation with religious Taoism was with the prolongation of life. Sought through internal alchemy, the quest was to become an 'immortal' (*hsien*), a mark of which was the ability to display magical powers, including the ability to fly.

Insight

Curiously, the quest for immortality did not involve an attempt to regain youth. Those heading for immortality continue to age – so that the 'immortals' are portrayed as being extremely old.

Awareness of breathing, as a form of meditation, has a long history, within both Taoism and Buddhism, but there developed in the 12th century a Taoist school called 'The Way of Realization of Truth' which gave it particular emphasis. It was believed that the air was the physical basis of the universe, and that it contained 'fine parts' which could be accumulated within the body, thus prolonging life. But it was also believed that a person had only a certain fixed number of breaths in this life, so that the faster a person breathed the sooner they would die, and conversely, retaining the breath for as long as possible would prolong life. This led to the practice of embryonic breathing (in other words, breathing like the embryo in the womb), which in practice requires the breath to be held for as long as possible.

We see here a basic, quantitative assessment of the Ch'i: there is only a fixed amount of breath, and one needs to take care to conserve it. Notice how very different this is from the natural flowing of energy in earlier Taoism.

Rude comment

In the rather literal approach taken by religious Taoism, the fixed amount of breath you have been given at birth has an unfortunate consequence. Not only does each breath via the mouth or nostrils go to exhaust your supply of Ch'i, but passing of wind in the other direction will also shorten your life. Perhaps this is one occasion where the generally individualistic approach of Taoism is at one with the Confucian emphasis on social etiquette!

SEXUALITY

Sexuality is bound to play an important role within Taoism, for as early as the *I Ching*, nature was seen as having a basic sexual polarity in nature – heaven is male and earth is female. Yin and yang, the very basic dual form of creative energy, also represents female and male. Neither can exist without the other. Therefore, logically, one would have thought that the sexual act between heterosexual partners is likely to be of great benefit in helping men and women to realize the Tao – part of the natural flow and balance of life, as promoted by philosophical Taoism. We know that Chuang Tzu, for example, was a married man, and that certainly did not count against him. Clearly, the whole basis of philosophical Taoism, therefore, was such that family life and sexuality could be seen as natural, in contrast to the Buddhist encouragement of monasticism.

When we turn to the later religious Taoism, however, we find that sexual intercourse created problems. In the quest for immortality, it was essential to conserve Ch'i energy, and it was feared that, in the sexual act, the woman would drain her partner of his basic yang (the masculine aspect of the Ch'i) which he needed to stay alive and that the emission of semen also involved a leaking away of a man's Ch'i. On the other hand, sexual stimulation itself was good for producing yang, and thus maintaining Ch'i.

Religious Taoism, with its very literal view of the need to preserve Ch'i, and the priority given to extending life, therefore faced a dilemma. How could the stimulation of yang be maintained without the resulting threat to a man's Ch'i? Within some Taoist circles, the way of overcoming this problem was by *coitus reservatus*. The man produces yang essence through becoming sexually aroused, but then he stops short of emission and reabsorbs the semen into his body, avoiding a loss of Ch'i. This, it seemed, offered men the best of both worlds!

Within one particular Taoist society, founded in the second century CE and named 'The Five Bushels of Rice Society' (after its alleged entry requirement), this was taken one step further with the practice of communal sex. To maximize the possibility of realizing Tao and yet retaining the maximum ch'i, it was argued that a man should have sex as often as possible, while retaining his semen. Hence, it became the custom to arrange for situations where men could enjoy frequent penetration of various partners but without emission. This was never widely accepted as part of Taoism, and it was clearly organized for the benefit of men rather than women. Nevertheless, it is interesting to see the logic that brought them to this point. Religious Taoism had focused on the preservation and maintenance of the vital essence at all costs in the quest for long life, and – ultimately – for immortality.

Nevertheless, setting aside the extremes to which this approach was taken, and the difference between the views of philosophical and religious Taoism in this respect, it is still the case that sexuality was generally regarded as a positive and natural thing.

Whether it is the conservation of semen or the conservation of breath, religious Taoism seems to be very far removed from the earlier tradition. Whereas death is natural for philosophical Taoism, in the later religious Taoism it is the enemy, to be staved off by all means, however unnatural they may seem.

Taoism and other philosophies

It is important to recognize the very fluid situation in China with regard to different religious and philosophical systems. We noted at the beginning of this chapter how, prior to the unification of China in the second century BCE, there were a number of different schools of thought. This continued to be the case. With the arrival of Buddhism, the three major philosophies – Taoism, Confucianism and Buddhism – coexisted and cross-fertilized to a considerable degree.

In particular it is important to recognize that Taoism provided a complementary philosophy to Confucianism. Confucianism continued to be largely concerned with people in their social context, with society as a whole and how it should be organized. Taoism is far more concerned with the way in which individuals understand their life and its changes. Social, political and cultural consequences follow from this, as we have seen, but they are a secondary consequence of Taoism, rather than its main concern.

Although the fundamental arguments are presented quite differently, the Taoist sense of constant flux and the denial of a fixed personal identity, found parallels in Buddhism. You will also notice that the simplicity and naturalness of Taoism is reflected in later Zen Buddhism.

During the last two thousand years, in varying degrees and at different times, all three main philosophies have influenced Chinese thought and culture, and they have also, in doing so, influenced one another.

10 THINGS TO REMEMBER

1 Taoism traditionally starts with the teaching of Lao Tzu, as set out in the *Tao Te Ching*.

2 The Tao (literally: path) expresses the natural way things are.

3 Although the Tao is seen as the natural source of everything, it is *not* the same as the western idea of God.

4 To return to the Tao is to live at one with the natural flow of things.

5 To follow the Tao gives a natural energy to fulfil one's potential.

6 Like Buddhism, Taoism sees everything as changing and impermanent.

7 Ying/yang, originating as a separate philosophy, expressed within Taoism a balance of male/female, light/dark.

8 Wu wei is the ideal of natural and spontaneous action.

9 Religious Taoism was concerned primarily with prolonging life and conserving vital energy.

10 Taoism, Confucianism and Buddhism influenced one another, but tended to focus on different aspects of life.

7

Tantra

In this chapter you will:
- *examine the background to Hindu and Buddhist Tantra*
- *consider the theory behind Tantric sexuality*
- *explore the part played by imagination and emotion in Tantra.*

Background

Tantra is the term used to describe a movement that developed within both the Hindu and Buddhist traditions, concerned with the use of images and rituals as a means of utilizing the energy generated by the emotions and sexuality in the quest for spiritual liberation and insight.

At one level Tantra may appear to be little more than magic and a crude attempt to manipulate the external world by means of ritual, at another it can be examined in terms of the psychological implications of the images and values exhibited within its practices. Much Tantric literature is concerned, directly or indirectly, with sex – a topic that often invites a superficial or sensationalist approach.

We may explore the implications of Tantric practices and the presuppositions of Tantric writers, but we are unlikely to find any rational exposition in Tantric texts of what Tantra is or how it relates to an overall understanding of life. So, when we approach Tantra in a book on Eastern philosophy, the first question to ask is, 'Can Tantra possibly be considered a philosophy?'

Philosophy is sometimes concerned with a limited range of intellectual questions, but equally it may set out to formulate an overall understanding of life and its meaning. In looking at Eastern philosophy, we have found that the latter task predominates, and it includes techniques (for example, meditation) to maintain an awareness of reality in the face of the human tendency to become immersed in the mundane and the limited. Without doubt, Tantra should be understood as a method of achieving such awareness, a method which – although not intellectual – is based on presuppositions and intuitions that are worth exploring and setting within an overall philosophical framework.

Within the Indian tradition, meditation, wisdom, morality and devotion are considered to be 'ways of release', ways of achieving the state of freedom, insight and bliss that is called *moksha* or *nirvana*. The problem is that these three ways require a great deal of time and effort – hence the ascetic tradition, in which a person on a spiritual quest leaves home and family in order to spend a life of simplicity and meditation.

However, Tantra offered a means by which – under the direction of a spiritual guide (a guru) – one might speed up the process of spiritual development, by harnessing emotional and sexual energy and by the use of the imagination alongside the intellect. Tantra is a broad tradition which embraces everything from the gestures used in Tibetan Buddhism, to the esoteric quest to gain spiritual benefit from sexual intercourse and the deliberate breaking of taboos.

Whereas the methods used may not be considered philosophy, it would seem quite appropriate for philosophy to explore the implications of using emotion and imagination in this way. What is more, the integration of intellect and emotion may have implications for an overall understanding of the self, and it sets the purely intellectual approach to philosophical problems within a broader human context. For this alone, it deserves to be considered within a book on Eastern philosophy.

Insight

If our understanding of life if shaped by our imagination and our emotions, then that in itself says something important about the way we understand life; intellectual theories are not the whole story. Tantric thought is never going to be crisp, clean, logical or straightforward, but it is likely to be both rich and instructive about the human condition.

The origins of Tantra cannot be determined with any precision, but some things that featured in later Tantra (specifically the use of mantras, see below) were known in India from about the second century CE. Many Tantric texts take the form of dialogues between the Hindu god Shiva and his consort Shakti (although 'Shakti' developed into a more general term for the feminine power within divinity). The potency of Shiva and Shakti had long been represented within Hinduism by the sexual symbols of the lingum and the yoni, and the image of Shiva goes back to the very earliest strand of Hinduism – possibly to the Indus Valley civilization before the Aryan invasions – so there are very ancient elements within what was later to be the sexual imagery of Tantra.

On the other hand, it is quite likely that Tantra developed during the 2nd and 3rd centuries CE within Mahayana Buddhist circles, and that Hindu practice was subsequently influenced by it and linked it to the already established sexual iconography of the worship of Shiva. We also know (see, for example, the introduction to Buddhist Tantra in A. Skilton's *A Brief History of Buddhism*) that Tantra went through different phases, from the earliest evidence of the use of mantras (sacred chants), through a period when it was studied in Buddhist universities and practised within the monastic community, to a later phase when there were individual, itinerant Tantric teachers, often accompanied by lower-caste partners with whom they could perform the Tantric rites.

All we can say with some certainly, however, is that Tantra developed progressively in India within both Buddhist and Hindu religious traditions.

THE SECRET TRADITION

Tantra has generally been kept secret, and those who try to read Tantric texts will find in them little that makes immediate sense. They appear sometimes to be stage instructions for a play, with cryptic hints at action and with words that seem to have no meaning.

This secrecy is partly because of the potential for misunderstanding the motives of those more extreme practitioners of Tantra who enjoyed (whether literally or imaginatively) sex as part of their practice, but more generally because it was believed that one could only benefit from Tantric practices if they were conducted under the instruction of a guru, and that one should be prepared for them by a process of initiation. There is a recognition that sexuality and the emotions are powerful forces and need to be carefully controlled, and that the means of doing this is by passing the tradition of Tantric ritual down from guru to pupil. Hence, in their written form they can appear quite bizarre and unintelligible, and this (even though done for the best of reasons) has only fuelled the sense of esoteric attractiveness that hovers over all Tantric practices.

Note

Since Tantric practices developed within both Hindu and Buddhist traditions, with some uncertainty about which influenced which in the early stages, the basic elements of Tantra are not specific to either tradition. In this chapter we shall first look at the basis of ritual and meditation and then at the Hindu background in Shiva and Shakti, before examining Tantric sexuality. Following that we shall look at the philosophical background to the Buddhist interpretation of Tantra – a tradition which has continued down to the present day within Tibetan Buddhism.

Rituals and meditation

VISUALIZATIONS

Visualization is the basic method used in Tantra for engaging the emotions. Both Hindu deities and Buddhist images of Buddhas and Bodhisattvas have rich iconography in terms of colours, clothes, hand positions, number of limbs, attendant creatures and so on, and these features can be rationalized and related to particular qualities that the deity represents.

But the analysis of images, as might be set out in a textbook, does little to show their place within the religion or their impact on the overall view of life taken by their devotees. What happens in a visualization is that a person who is familiar with a particular image is able to reconstruct that image imaginatively at will. Images can appear in the mind's eye and then dissolve again, and particular features of the image can be mentally enhanced and appreciated. In doing this, the worshipper may start to 'see' the deity not as an external image, but as a living person with whom he or she can have a relationship.

This is, of course, common to many religious traditions, but what is distinctive about Tantra is that a person may then go on to visualize himself or herself as the deity. In other words, in the process of visualization and meditation a person imaginatively adopts those qualities that are admired in the deity.

Through visualization you explore imaginatively what it would feel like to be that Buddha or Bodhisattva or deity. You take a short-cut to enlightenment by imagining what it would be like to be enlightened. Is that cheating? Is it the deliberate acceptance of illusion as fact? Well, consider the nature of self-understanding generally. It may be partly based on reason and an objective assessment of one's situation, but one's aspirations, values and fears, one's inherited characteristics even, play a large part in the interpretation of reality. A person changes as they engage emotionally in various situations in life. Why then, in principle, should it not be a valid exercise to engage imaginatively with an image that represents one's highest ideals?

Insight

Even if philosophers do not appreciate the importance of imaginative identification with images, those who control media advertising certainly do! If you were this sort of person, what sort of coffee would you be drinking or what sort of car would you be driving? An advertisement invites you to enter imaginatively into a fantasy realm in which certain values are suggested and (if the advert works as intended) this influences your subsequent choices in terms of buying coffee or cars. In this respect, a visualization is like a successful TV advert.

There are four levels of Tantra. The first three are Action Tantra, Performance Tantra and Yoga Tantra. They involve ritual actions and are referred to as the Lower Tantras. The fourth is the *Anuttara* (Highest) Tantra, and requires no external action – everything takes place in terms of visualization. And, of course, such meditations were considered only suitable for those who had received formal initiations into the appropriate level. Without that, Tantric visualizations could be considered at best ineffective and at worst, harmful.

MANDALAS

A *mandala* is a pattern which integrates its various elements to form a single unified whole. So, for example, you can have the Buddhist mandala of the five Buddhas, where each of the Buddha images is set in relation to the others, so that together they form a total view of spiritual reality. A mandala may simply be viewed and visualized, or the value may be in the constructing of it. Even very elaborate mandalas may be constructed on a temporary basis. After many hours spent creating a mandala out of coloured sand, it may simply be discarded after use – which itself becomes a symbol of the transience of all life.

Insight

In terms of emotional engagement, the mandala may promote a sense of wholeness and integrity, serving as a spiritual map.

MUDRAS

Images of Buddhas, bodhisattvas or deities generally convey their meaning through the position of the hands (the *mudra*) – meditation, generosity, fearlessness and so on. It is natural therefore that in Tantric ritual the worshipper should adopt the same mudras. By making the gesture representing fearlessness and determination, the practitioner generates those emotions.

This is of central importance for the place of Tantra within philosophy as a whole. Whereas most philosophy is an intellectual process of examining questions that arise as a result of our encounter with life – questions of what we can know for certain, what is the nature of the self, what does it mean to say something is just, or true or beautiful – Tantra seeks to manipulate life itself. Tantra is not a process of observation and reflection, but one of engagement.

Insight

Tantric rituals seek to engage the emotions and imagination to create a new relationship to life, rather than just think about it. But Tantra also sets what it creates within an overall context of meaning – and that is what may enable it to be considered as a philosophy, rather than a therapy.

Shiva and Shakti

In the chapter on Hinduism, we saw that ultimate reality was represented by a triad of gods – Brahma, Vishnu and Shiva. Shiva was there described as the destroyer, but that is only a small part of what he represents.

Long before Tantra developed, there had been an established tradition of energy and balance within Shaivite iconography – seen particularly in the image of Shiva Nataraja. Shiva dances within a circle of flames, treading upon a demon. He expresses a balance of creation and destruction, holding chaos in check.

There are many aspects of Shiva. He is shown as an ascetic, and also as the 'Lord of Animals', ruling in the natural sphere. But, alongside this, he is generally represented by the lingum – representing the sexual power of the erect penis, and it is this sexual iconography which relates the older Shaivite tradition to Tantra.

SEXUALITY AND ASCETICISM

Shiva is presented as having a consort, representing female creative energy. This energy is generally referred to as Shakti, which at one level can refer to a goddess and at another to the general sense of feminine power.

But there is a curious polarity within this Shiva/Shakti tradition. On the one hand they represent the sexual pair, and on the other, Shiva is seen as the ascetic who disengages himself from sexual and other domestic concerns. How can such asceticism be related to sexuality?

It is in the elements of balance and control that sexuality is able to be employed as a means of self-discipline. This is seen, for example, in the retention of semen following sexual arousal – a tradition which, from quite another philosophical starting point, was also practised in some Taoist circles (see Chapter 6). Sexuality may therefore be seen as an area of life within which there are powerful forces, the understanding, sublimation and control of which may bring spiritual benefits.

In terms of Tantric philosophy, the essential element taken over from the older Shaivite tradition would seem to be the idea that Shiva is able to utilize the power represented in sexuality in his pursuit of the ascetic path. Sex is not denied, but is utilized, transformed and transcended.

KUNDALINI

Within the Hindu Tantric tradition, it was believed that the power of the feminine resided in a point at the base of the spine, and that, with appropriate ritual, this 'kundalini' could become active. Unlocking this power therefore became a key feature of Tantric yoga.

The problem with any philosophy that appears to be based on human biology is that, with the advance of scientific knowledge, it may appear dated or plain wrong. The point for awakening feminine power is unlikely to be located at the base of the spine, but the idea might today be phrased in Jungian terms as an integration of the anima. On the other hand, in meditation a practitioner may become aware of various *chacras*, or circles at different parts of the body. Language about raising the kundalini from the base of the spine is therefore more likely to make sense in terms of a meditator's centres of awareness rather than straight biology.

Philosophically, however, this is of little importance. The key feature, as far as an appreciation of Tantra is concerned, is the need for a balance between male and female energies – a balance that finds parallels with the ancient Chinese yin/yang tradition.

THE UNION OF MATTER AND SPIRIT

Notice one important metaphysical assumption in this approach – the union of matter and spirit. Spirituality is here explored *within* the physical world, not by escaping from it. Compare this with Sankhya philosophy (see Chapter 3), where we have a metaphysics which presents the world as a union of *prakriti* (matter – feminine) and *purusha* (soul – masculine). But, for Sankhya, the aim is for a release in which the soul extricates itself from matter. Thus, within that tradition, you have a dualism in which the spirit is effectively trapped within the material and seeks to escape from it.

The implications of Tantric ritual are quite different. On the one hand, physical actions are thought to bring about spiritual change; on the other, spiritual intentions are thought to have a literal and therefore physical effect on the material world. In other words, Tantra integrates spirit and matter – they are part of an interconnected whole. Hence one could describe the basic metaphysics of Tantra as monistic, rather than dualistic.

If Tantric rituals are to work, they imply that there is a single reality, encompassing both what we would normally think of as the separate realms of the material world and the personal, spiritual or human world of people's aspirations and desires. Tantric ritual therefore implies a complete, single, interconnected world, where physical, mental and emotional reality reflect and influence one another.

Tantric Sex

Tantric texts, as we have them today, are very difficult to interpret – and deliberately so, since what they contain is meant to be reserved for the initiated and interpreted by a guru. Some of them describe sexual acts of different kinds, and do so in ways that leave the reader in little doubt about what is happening. On the other hand, some writers suggest that the actions described should be interpreted symbolically, and would not generally have been acted out physically. Others point to the texts as giving a script for visualization – so that the Tantric practitioner enters into what amounts to a guided fantasy.

This may be interpreted in ways that are valid and appropriate for the spiritual traditions of both Hinduism and Buddhism. The act of copulation (*maituna*) may indeed be symbolic, representing (depending on your tradition) either the integrative power of matter and spirit or of wisdom and compassion. While it is clearly the case that this (and all similar iconography) can be used as the basis of meditation and visualization, the question remains as to whether, and how widely, the sexual rites described took place literally.

What seems clear is that there were levels of Tantra in which sexual intercourse took place as part of the rituals, and probably involved lower caste women who were effectively working as prostitutes. There is also the tradition within Tantra of married gurus who are able to act out the Tantric rites with their wives.

Western

The physical and literal nature of much of what is described seems obvious – techniques for maintaining an erection while avoiding ejaculation are hardly necessary in an entirely symbolic context! But that should not detract from the philosophical significance of what is taking place. Participating in the sexual act, in a narrowly Western context, is neither part of religion nor philosophy. But within Tantra, such participation has profound significance. It is not that sex trivializes philosophy and religion (as might be imagined from a Western perspective, for example from the standpoint of Natural Law, where the sexual act is only justified if it is done with the intention of, or at least being open to the possibility of, the conception of children), but that a narrow appreciation of the scope of philosophy and religion trivializes sex!

Tantra is a form of yoga – but one that has elements which can be practised with a partner rather than individually. Although, as we have seen, part of the idea of Tantra is to break down conventional thinking and taboos, there are also guidelines for how it should be practised, no doubt set down in an attempt to regulate the potential misunderstandings and excesses of the practice. The Mahanirvana Tantra, for example, specifies that the sexual practices should only be performed with one's own spouse.

Insight

If it is beneficial to calm one's mind through giving attention to one's breathing, or gently observing the arising of emotions or thoughts, why should it not also be beneficial to enhance the awareness of the balance of male and female energies in life through an appreciation of physical sexuality?

What you have here is an identification of the cosmic process with those forces that shape the individual. The expression of the awareness of oneself and one's partner in the sexual act parallels the balance of creativity and asceticism and of wisdom and compassion – and this, in turn, is seen as reflecting a balance throughout nature as, for example, in the image of Shiva Nataraja dancing creation and destruction, and holding chaos in check by doing so.

Western

In Western thought, the Natural Law approach to sexuality sees the purpose and therefore only justification of the sexual act as the potential it has for the conception of children, since that is the final 'end' it has within the overall scheme of things, ordained by God. By contrast, within Tantra, the sexual act may be seen as participating in and representing forces that are universal – whether it is the balance of Shiva and Shakti, or the Buddhist concepts of compassion and wisdom. Both Western and Eastern approaches here relate the particular action to its universal significance, but the Western approach is entirely biological in significance, whereas the Eastern explores the balance of emotional as well as physical energies.

Buddhist Tantra

In terms of its basic philosophy, Tantra took over the key
features of the Mahayana Buddhism within which it developed.
In the Madhyamaka tradition we saw that there was the initially
surprising claim that the ever-changing world of samsara was
also nirvana (in other words, there is only one world, and it can
appear simultaneously as samsara and nirvana). There was also
the important idea that every creature has an indwelling Buddha
nature (the Tathagatagarbha doctrine). Together, these ideas enabled
Buddhist practitioners to see present physical reality as a stage on
which the aspiration of enlightenment could be acted out.

In other words: if you already have a Buddha nature, and if this world
of samsara can also be experienced as nirvana, then it follows that
you can use physical actions as a means of expressing and realizing the
enlightened state.

The Tantric tradition in Buddhism is generally known as the
Vajrayana. Vajra is a word that has two meanings: a diamond or
a thunderbolt. Both are appropriate, since the Vajrayana tradition
seems to engage directly and immediately in experience, rather than
use logical argument or discursive thought. It is therefore seen as
powerful and threatening, hard and precious.

The term 'vajra' is also used for an object used in Tantric ritual.
Vajras are generally small enough to be held in the hand. They
comprise a central sphere, out of which, at each of the opposite
poles, there come five shoots – like the petals of a lotus – curving
outwards and then coming together again in a point. Each part of the
vajra is symbolic. The sphere is a symbol of purity, and thus of the
enlightened self. At the one pole, the lotus petals represent the five
poisons (infatuation, aversion, conceit, passion and envy), and at the
other, five perfections represented by five Buddhas. Taken as a whole,
therefore, the vajra is a symbol of transformation – the poisons
that can impede one's progress being transformed into the very
perfections one seeks. But its shape also reflects the unified view of
Tantric Buddhism, namely that both the poisons and the perfections
spring from the same central reality.

A basic assumption in Buddhist tantra – and indeed throughout
Buddhism in all its forms – is that there are not two separate worlds,

A vajra and a bell with a vajra handle.

an objective world 'out there' and another private, secret world of the inner self. Ultimately, for Buddhism, there is no self; the idea of a 'self' is simply a conventional term and not one that can stand careful analysis. The most fundamental philosophical assumption of Tantra reflects this, in that it sees the forces at work throughout the universe as also to be experienced within the human heart.

Another important feature of Mahayana philosophy for an understanding of Tantra is the claim, made in Yogacara philosophy (see Chapter 4) is that all reality is mental – what we know of the world, we know only in the form of experiences gained and assimilated through our own mind. Our perception of the world is therefore a mental phenomenon. The implication of this is that as we change, so our perception, and therefore the reality of the world as we know it, also changes.

This led, within Tantra, to a two-way relationship between what (in the West) we would call the inner and outer realities of the mind and the physical world. On the one hand, Tantra saw what happened mentally as having a profound effect on the external world. On the other, external actions and rituals could be a means of transforming one's mental state.

Tantra and magic

Magic is the attempt to change external reality through mental activity – for example, by means of a particular chant, prayer or invocation of a deity. Religion is sometimes dismissed as magic when it claims to effect change in this way. On the other hand, if ritual, prayers, chants and invocations are simply means of spiritual self-development – effective because enabling the self to be better aligned to fundamental realities – then no magic is involved.

But this reflects a very Western view of the self and the world – mind and matter – as separate things. Buddhism, in particular, rejects this – everything is anatta, it lacks separate inherent existence, it interconnects. The crucial question for Tantra, therefore, is: Is an experienced change the same thing as an actual change?

Through various practices, one may experience the world differently. But does that actually make the world different? To put the question crudely and from a Western perspective: On a sunny day, one may become accustomed to the more comfortable view through sunglasses, but has the sun thereby been dimmed?

WISDOM AND COMPASSION

The Buddhist interpretation of what is represented by the sexual pair is very different from the Hindu. For Hinduism they were two fundamental forces within nature. For Buddhism, the male represents compassion (and also 'skilful means') and the female represents wisdom, the union of the two producing the ultimate goal of enlightenment.

Within Buddhist iconography, this union is represented by what are generally known as the *Yab-Yum* (literally 'Father-Mother') images, in which male and female are locked in sexual embrace facing one another, the male in the traditional posture of meditation with the female sitting in his lap with her legs locked round his body. The image often portrays one of the archetypal Buddhas, for example

Buddha Akshobya with his consort Lochana, representing aspects of clear-sighted wisdom.

Akshobya

Akshobya is one of the archetypal Buddhas represented in 'The Mandala of the Five Buddhas'. His particular wisdom is 'mirror-like' – seeing reality just as it is. The philosophical implication of this is that conventional wisdom sees only distortions, brought about by a false idea of the self, but the removal of those distortions leads to the natural, primordial state of wisdom. In what is known as 'The Great Seal Tradition', the pure mind is thought of as an undistorted mirror, reflecting exactly what is before it – which is exactly the role played by Akshobya in Buddhist iconography.

Within the overall Buddhist philosophy the implication here is that insight and wisdom (represented by the female partner in the image) only leads to the spiritual goal when it is in union with appropriate action or skilful means (represented by the male). Within the Buddhist tradition, sexuality can be a cause of craving (*tanha*), which is the root of suffering. Therefore the challenge for Buddhist Tantra is to engage in sexuality without allowing this to be motivated by craving. It is sex without craving that is considered to lead to insight – again, in a union of wisdom and action.

Insight

Pornography turns sex into an object to be possessed or consumed. It encourages separateness; sex is 'out there' to be sought. By contrast, Tantric sex, by seeking to overcome the illusion of a separate self, also allows sexual energy to be channelled into the quest for enlightenment and the sense of universal interrelatedness. It enjoys without possession.

Buddhist Tantra sought to channel the energy of destructive urges into the removal of hindrances to enlightenment. Hence, images of violent, threatening Buddhas and bodhisattvas express the forcefulness with which a person is to break through all that limits his or her progress. In this spiritualization of the sexual and violent urges, Tantric Buddhism saw the potential of sexual power to create the moment when the mind is able to develop the *bodhicitta* (the mind/heart determined to seek enlightenment), rather than the crude physical production of semen. The moment of sexual climax, prolonged by avoiding emission, becomes the moment of the *mahasukha* – the great bliss.

As was noted at the beginning of this chapter, the development of Tantra within Buddhism is complex, and went through a number of phases, from the appearance of written records of mantric chanting from about the 2nd century CE through to the appearance of independent non-monastic Tantric gurus who travelled about giving Tantric initiations. But this final stage was not reached until probably the 9th century. It is not possible, therefore, to give a straightforward account of Tantric philosophy, because at each stage it simply built upon existing philosophical ideas, integrating them into the understanding of its rituals.

The Tantric tradition and philosophy is found mainly in Tibetan Buddhism, and also in Japanese Shingon Buddhism, although it should be noted that the Japanese form never accepted the sexual rites of the later (yogottara) Tantra, and anyone seeking for the more extreme Tantric practices within modern Tibetan Buddhism is likely to be disappointed.

Note on Tibetan Buddhism

Buddhism had spread into China by the 1st century CE and into Japan by the 5th. These countries therefore received and developed a broadly Mahayana form of Buddhist philosophy. But, although there had been earlier Buddhist influence from both India and China, Buddhism really only made headway in Tibet from the 8th and 9th centuries, and by that time Tantra was well developed within India. So, for example, Padmasambhava, who arrived in Tibet in 747 CE and is generally seen as the teacher who established Tibetan Buddhism, was already well known as a Tantric adept in India. Then, following a period of the suppression of Buddhism in Tibet (from the time of the ending of the Tibetan monarchy in 838 CE) it was introduced again in the 11th and 12th centuries. Hence, Tibetan Buddhism developed from the whole range of Indian Buddhist traditions, and preserved them once Buddhism had died out in India. Tibetan Buddhism should not simply be identified with Tantra, but it is the one major branch of Buddhism which displays Tantric as well as earlier philosophies.

An important feature of Tibetan Buddhist literature is the *lam rim* tradition, which sees a cumulative progression from the earlier traditions to the later Tantric ones. In other words, Tibetan Buddhism is early (Hinayana) Buddhism, plus the Mahayana developments, plus the Tantric elements (Vajrayana).

SOME PHILOSOPHICAL IMPLICATIONS OF TANTRIC SEXUAL INTEGRATION

Within Buddhism, the aim of most spiritual practice is to break down the false notion of a separate self, and to overcome the craving associated with seeing the world 'out there' as a separate entity to be grasped and used. This is reflected in an awareness of a fundamental unity between inner and outer, between what is experienced personally and that which is universal – all things lack inherent existence, all arise in dependence upon conditions.

The integration of the sexual imagery into that overall view of reality is therefore part of that process of breaking down the sense of self. Whereas the conventional 'self' is likely to be possessive and craving in terms of sexuality, the enlightened self finds in the sexual act a natural blending of wisdom (which, for the Mahayana, is practically identified with the sense of shunyata, 'emptiness') and compassion – a dispassionate affirmation of the other person.

Insight

In the sexual act, wisdom and compassion come together. Wisdom recognizes the falseness of seeing separate selves; compassion is the emotionally positive response to that wisdom, going out to others because all are interconnected. Although generally practised through visualization, Tantric sex seems to have much to contribute to a positive, healthy attitude to ordinary physical relationships.

But, as we have already seen, integration is represented in other aspects of Tantric iconography as well. Thus the image of the vajra – with both poisons and perfections springing out from opposite sides of the central sphere – represents the power to transform even those things that would generally be considered poisonous.

Tantra touches on a fundamental issue for all philosophy. Intellectual debate depends upon concepts, and concepts depend on seeing objects as discrete entities to be related to one another. Buddhist philosophy describes this process as being merely conventional and argues that, at a deeper level, all things interpenetrate, and that none possesses separate or inherent existence. In the earlier Buddhist traditions enlightenment was seen as the final goal at the end of a long process of spiritual development. It required study, discipline and meditation. Tantra short-circuits this process by entering imaginatively into the situation of being a Buddha, and thus goes beyond what is possible by intellectual effort alone.

The moment of sexual release, described in Tantric texts as the moment of 'great bliss', coming about (in the cryptic language used in the texts) through the union of the *vajra* (penis) and the *lotus* (vagina), strives – whether literally (if the act is to be performed) or mentally (if this is used in meditation) – to enter imaginatively into a situation of union, and use that as a basis for a universal awareness.

Western

In the West, it is rather assumed that one's behaviour should follow from one's beliefs and should be justified subsequently in terms of them. Emotion and action follow thought. The problem with this is that, in everyday experience, thought is often led by emotion and action, rather than the other way round. By contrast, in the East – and particularly in Tantra – emotions and actions enable reality to be engaged and understood at a level that is deeper than that of conceptual thought. Concepts follow along afterwards, and (from a Buddhist point of view) are merely conventional.

In the West the moment of orgasm has been described as 'the little death', but it is also the potential starting point of life. The sexual act would seem to be exactly suitable as a vehicle for exploring this view of reality.

Perhaps the nearest Western philosophy gets to Tantra is in the area of Aesthetics, where it explores what it is that can be considered beautiful, since that process is dependent upon the natural attractiveness of certain things that leads them to be called 'beautiful' in the first place, or the power of an image that leads it to be considered a work of art.

> Philosophy thus stands back from and comments upon a process
> that most obviously is not based on reason alone, but on reason as
> interpreting emotional and intuitive resonance.

ONE MIND

Tantric Buddhism sees sense experience as essentially an illusion and reality as One Mind – and in this it follows Yogacara philosophy. But in probing the idea of One Mind, we find that it reveals another way into fundamental Buddhist philosophy:

▶ One Mind is a predicateless unity. In other words, the experience of 'One Mind' is an awareness of reality that goes beyond all distinctions, beyond the separation of one thing from another, and therefore beyond the conventional perception of time and space.

▶ One Mind is therefore timeless, changeless, eternal. One Mind represents total reality, before it is subsequently divided up by our conventional experience of it. It also gets beyond the self/ non-self division.

▶ Entering into the experience of One Mind is therefore self-liberation, since it takes a person beyond those things in the world of samsara that cause suffering.

In Tantric visualization, a person enters into a relationship with the visualized image of his or her personal deity (*yidam*), and this might give rise to the impression that there is a separation between the deity and oneself. But the Tantric tradition insists that one should not become over-enthusiastic about the visions of the yidam, since they are only manifestations of one's own mind.

Thus, even in those aspects of Tantric Buddhism that make it resemble a conventional religion with worship of gods and goddesses, there is the reminder that this is simply a process of mental cultivation. But this should not be emphasized as being 'only' in the mind – since that would be to make the self/non-self division that Buddhism as a whole wants to get beyond. There is a single reality, and one's mind is part of it. However elaborate Tantric ritual and language may become, it still relates back to the fundamental Buddhist perspective.

From a Westerner's point of view, however, there is something rather unsettling about the 'mind only' recognition that there is no separate, external reality corresponding to your visualized images, even if the experience is real for you. Engagement with a visualized image finds parallels with the involvement of digital avatars in virtual environments. The question is: Can this visualization become obsessive? If so, can it lead to a neglect of practical and moral issues in the non-visualized, mundane world? This is not a philosophical question, merely a recognition that every philosophy (and method of engagement with it) has ethical and practical implications.

MILAREPA (1052–1135)

Milarepa – the second part of whose name means 'cotton clad', a title given to Mila because he is said to have practised a form of heat yoga that enabled him to wear only light clothing even in conditions of extreme cold – was an ascetic, a philosopher and also a poet. He brought together Madhyamaka and Yogacara philosophies into his practice and outlook, insisting on both the emptiness (shunyata) of individual things and also the absolute nature of mind. In what is called the Mahamudra Yoga, he sets out four stages:

1 Establishing inner focus and quietness.
2 Moving beyond conceptual thought to direct experience of reality.
3 Singleness of purpose as the infinite is experienced in and through everything.
4 The ending of practice, as meditator and meditation become one and the same and one goes beyond even the idea of spiritual practice.

After enlightenment, all separate objects are seen as shadow plays, devoid of inherent existence, but at the same time they become 'helpful friends' in that they can assist one to make progress. It is described as a point in which there is no fear of death or of anything in life.

Western

Notice the parallels here with Plato and the simile of the cave in *The Republic*. Like Milarepa, the prisoner who is freed from the restraints that previously kept him bound in the cave, emerges into the daylight and realizes that all he had previously known and taken for reality was no more than a sequence of shadows.

Seeing the infinite in and through the finite is also a key theme of Schleiermacher's view of the purpose of religion.

Conclusion

Inevitably, perhaps, this chapter has focused on the sexual elements within Tantra, partly because it is so different from any Western philosophy, and also because it highlights issues that are there for all human action and emotion *vis-a-vis* an intellectual view of reality.

Nevertheless, if there is one single thing to grasp in terms of the importance of Tantra for philosophy it is this: that without Tantra it is possible to have an idea of the self that is forever a spectator – looking out at and trying to analyse an external world. That same spectator tries then to look inwards and objectify his or her own emotions, making them, too, part of an external world. And in the midst of all that, the self becomes lost, it vanishes. It appears to have no reality, because the elusive 'I' cannot become simultaneously an observer and part of the observed world.

Tantra will have nothing of this. For Tantra, the self and the world, emotions and experience, are part of one and the same process, and between the two aspects of that process there is a constant interaction.

Shunyata, the fundamental Mahayana concept, is here experienced directly. There are no boundaries between one thing and another, or between the human heart and the external world – all interpenetrate, and all therefore influence one another. Sexual or destructive urges, which from the perspective of the limited, false self can lead to suffering, can, from the perspective of the shunyata doctrine, become a vehicle for the harmonious balance of the inner and outer parts of reality.

Perhaps the last word here should be from Lama Anagarika Govinda, a great 20th-century practitioner and writer on Vajrayana Buddhism.

Here he points to the effect of a changed vision that comes through meditation:

> *By seeing the world from the perspective of our limited little ego and our ephemeral aims and desires, we not only distort it; we make it a prison that separates us from our fellow beings and from the very sources of life. But the moment we become truly selfless, by emptying ourselves of all ego-tendencies, of our power hunger and all possessiveness and craving, we break down the walls of our self-created prison and become conscious of the immensity and boundlessness of our true being.*

> (*Creative Meditation and Multi-Dimensional Consciousness*, 1976, p. 104)

This, of course, is religious vision rather than philosophy. But look at the implication of that vision. Govinda is arguing in effect that it is only once one's narrow self-view is surrendered to something wider in the practice of meditation, that one can understand the true nature of the self. In other words, experience rather than rationality is the starting point of the journey of self-discovery.

This, then, is the justification of examining Tantra within a book on philosophy. Tantra raises the fundamental question about the adequacy of rationality alone for understanding either oneself or the world. It recognizes that human beings are psycho-physical entities, for whom sexuality and aggression are important features to be taken into account, as well as energies to be harnessed.

10 THINGS TO REMEMBER

1 Tantra is found in both Hinduism and Buddhism

2 The Vajrayana vehicle builds on the earlier traditions.

3 Visualization and ritual are key features of Tantra.

4 Mandalas act as spiritual maps.

5 Tantric elements are found in early images of Shiva.

6 Tantra integrates sexuality into the spiritual quest.

7 Buddhist Tantra takes up and develops Mahayana philosophy.

8 The mother-father images represent the integration of wisdom and compassion.

9 Tantra deliberately uses and transforms what is potentially dangerous and destructive.

10 Tantra seeks to engage the whole self, not just the intellect.

8

Zen

In this chapter you will:
- *examine the origins and development of Zen*
- *explore key features of Zen Buddhism*
- *consider some 20th-century attempts to relate Zen to Western thought.*

Introduction

All Buddhist traditions use meditation as a tool for spiritual development, adopting what had already become a feature of the Hindu religious milieu. The Chinese term for meditation is *Ch'an*, and the Japanese form of this is *Zen*. Zen simply means 'meditation'.

As we shall see, however, Zen goes beyond other traditions in that it rejects the possibility of using concepts to describe what is perceived in a moment of insight. Zen is the quest to break down our tendency to conceptualize, encouraging us to deal with reality directly.

It might be tempting, therefore, to ask what Zen is doing in a book on Eastern philosophy, since philosophy is primarily about the use of concepts. There are three reasons why it should be included:

▶ It explores the parameters of logical thought. By showing what concepts cannot do, it points to their proper use.
▶ It is a reminder that 'wisdom' – the true object of philosophy – is not simply conceptual, and in doing this it reinforces the breadth of understanding of wisdom in the East, in contrast to the more narrowly defined function of philosophy in a Western academic context.

▶ It has influenced a number of thinkers who have consciously attempted to develop Eastern philosophy in ways that relate it to Western thought.

Origins and development

KASYAPA'S SMILE

Although the practice of Zen might be geographically and historically far removed from the teachings of Siddhartha Gautama, it claims to trace its origins to an incident that occurred while the Buddha was teaching. Instead of attempting to explain the Dharma in words, the Buddha was said simply to have held up a flower, turning it in his hand. Kasyapa, one of the disciples present on that occasion, saw the flower and smiled. That smile, devoid of all concepts or explanation, is claimed as the origin of Zen – a direct perception of the nature of reality.

Zen, therefore, claims to be a tradition of teaching going back to the Buddha himself, but one that was handed on verbally, by way of a tradition of training passed on from teacher to disciple, and not committed to writing. Indeed, Zen does not require acceptance of any written tradition, only the following of a pattern of spiritual teaching.

BODHIDHARMA

By tradition, Ch'an (Zen) was brought to China in 520 CE by Bodhidharma, to whom is attributed what amounts to a definition of Zen as a 'direct transmission of awakened consciousness, outside tradition and outside scripture.' He was the first of a line of Ch'an teachers, referred to as the patriarchs. He is portrayed as a fierce character with staring eyes, and a number of legendary stories have gathered around him, including one that he sat in meditation facing a wall until his legs dropped off, and another that he cut off his eyelids to stop himself from dozing! What is clear, however, is that he did not initiate a totally new form of Buddhism, but rather developed aspects of meditation from Indian Mahayana Buddhism.

On the other hand, it was characteristic of Bodhidharma, and later Ch'an and Zen, to present the Dharma in a slightly shocking way, breaking down conventional assumptions. Thus, when asked to give a summary of Buddhism, Bodhidharma is said to have replied 'Vast emptiness, nothing holy.'

Hui-Neng was the Sixth Patriarch in succession to Bodhidharma. A key feature of his philosophy was a rejection of all rituals as a means to salvation, or enlightenment. He also emphasized the possibility of sudden enlightenment. This was a departure from the earlier tradition, following the Indian approach, where enlightenment was thought to come gradually as a result of long training.

He presented important features of what developed as the Zen tradition – that nothing exists permanently, separately or independently (we saw this as a fundamental feature of all Buddhist traditions), but he took this a step further by claiming, as an implication of this, that nothing could be conceptualized correctly.

Insight

This is the logical conclusion of a loss of separate existence, since concepts discriminate between one thing and another. Once you start using concepts you divide your world up into separate entities. This, according to Hui-Neng, went against the fundamental idea of shunyata.

He believed that people were habitually attached to the notion of separate objects, and this obscured their light, like clouds obscuring the sun or the moon. What he sought to do was to get beneath the superficiality of concepts to a self-nature that was also pure Buddha nature.

But what could be known in such a state? What can be conveyed if concepts cannot be used? Hui-Neng's answer is that one knows that there is nothing to be known. There is a sudden lightness and clarity; everything is empty.

Key features of Zen

When compared with other Buddhist philosophies, Zen has three important features which, as was said above, were originally attributed to Bodhidharma:

- ▶ It depends on verbal transmission: it passes directly from mind to mind.
- ▶ It does not rely on scriptures.
- ▶ It offers a method of dealing directly with each person's experience.

And to this we have now added the central features of Hui-Neng's teaching, namely, that it goes beyond all concepts, and that it is discovery of the Buddha Mind. Before looking at the two main branches of Zen and the techniques used, we need to clarify these two points.

INTUITIVE PRAJNA

To appreciate Zen, one needs to remember two features of Buddhism in general:

▶ That suffering results from grasping, and that it is possible to grasp and cling to ideas and concepts as well as to particular things. To attempt to systematize, categorize and conceptualize the world is to grasp at it, and that is to miss the point of the fundamental Buddhist intuition.

▶ That everything is impermanent and is 'empty' of inherent existence (the idea of shunyata).

Once you start to think of yourself as separate from others things, once you start to rationalize and set out your world in terms of individual things, differentiating between them, then your thinking is conventional and not absolute. In absolute terms, everything is shunyata.

Enlightenment requires getting beyond the clutter of conventional thinking and having a direct perception of reality. But how is that to be done? Certainly not by forming concepts and arguments about the nature of existence, for such arguments only drag you further into the quagmire of conceptual thought and conventional differentiation and analysis.

How, then, can you think the unthinkable? Zen cannot tell you how to do that, but it can offer a set of practices that can shock the mind out of its conventional patterns, in the hope that *satori* (a moment of insight) will occur.

Western

The nearest parallel in Western thought to this deliberate setting aside of all conceptual thought and simply accepting the whole universe just as it is, can be found in religious mysticism rather than philosophy.

In exploring any parallels with Western mysticism, however, it should be remembered that, like all Buddhist philosophies, Zen does not use the concept of God. Thus the experience that a Western mystic would describe in terms of union with God, a Zen practitioner might want to describe as the discovery of his or her own Buddha nature, or awareness of a vast nothingness.

What you have in Zen, therefore, is a form of intuitive wisdom. It can be communicated without words (a tradition that goes back to Kasyapa's smile), it leads to spontaneous behaviour and a sense of immediacy, and it shows little respect for tradition.

ONE MIND

In the Zen tradition (as in all Buddhism) the main obstacle to enlightenment is the way in which our superficial ego relates to life, both by grasping and in its thinking. This is, as we have seen, the result of the false notion of the self as a separate, self-existing entity. But Zen sees this small, surface mind as something that we acquire after birth. It is conventional, based on what we learn from others, influenced by our feelings and needs. In contrast to this, it sees the Buddha mind as innate. We do not acquire a Buddha mind, it is ours already; we only have to become aware of it.

In narrowly egocentric, conceptual thinking, we are not content just to experience something, but must immediately start to conceptualize it, to love or hate it, to ask how it relates to us and to give it a particular value in our scheme of things. In this way, reality is lost in our clutter of thoughts and feelings. Once the superficiality of this way of thinking is realized and discarded, however, the Buddha mind sees everything immediately and intuitively, just as it is. How, then, do we get beyond our small mind and start to use the Buddha mind? How, in other words, do we get to that state of awareness that Buddhism generally refers to as enlightenment?

In the Zen tradition, enlightenment varies in the way it is described, as do the techniques used for achieving it, between the two main branches of Zen: Rinzai and Soto. Rinzai emphasizes the use of koans, mental challenges to conventional thinking, and looks for sudden moments of insight (satori), whereas Soto Zen concentrates on the more gradual process of zazen, or sitting meditation, leading to an enlightened state.

The language used contrasts the small mind (one's own) with the universal, or Buddha, mind. In some ways this comes close to the earlier Yogacara traditions of all reality being mental. The state of enlightenment is one of transcending the self to the point at which one's own small mind is seen as at one with (and, indeed, *is*) the universal mind. In enlightenment, the self and Buddha are no longer seen as two separate things. The Buddha nature is within everything, therefore seeing your own nature is also to realize Buddhahood.

Dogen (see below) said that what Buddhas call the self is the entire universe. In other words, the true self is not the surface ego; the true self is the 'original face' that a person has before he or she is born.

Comment

The 'original face' concept is central to this whole approach. Once we get a 'face' we become an individual, distinguishable from others. We think of ourselves as separate from the world out there, and from that comes the whole problem of facing our own fragility and the suffering and grasping that comes from it – the problem that represents the starting point of the whole of Buddhist philosophy.

Our 'original face' before we were born relates the idea we have of ourselves to the whole undifferentiated world out of which we have emerged. The original face represents the loss of ego, the universal perspective and the Buddha nature. Our original face cannot be described in concepts; cannot be distinguished. If we strain after it, we fail to grasp it. We are thrown back on recognizing the superficial and temporary nature of what we conventionally see as ourselves.

Rinzai Zen

Before its arrival in Japan, Chinese Ch'an had already divided into different traditions. Two of which were Lin chi (which became Japanese Rinzai Zen) and Ts'ong tung (which became Japanese Soto Zen). Lin chi is named after a teacher who died in the 9th century, best known for his provocative saying: 'If you see the Buddha on the road, kill him.'

This, as we shall see later, is absolutely typical of the approach of Rinzai Zen, which aims to shock a person out of conventional thinking to a sudden realization of a deeper truth. In this case, of course, the idea is that one should not identify the Buddha with any particular thing, or teacher, or idea, or scripture that one might encounter on life's journey. Any such identification destroys the idea of directly seeing reality as it is, limiting one's view. Therefore, in order to get beyond them, all such Buddhas should be killed.

EISAI (1141–1215)

Eisai, who is regarded as the founder of this form of Zen, originally studied Tendai Buddhism, a form that involves a wide variety of Buddhist practices, and used meditation (Ch'an), as it had been developed in China, as part of his overall Tendai approach. However, as this particular practice became dominant, Rinzai Zen developed as a separate tradition. This form of Zen, established with the first setting up of a temple in Japan in 1184, quickly established itself with the ruling Samurai.

HAKUIN (1685–1769)

Hakuin revived Rinzai Zen after a period during which it had gradually become more of a cultural and artistic phenomenon than a philosophical and religious one. He seems to have been a ferocious and determined man, and yet one who was sensitive and artistic, producing calligraphy and a large number of paintings.

The starting point of Hakuin's philosophy is basic Zen: the world of ordinary experience is delusion; reality itself is a divisionless unity; no concepts can apply to this ultimate truth; the self/non-self division is ultimately unreal and is the cause of suffering. He also insisted that we could all experience reality itself, simply because we are part of that reality. Our Buddha nature is our real nature, it is our original face, hidden beneath the clutter of conceptual thought and conventional ways of seeing.

The goal of Zen is 'no-mind'. This does *not* mean extinction, but rather achieving a level of awareness that goes beyond the ego-centred mind. We are all potential Buddhas, for we are all theoretically capable of seeing reality as it is. He uses the image of water turning into ice to illustrate this:

All beings are primarily Buddhas.
Like water and ice
There is no ice apart from water;
There are no Buddhas apart from beings.

(from the opening of
Zazen Wasan, 'The Song of Zazen')

Like all Buddhists, he practised meditation, and extended it into all of life, suggesting that the whole universe should become one's meditation cave. He saw enlightenment as a state of absolute peace, absolute fearlessness and absolute joy.

But Hakuin is probably best known for promoting the use of koans to challenge conventional thinking and enable moments of satori (insight), which are a distinctive feature of the Rinzai approach.

KOANS

A *koan* is a recorded question or saying attributed to one of the Zen masters. It is designed to shatter one's conventional thinking and show our inability of find an answer by conceptual thought. Insight is produced once the mind lets go of the attempt to make sense of the koan.

As well as gathering together existing koans, Hakuin created his own. His most famous is generally abbreviated to the single question:

'What is the sound of one hand clapping?'

Hakuin argued that, as you investigate your koan, you find that your ego-based thoughts are challenged and you may come a point at which you face a 'vast abyss' in which you feel suddenly free, and in which you let go of both your body and your mind. So the more you think about the idea of clapping, the more you find the concept of a single hand clapping to be meaningless. There is no solution to the dilemma of what the single hand clapping can be.

The effect of a koan can be quite startling. Hakuin describes hearing another famous koan attributed to Joshu (778–897 CE):

A monk asked Joshu, a Chinese Zen master:
"Has a dog a Buddha nature or not?"
Joshu answered "Wu".

('Wu' – or 'Mu' – does not simply mean 'No'. Joshu was not saying that a dog does not have a Buddha nature, rather he was barking back a 'nothing' indicating that the question itself is flawed. And, of course 'Wu!' is very much what a dog would say, if asked!)

Hakuin says that the effect this had on him was like being frozen in a sheet of ice extending thousands of miles in each direction, so that he was quite unable to move. He was quite out of his mind, just hearing the single word 'Wu'. Then suddenly he was brought out of this state by the sound of a temple bell, and achieved satori. Once the koan has done its job, it can be set aside.

Insight

Koans, can easily be taken superficially and misunderstood. Someone might feel that they have found a logical answer, for example; in which case the koan has failed to produce the right result. For this reason koans are generally studied only under the guidance of a trained and experienced Zen teacher.

Alongside koans, Zen Buddhists explore their traditions through the recounted stories of the Zen masters, which often take the form of question and answer sessions between master and student. Such stories are generally termed *mondo*. As with the koan, the mondo is not to be treated as a scripture, but simply as the recording of a particular example of the teaching of a master, which one can appropriate by reading and reflecting. But again, as throughout Zen, it is considered best to do everything under the guidance of a *roshi*, or Zen master.

SATORI

We have already used the term satori several times; it is the word used in Rinzai Zen for a moment of enlightenment. This is not seen as a once-for-all event, but a fleeting glimpse of reality. It is described only in the most oblique way, as a sense of unity, of peace and of being beyond time and space, of suddenly knowing the truth. But if you can describe satori, it is not satori that you have described.

The only distinctive thing to be aware of is that satori is described as a flash of insight that can happen unexpectedly as a result of Zen practice. A person can have several of these moments of satori. This contrasts with the more general term 'enlightenment', which is used in other forms Buddhism for the general and on-going state of awareness of reality as it is.

D. T. SUZUKI (1870–1966)

Suzuki was particular known for his *Essays in Zen Buddhism*, of which the first edition appeared in 1927. He followed the teaching of Hakuin, in seeing reality as non-dual, and insisting that all conceptual frameworks of space, time and identity are false, and are imposed on undifferentiated reality by the mind. Apprehension of reality is satori, and satori cannot be communicated, only experienced. In that book he sets out eight properties of satori:

▶ Irrationality – it cannot be achieved by reasoning, nor can it be described rationally.

▶ Noetic quality – it is not simply a void, but has content, although that content cannot be communicated in words.

▶ Authoritativeness – it is absolute and authoritative for the person who has it and, of course, it cannot be refuted logically.

▶ Affirmation – although it goes beyond conventional awareness, it is certainly not a negative experience, but gives a very positive view.

▶ Sense of the 'beyond' – it goes beyond the normal distinction between self and other, although to try to take is further and describe the 'beyond' as 'God' or 'the Absolute' would be to try to bring concepts into what cannot be conceptualized.

▶ Impersonal tone – it is definitely not like a personal encounter; what is experienced in satori is positive but impersonal.

▶ Feeling of exaltation – this is the result of all the conventional hindrances falling away, giving direct awareness.

▶ Momentariness – it happens suddenly, and is 'out of time'.

The last of these is particularly important, as the experience of satori is described as 'one thought'; it is a single insight, with no sense of one thing leading on to another. It is a moment that disrupts the normal awareness of the passing of time. In this sense it is 'eternal'.

Notice that Suzuki has not done the impossible. He has not *described* satori, only spoken about *what it is like* to have satori. The content itself can be experienced, but not described.

Western

There are interesting parallels here with the moments of insight claimed by Western mystics. Suzuki himself explored these in a later work entitled *Mysticism, Christian and Buddhist* (1957).

Soto Zen

In contrast to Rinzai Zen, with its challenging koans and sudden satori, Soto Zen placed its emphasis on enlightenment through the practice of sitting meditation – *zazen*. The key figure in the development of this tradition was Dogen.

DOGEN (1200–1253)

Tendai, a form of Buddhism practised in Japan at the time when both Eisai and Dogen were developing their particular forms of Zen, had taught that people were originally enlightened, but that their enlightened nature (Buddha nature) was obscured. This led to the question: Why, if one is fundamentally enlightened, should one need to practise religion or asceticism at all? Should the enlightened state not be the natural one?

Having travelled in China and encountered the Ts'ong tung tradition, Dogen, returned to Japan to develop it there as Soto Zen. He believed that sitting meditation (zazen) was the right way to practise Buddhism and that, as a person sitting in meditation, he or she was able to realize the enlightened nature. Nothing else was needed for enlightenment, so one could dispense with other religious or ascetic practices.

In coming to this conclusion, he did not see Zen as something new or different from the earlier forms of Buddhism, just the result of placing emphasis on a particular means of practising it. He also argued that everyday activities should be the basis of meditation leading to the exploration of the Buddha nature. Thus one could find realization *through practice itself*, not just as a result of having *done* the practice. For Dogen, the realization of the Buddha nature, and the practice of zazan that aimed to bring it about, were actually one and the same. To put it simply: sitting in meditation is being enlightened – you don't develop awareness in meditation in order to move on to some other state afterwards.

Insight

A key thing to remember here is that Dogen did not think of the Buddha nature as something that a person could possess, as though it were some spiritual object. Rather, he saw the whole of being as the Buddha nature – something to be realized here and now, once superficial distractions are removed and one can see clearly.

Dogen saw *mujo* (impermanence) as the Buddha nature. If you realize the one, you realize the other. In this way he sought to get beyond both samsara (the world of change) and nirvana (the original goal of peace and serenity for one who had gone beyond change). A person should not stay in either state, but, experiencing nirvana, should then freely enter into the ever-changing world of samsara again. But such a person will be enlightened – in other words, he or she will see and recognize the world of samsara for what it is.

Dogen and time

In *Shobogenzo Uji*, his main work, Dogen claimed that time, just as it is, is being and that being is all time. In other words, all phenomena – mountains and seas included – are a feature of time. They would not exist without time. All beings are impermanent, and all have Buddha nature, therefore even the Buddha nature itself is not unchanging.

He uses this argument for equating being and time:

- ▶ Time cannot be something that flies past, something that happens.
- ▶ If it were, it could only be known if it had gaps in it. In other words, you would need to see one thing and then another, and then point to time as being the means of moving from one to another. But actually reality is not sliced up in that way.
- ▶ There is no passage from one state to the next – no gap that is created by something external called 'time'.
- ▶ Rather, time is the 'passageless passage' as one state flows into the next.
- ▶ So time is the name we give to the flow of being.

He also considered that the Buddha nature, being fundamental reality, is always manifested in the present. In other words: the real is always present.

Hence, rather than have two separate entities – being and time – he has the single ever-changing and flowing entity, 'being-time'. There is no 'eternal' realm other than this present realm in which things change. Everything is manifested here and now. Every moment manifests eternity, for every moment reveals the passageless passage of time.

It would be interesting to speculate on what Dogen would have made of the Theory of Relativity – sadly, he lived 700 years too early.

There are also parallels here with Process Philosophy, where the traditional, Western 'eternalist' approach is up against the reality of time and change. There are connections here all the way from Heraclitus through to Bergson and Whitehead and, on the theological side, with Teilhard de Chardin.

But most interesting are the possible parallels between his thought and that of Heidegger in his *Being and Time*.

Insight

If everything in the cosmos is impermanent and changing, time is simply the name we give to that process. The unity and ultimate nature of the universe is not something known by getting outside or above that process, as theistic religions seem to suggest with their idea of God, but by recognizing the universal nature of change itself. Dogen sees the logical outcome of the original Buddhist view of impermanence as a single space–time continuum in which everything interpenetrates.

Philosophically, it is interesting to put together this Soto Zen approach with the Rinzai view of satori, as it has been outlined above by Suzuki. For Suzuki, the moment of satori is outside time, whereas for Dogen awareness is of everything flowing through time, or being part of a process we call time. These seem to be contradictory, but need not be so. The moment of insight is a single thought, and the singularity of that thought takes us beyond all distinctions and therefore beyond time and space. On the other hand, the *content* of experience on which this single thought subsequently comes to bear – the result of that thought, in other words – would seem to be the universal awareness of the changing, flowing nature of reality.

ZAZEN

Zazen is generally performed sitting facing a blank wall. Sessions of zazen are interspersed with some walking meditation (*kinhin*). The task is just to sit with an absolutely clear, bright mind. This is far from easy, since the untrained mind naturally becomes cluttered with thoughts. To overcome this clutter, it is necessary to have some object upon which to focus one's attention. In zazen it is common to focus on the process of breathing (in other words, just giving attention to the flow of air in and out of the lungs), and on the passing of thoughts (noting them as they arise, allowing them to drop) as a means of entering into the calm, thoughtless state within which a direct, clear experience of reality can arise.

An image used for Zazen is the clearing of a pool of muddy water. One's reflection is only seen once the water is clear and still. Zazan does not determine the content of the reflection, it merely clears the water so that a reflection can be seen, but the clearing of the water and the seeing of the reflection happen simultaneously, so sitting in zazen is the process of becoming enlightened.

ENLIGHTENMENT IN MEDITATION

Unlike Rinzai Zen, which spoke mainly of moments of insight (satori) in which there is a sudden breaking through to a new form of awareness, Soto Zen emphasizes that, as one sits in meditation, one is already a Buddha. In other words, in meditation one becomes aware of one's true nature – one's Buddha nature. Therefore, enlightenment is not something to be gained at the end of a long process of spiritual development, but is a present experience. To the extent to which a person practises meditation, to that extent he or she is already Buddha.

Insight
Remember that the goal here is not something to be grasped or possessed. Indeed, the very attempt to do so only reinforces the false idea of the self. Enlightenment happens as if by accident. What is sought is the clarity of mind that can allow it to happen.

The Buddha nature

What has been said above about both the Rinzai and Soto approaches to Zen has brought out two features of the nature of the self in relation to Buddhism – characterized by the term 'Buddha nature'.

INTROSPECTION

The first key feature is that the Buddha, and our Buddha nature, is not separate from our own self. If we see the Buddha on the road, we are to kill him! Buddha nature, whether revealed as a moment of satori, provoked by a koan, or as a result of zazen, is essentially our own true nature, once the illusion of a separate self has been set aside. The self and its Buddha nature are therefore known through introspection (although through an unconscious form of introspection, rather than a conscious analysis of self, which would be quite contrary to Zen), not through any external doctrines. It is the clearing of water that has formerly been muddied, the revealing of what has always been there, not the discovery of something new.

SPONTANEITY

The Buddha nature is revealed through spontaneity, the second key feature. That is the key to recognizing the difference between self-consciousness and Buddha consciousness. Spontaneity is action that takes place prior to any consideration of the illusory separate self. Devoid of self-consciousness, it accords with the general Buddhist view of the world, in which everything is connected to everything else and arises in dependence upon conditions. Recognition of this gives a lightness of touch, almost a playfulness, in all creative activity. As we shall see, this has a profound influence on Zen practice, and in particular on the Zen view of the arts.

Zen practice

ANARCHY AND DISCIPLINE

Zen morality follows from its basic view of the mind. All evil actions are seen as the result of acting on the basis of the selfish ego-mind. The Buddha mind, being universal, cannot be selfish.

This is sometimes referred to as living in the 'unborn' – in other words, being at one with the One Mind that is beyond the changing surface of things. A person who dwells in the unborn, who has developed 'no-mind', will be totally spontaneous.

Whatever you are doing, once you stop and think about it, you become self-conscious and the absolute and spontaneous nature of that action is lost. To shoot an arrow perfectly, one should not be conscious of an 'I' that shoots at all, at the appropriate moment the arrow shoots itself – the mind is beyond the self, beyond that arrow and beyond the target.

Clearly, Zen requires great discipline, whether in the efforts to break down conventional thinking in the Rinzai tradition or in the disciplined sitting in Soto Zen. But the result of insight is that a person is freed to behave quite spontaneously. (Indeed, it no longer feels like 'a person behaving' but more like 'action taking place'.) This makes Zen action unpredictable and unconventional. Indeed, convention is the very enemy of Zen, for the conventional, by definition, has lost its spontaneity. Zen morality is certainly not based on rules, but on insight and intuitive response. In a way, that is anarchy. But it is not selfish anarchy, but rather a totally selfless unpredictability, born out of the disciplines that help a person get beyond the narrow view of self.

Western

In moral terms, this is rather like Augustine's view that one should 'love and do what you want'. For Augustine, of course, to love was to know the mind of God and therefore all action that flowed from love was morally good. Zen has a similar approach, but substituting 'love' and 'God' for 'egoless no-mind' and 'the unborn' or 'Buddha mind'. Both recognize the limits of conventional morality.

As with all Zen, the conventional is challenged in a very direct way. Here are verses from *Honshin no uta*, 'The Song of the Original Mind' (1653), by Bankei Yotaku:

> *You think that good*
> *Means hating what is bad*
> *What's bad is*
> *The hating mind itself.*
> *Good, you say,*
> *Means doing good.*
> *Bad indeed*
> *The mind that says so!*

Such verses reflect the paradoxical and challenging nature of Zen, always breaking down conventional patterns of thought.

Yet this feature of Zen might lead to the quite false impression that Zen is concerned in a narrow way with the self and not with issues of the wider world. But the aim of Zen is to return a person to the everyday world with a new sense of clarity and selfless action. Two things might illustrate this aspiration:

▶ The 12th-century Chinese Ch'an master Kakuan devised a set of ten pictures depicting bulls (sometimes referred to as the 'The Bulls' and sometimes as 'The Ox-herding pictures'). In these, the relationship between the man and the bull depicts the human being and the Buddha nature. The herder spies the bull, goes after it, catches it, brings it back. But then both bull and self are forgotten, and in the last image the person returns to the market place of life, giving the sense of seeing everything alive and new and providing blessings on everyone he sees.

▶ There is also the traditional prayer used after evening zazen:

Sentient beings are numberless,
I vow to save them;
Desires are inexhaustible,
I vow to put an end to them;
The Dharmas are boundless,
I vow to master them.
The Buddha way in unsurpassable,
I vow to attain it.

Both in the mastery of the dharmas (in other words, understanding reality and gaining skills in dealing with it) and in the desire to save the innumerable beings, there is a sense of the ultimate altruism that comes once the self is transcended.

The result of Zen practice should be unselfconsciousness, spontaneity and altruism. But if you simply aspire to become unselfconscious, spontaneous and altruistic, you may fail to do so simply because you are grasping at them as qualities to enhance the self (a subtle form of selfishness). So, to counter this, Zen provides techniques to break down the notion of self, following which unselfconsciousness, spontaneity and altruism may arise quite naturally.

ZEN AND THE ARTS

In the idea of hua yen (interpenetration), every spec of dust in the universe contains the whole universe. Everything is within everything else; separateness is illusion. Therefore the whole of Buddhahood can be found in a simple action. Whatever is done naturally and spontaneously flows from our own Buddha nature.

In Zen, the arts give an opportunity for natural expression and are therefore vehicles for spiritual development. A simple flower, a sand garden, the naturally flowing and unselfconscious actions of the tea ceremony – all these are attempts to get beyond the self, to act at one with the universal Buddha nature. Zen has therefore influenced calligraphy, music, poetry, painting and gardening.

The wonderful, precise simplicity of Zen arts are beyond description, but need to be encountered with an open mind, free from the temptations of intellectual analysis.

Insight

Notice the parallels here with Taoism. One could almost say of a Zen creation that it is the product of wu wei (non-action), because it is free from any conscious imposition of the self upon the material with which it works.

East meets West

Modern Buddhist philosophers have been concerned to explore parallels and differences between their own views and Western philosophy. D.T. Suzuki, for example, was critical of the dualistic, analytical and conceptual framework within which Western philosophy was couched. He pointed out how very different this was from Zen, which sought an insight that was non-dualistic and therefore beyond concepts. Contrasts in Western thought – between man and God, for example, or between faith and reason – simply do not apply to Zen.

In *Reason and Intuition in Buddhist Philosophy* (1951) he made an important distinction between two terms – *vijnana* and *prajna*.

▶ Vijnana is best translated as 'reason'. It is essentially analytical. In the West, philosophy is primarily concerned with vijnana.
▶ Prajna is 'wisdom'. Far from being analytic, its chief function is to integrate – to achieve awareness as a whole, going beyond conventional distinctions.

Insight

The meeting of East and West in philosophy is essentially a dialogue between vijnana and prajna. From the Western point of view, Eastern prajna is too much bound up with religion, morals, culture and so on. From an Eastern point of view, Western analytic vijnana never gets beyond the conventional distinctions within which rationality is forced to operate.

NISHIDA KITARO (1870–1945)

From the mid-19th century Japan came out of a period of cultural isolation, and its philosophers were able to study Western philosophy and to assess its relationship to their own tradition. This process is particularly well illustrated by the work of Nishida, who was Professor of Philosophy at Kyoto University from 1913 to 1928.

Nishida's work went through various phases as he took first one and then another set of Western concepts through which to articulate his thought. Basically he was trying to see if Zen could be articulated using concepts and, if so, whether Western philosophy could provide a conceptual framework for doing this.

Insight

Notice what a difficult task Nishida set himself. Zen, like Western mysticism, is inherently non-conceptual. It works by breaking down conventional thinking. How, then, can concepts be used to illustrate it without at the same time destroying it?

His first approach was based in part on an interpretation of Hegel. In Hegel's 'dialectic' you have a process whereby thesis and antithesis are resolved in a synthesis. But that synthesis in turn moves on to become another thesis, and so on. At the risk of gross oversimplification, we may say that what he took from Hegel was the sense of the universe as a constantly moving process which works by the resolution of opposites.

Now Nishida's basic question was how it could be that we experience the world in terms of the changes and contradictions of ordinary experience, given that Zen points to an underlying unity. In *An Inquiry into the Good* (1911) he suggested that reality is pure experience – prior to any subject/object division, prior to any division between mind and matter, prior even to any sense of time. But, of course, the way we normally experience reality is not like that at all; such pure experience would be satori, or enlightenment. What we actually see is a universe that goes through a process of change, but beneath that we can be aware of a fundamental unity.

Nishida's idea of 'pure experience' as the basic way of getting beyond the subject/object division can be related to such Western thinkers as Henri Bergson and William James, who took experience as the starting point out of which can come philosophical concepts and distinctions. And his question reflects Kant's distinction between things as they are in themselves and things as we know them to be through experience.

He then takes a bold step and introduces the concept of God (*An Enquiry into the Good*, p. 79). He argues that God is not something that transcends reality, but is the basis of reality – something which dissolves the distinction between subjectivity and objectivity, spirit and nature. Our 'true self' is the ultimate reality of the universe, and to know one's true self is therefore to be united with the will of God. The 'Good' which he seeks is the realization of that true self.

Insight

What you have here is a very bold attempt to bring together the Eastern, non-conceptual experience found in Zen with Western concepts, thereby opening up the possibility of a global philosophy.

By 1917, Nishida was moving away from the idea of 'pure experience' as the basis for his work, towards 'absolute free will' and then to 'the place of nothingness'. From 1927 he was much occupied with trying to develop a form of logic that went beyond Aristotle. This is fundamental to any appreciation of the dilemma of wedding Western and Eastern thought. For Aristotle, there are two very basic logical principles:

▶ a thing is itself and not something else
▶ 'p' and 'non p' cannot both be true at one and the same time.

But we have seen that the approach of Zen is exactly to break down the habitual use of this kind of logic. It relies on paradox and opposition in order to force the mind to go beyond conventional analysis. What Nishida insists on is that the real is both one and many at the same time.

Nishida attempted to replace Aristotelian logic with what he called 'place or field logic'. Subjects are determined by their place. But that which is ultimate can have no place – it is therefore 'nothingness' (which is, of course, an absolutely central Buddhist concept for Mahayana Buddhism). In *The Logic of the Place of Nothingness and the Religious World View* (1945) he argued that religion is fundamentally about the true self and its relation to reality. He thought that religious consciousness is universal and that God and the 'true self' are identical. In this, he was reaffirming a basic Zen concept that the Buddha nature is present in everyone.

The key concept here is 'absolute nothingness', which Nishida sees as true reality. This is not a relative nothingness, which simply negates a particular being (i.e. 'Is it here or not?'), but an absolute nothingness that denies absolute reality to individual beings. This reflects the most fundamental feature of Buddhism, namely that everything lacks inherent selfhood (anatta in early and Theravadin Buddhism), depends for its existence on everything else and is interconnected. This 'nothingness' (shunyata in the Mahayana tradition) is central to the Buddhist view of reality, and so, in relating his thought to Western concepts, Nishida emphasizes the 'place of nothingness'.

In other words, if you tried to make 'God' (or reality) 'absolute being', you would start to describe it – and, as soon as you did that, it would no longer be 'absolute being', for once you define it, you objectivize it and limit it. Such an idea needs, therefore, to be balanced by making reality 'absolute nothingness'. This is not a negative thing, but a very positive affirmation of reality. It is that which is beyond objectivity and concepts. You can only have absolute being in terms of absolute nothingness. You have what Nishida called an 'identity of absolute contradiction'. Very Zen!

Western

Nishida's concept of God, as both transcendent and immanent, is probably closest to the Western concept of panentheism. It sounds, at times, as though Nishida wants a pantheism, with reality within everything, but yet, through the idea of 'absolute nothingness' this is always negated. He is using Mahayana Buddhist concepts to articulate a basic tension that is also found in Western concepts of God – as something that is said to exist, and yet to be beyond the existence that we would predicate of individual things.

One might explore Heidegger's idea of the nature of 'Being', and also the theology of Paul Tillich with his concept of God as 'Being itself'. There is also the 'Death of God' theology of Van Buren and others. These were Western attempts to prevent the concept of God being objectivized and limited. Nishida tries to accomplish the same thing using the basic Buddhist concept of 'shunyata'.

The Buddhist concept of shunyata can be applied to a whole range of Western problems including, for example, the elusive nature of the self. (In the spontaneity of Zen, the self both vanishes and acts at the same time.)

Much of Nishida's work concerned the mystical and personal aspects of reality, taking little note of the political and social dimensions, which probably reflected the concerns of the Western thinkers with whom his philosophy entered into dialogue. This lack was corrected by a follower of Nishida within the Kyoto School of Philosophy, Tanabe Majima (1885–1962), who insisted that individuals did not connect with the absolute directly, but did so through the medium of social and political structures. His earlier work was particulary concerned with the place of the nation state, but later he was more concerned with surrendering the self as a response to the past, and moving towards receiving power from the 'other power', identified again with the ultimate reality, which he related to the idea of Amida Buddha.

In its ethics, the Kyoto school emphasized the need to negate the self absolutely – and that can work on two levels, either through losing the self by becoming integrated into society, or more generally as an experience of the 'nothingness' of the self. There are interesting parallels here with the Taoist idea of wu wei ('no action'), as a description of what is done most naturally and spontaneously. Interestingly, the ethical thinking from within the Kyoto school emphasized the role of society, criticizing Heidegger for being too individualistic. This perhaps reflects a very important East Asian contribution also to Buddhist thought, which at times has been portrayed as being overly individualistic.

Beyond concepts

Zen pushes philosophy to its limits, because Zen involves going beyond concepts and rational thoughts and aims at direct awareness. Many of the activities associated with Zen, along with the practices designed to deepen a person's appreciation of it, aim to break down conventional thinking and reasoning.

Having said that, Zen is an absolutely essential part of any appreciation of Eastern philosophy, firstly because it is rigorous in setting the limits of what can be articulated, and secondly because it is from within a broadly Zen tradition that there have been these interesting attempts to articulate Eastern spiritual insights using Western concepts. The subject of Zen and Western thought deserves far greater coverage than is possible here, all we have attempted to do is look briefly at some of the great thinkers in this tradition, the key elements that form the distinctively Zen approach to Buddhist philosophy, and at Nishida, whose work established the Kyoto school of philosophy, which has most obviously worked towards not just the interpretation of Eastern thought for the West (a task that had been undertaken particularly by Suzuki) but in actually forming a global philosophy, utilizing concepts from both hemispheres.

In most of the material we have looked at in this book, it has been clear that the concepts and background are culturally conditioned, and that parallels with Western thought can appear to be rather tenuous, simply because Western philosophers approach similar questions from a very different point of view. Naturally this is also true to some extent with Zen, which has influenced and been influenced by Japanese culture. On the other hand, in its attempt to get *beyond* concepts, and in its rejection of doctrines and rituals, Zen offers the possibility of a philosophy that can claim to be genuinely global.

10 THINGS TO REMEMBER

1 Zen means 'meditation'.

2 It traces its origin to the teachings of the Buddha.

3 It is based on verbal transmission not written traditions or scriptures.

4 Rinzai Zen uses koans to break down traditional thinking.

5 Hakuin considered ordinary experience to be delusion, and reality to be beyond concepts.

6 A moment of enlightened awareness is called 'satori'.

7 Soto Zen is based on meditation.

8 Zazen (sitting meditation) aims to clear the mind of distractions.

9 Everyone is considered to have a Buddha nature.

10 The Kyoto school of philosophy sought to bring together Eastern and Western thought.

Postscript

This postscript is both an apology and an invitation.

An apology, because it is folly to try to give an overview of the whole range of Eastern philosophy in a book of this length. Inevitably, ideas of subtlety and depth have received no more than a cursory mention or a brief sketch. I hope those who are coming to Eastern philosophy for the first time will not take this book as the last word on any of the traditions included, and that those who have already studied this material will excuse the inevitable lacunae and accept it in the light of its intended purpose.

Which brings me to the invitation.

The purpose of this book has been to whet the appetite for Eastern philosophy. Every one of the traditions outlined here could repay a lifetime of study and reflection. It is enriching both to see something of the ideas that have shaped cultures which now contribute so extensively to our global humanity, and also to have our own thoughts and assumptions challenged by those who may come to familiar topics from perspectives very different from our own.

In a world where communications and economic influences are global, where ideologies, political or religious, impact on one another, sometimes in the most brutal way, it is both unrealistic and dangerous to divide up philosophy too rigidly. Unrealistic, because there are basic questions about life that transcend conventional cultural and religious differences; dangerous, because failure to recognize common concerns across a range of philosophies, religions or ideologies may too easily lead to an 'us/them' view and an inability to appreciate the motives and aspirations of others.

The recognition of interconnectedness will come as no surprise to those who reflect on Buddhist philosophy, for cultures as much as individuals are temporary and 'put together' from elements that are found everywhere. The division of philosophy between East and West is no more than a conventional convenience, whereas the activity of thinking and asking questions is global.

This book is now in its third edition. The fundamentals of each tradition of Eastern philosophy remain unchanged, so much of the text of the earlier editions has remained substantially the same. What has continued to change over the last decade, however, is the speed with which the globalization of our economic, financial and cultural systems has progressed. It is now more important than ever – if we are to live sensitively in this interconnected world – to appreciate and celebrate cultural differences while exploring our common fund of ideas.

Mel Thompson

Taking it further

Further reading

For those who want to follow up on any branch of Eastern Philosophy with an authoritative, academic but readable survey of scholarship:

The Companion Encyclopedia of Asian Philosophy, ed. Brian Carr and Indira Mahalingam, Routledge, 1997

There are also concise entries on a wide range of Eastern philosophers and philosophies in:

The Oxford Companion to Philosophy, ed. T. Honderich, OUP, 1995

The Concise Routledge Encyclopedia of Philosophy, Routledge, 2000

And for books that give a global perspective, and therefore include Eastern Philosophy, try:

Chambers Dictionary of Beliefs and Religions, ed. Mark Vernon, Chambers, 2009 (Although this is mainly concerned with religion, there are entries which outline Eastern philosophical traditions.)

A Companion to World Philosophies, ed. Deutsch and Bontekoe, Blackwell, 1997

World Philosophies, Ninian Smart, Routledge, 1999

World Philosophy, ed. D. Appelbaum and M. Thompson, Vega, 2002

For general books on Eastern philosophy and religion:

Key Concepts in Eastern Philosophy, Oliver Leaman, Routledge, 1999 (A great book for revision of key terms, very straightforward and clearly written.)

Oriental Philosophies, John M. Koller, Macmillan, 1985

The Sacred East, ed. C. Scott Littleton, Macmillan, 1996

The Illustrated Encyclopedia of World Religions, ed. C. Richards, Element Books, 1997

Thirty-Five Oriental Philosophers, Diané Collinson and Robert Wilkinson, Routledge, 1994

Understanding Eastern Philosophy, Ray Billington, Routledge, 1997

There are classic texts in a variety of translations. Try, for example:

The Analects, Confucius, OUP, World's Classics Series, 1993

That Which Is (the Tattvartha Sutra), Umasvati (trans. Nathmal Tatia), HarperCollins 1994 (This book gives a very clear exposition of Jain philosophy, as well as a translation of the principal Jain scripture.)

Buddhist and Hindu texts are available in a number of translations, including Penguin Classics. Or you can find translations of many classic texts freely available on the internet.

There are a vast number of books on each of the philosophies included in this volume. Most examine them from a mainly religious perspective, but they will nevertheless include expositions of the underlying philosophy, and – as has been pointed out many times – it is difficult to separate out the religious from the philosophical in Eastern thought. Of the many books on branches of Eastern philosophy, try:

An Introduction to Hinduism, G. Flood, CUP, 1996

A Short Introduction to Hinduism, K. K. Klostermaier, Oneworld, 1998

An Introduction to Buddhist Ethics, Peter Harvey, CUP, 2000

Buddhist Thought, Paul Williams, Routledge, 2000

Buddhism as Philosophy, Mark Siderits, Ashgate, 2007 (This is a wonderful book for engaging in philosophical dialogue with the whole range of Buddhist ideas. It is written by a philosopher as philosophy, rather than just giving an exposition of traditional arguments.)

Classical Hindu Thought: an introduction, Arvind Sharma, OUP, 2000

Concise History of Buddhism, A, Andrew Skilton, Windhorse, 1994

Early Buddhism: a new approach, Sue Hamilton, Curzon Press, 2000

Heart of the Buddha's Teaching, The, Thich Nhat Hanh, Rider, 1998

History of Buddhist Philosophy, David J. Kalupahana, University of Hawaii Press, 1992

Indian Philosophy: a very short introduction, Sue Hamilton, Oxford, 2001

Living Zen, Michael Paul, Francis Lincoln, 2000 (This and similar illustrated books – see *Zen: images, texts and teachings* below – often convey the essence of Zen in a way that usefully supplements more academic surveys.)

Mahayana Tantra, Shri Dharmakirti, Penguin, 2002 (This book gives useful insight into the practice of Tantra, but you should recognize that this is written from within a religious commitment to this tradition.)

Philosophy in Classical India, J. Ganeri, Routledge, 2001

Tantra: the Search for Ecstasy, Indra Sinha, Hamlyn, 1993

The Foundations of Buddhism, Rupert Gethin, OUP, 1998

Zen in English Literature and Oriental Classics, R. H. Blyth, The Hokoseido Press, 1942 (This is an amazing resource for anyone wanting to explore parallels between Zen and literature.)

Zen: images, texts and teachings, introduced by Miriam Levering, Duncan Baird Publishers, 2000

On the web

There is plenty of material on Eastern philosophy available on the internet, and previous editions of this book have included recommended websites. However, links to particular pages can quickly become dated. Suggestions for websites to follow up on topics covered in this book are therefore included on the author's website, along with a range of other books that may interest you. Just log on to www.philosophyandethics.com and either explore the Buddhism topic page, or select Eastern Philosophy from the 'My Books' link.

Glossary

Hindu

advaita Non-dualist philosophy. Brahman/Atman is ultimately real; all else is illusion.

ahankara The individual ego (in Sankhya philosophy).

ahimsa Non-violence.

ananda Bliss (one of the three qualities of Brahman).

aparigraha Avoiding avarice (last of the yamas).

asrama Stages of life.

asteya Not stealing (third of the five yamas).

astika 'Orthodox', used of schools or philosophies (c.f. nastika – unorthodox).

Atman Self of soul.

avidya Ignorance.

bhakti Devotion (one of the paths to liberation).

Brahman The absolute reality.

bramacarya Student stage of life.

Charvaka *See* 'Lokayata'.

cit Mind or consciousness (also quality of Brahman).

darshana 'Viewing', used in Hindu religion for the act of viewing the image of a god (a murti) or a spiritual teacher. It is also used in the sense of a 'view' or 'philosophy', a particular tradition of teaching leading to insight.

Dharma *See* Sanatana Dharma.

dvaita Dualist philosophy.

grhasta Householder stage of life.

gunas Three aspects of the material universe (Sankhya philosophy).

guru Spiritual teacher.

Isvara One's personal deity.

jnana knowledge.

jiva The individual person.

karma Literally 'action', used of actions that produce spiritual results (found in Hinduism and Buddhism).

Lokayata an unorthodox, materialist and hedonist philosophy, probably originating in the 6th century BCE

marga Way (of release) – of which there are three: karmamarga (based on action), jnanamarga (based on understanding) and bhaktimarga (based on devotion).

Mimamsa Branch of Hindu philosophy.

moksha Spiritual liberation, the goal of the Hindu life.

nastika 'Unorthodox', used of schools of philosophy

Nirguna Brahman Ultimate reality, pure consciousness, beyond description.

prajna Wisdom.

prakrti The material universe (in Sankhya philosophy).

purusa The spiritual element, which (with Prakrti) makes up the universe within Sankhya philosophy. Used also of the original 'cosmic man' out of whose body the various varnas are formed.

rta Early term for the principle of order within the universe.

Saccitananda 'Truth, Consciousness and Bliss' – spiritual goal.

Saguna Brahman Ultimate reality as it is manifested in and though things that can be directly known and experienced (as opposed to Nirguna Brahman).

samsara The ordinary world as it is experienced, constantly changing.

Sanatana Dharma 'The eternal Law; the way things are ordered in the universe.

Sankhya Branch of Hindu philosophy.

sannyasa A renunciate or ascetic, the final stage in life.

sat Truth (quality of Brahman, also used in many other contexts).

satcitananda 'Truth, Consciousness and Bliss', spiritual goal.

Shakti Feminine power, personified in goddesses.

shruti Literally: what is heard. Knowledge gained through hearing Vedic texts recited, believed to be of divine origin.

smriti Literally: what is remembered. Knowledge that comes from texts or traditions; used of the study of texts other than the Vedas.

Upanishads Final part of the Vedic scriptures, giving teachings aimed at those who 'sit near' to the teacher.

varnasramadharma Duty established according to one's stage in life and by one's 'colour' or class.

varna 'Colour'; used of the basic class groups.

vanaprasta The retirement stage of life.

veda 'Knowledge', used of the Hindu scriptures.

Vedanta Hindu philosophy, concerned with interpreting the Vedas.

Visistadvaita Qualified non-dualism; it affirmed the existence of the world, a personal God, the individual souls.

Yoga Disciplines aimed at achieving liberation.

Jain

ahimsa Non-violence.

anekantavada The Jain refusal to accept any proposition as absolute truth because subject to a particular perspective.

Digambara Monastic sect within Jainism.

jina Conqueror (used of Mahavira and the other ford-makers).

jiva Soul (found within everything).

karma-vada The Jain interpretation of the general Hindu view of Karma.

kavala The state of recognizing that one's spirit is in fact the same as absolute reality.

moksha Liberation.

Nigantha Nataputta Title used of Mahavira in Buddhist scriptures (and the Jains are termed Niganthas).

sallekhana Preparing for imminent death by meditation and voluntary starvation.

samsara The ever-changing world we experience.

shramana Independent spiritual teacher.

siddha 'Perfect one'; a person who recognizes the self as the absolute reality and who is said to have infinite knowledge, vision, strength and bliss.

Svetambara Monastic sect within Jainism.

tirthankaras 'Ford-makers', Jain teachers, the last of whom was the historical Mahavira.

Buddhist

Abhidharma Philosophical analysis of the Dhamra.

alaya-vignana 'Store' consciousness; mechanism by which we remember and are affected by events in the past.

anatta 'No inherently existing or independent self'; one of the three marks of conditioned existence.

anicca The first mark of conditioned existence, that all things are subject to change.

Arhat 'Worthy one', used of those who gained enlightenment following the Buddha's teaching.

avidya Spiritual blindness.

Bardo Used of a transitional state, especially that between one life and the next.

bhikku (bhikkuni) Buddhist monk (nun), used within the Theravada tradition.

bodhicitta 'The mind of enlightenment', used of the spiritual state in which a person is determined to follow the path towards enlightenment.

bodhisattva 'Being of enlightenment', used of Gautama prior to his enlightenment; also of other spiritual beings that aid enlightenment in Mahayana Buddhism.

dhyana meditation; also used of the various spiritual states achieved during meditation.

dukkha Suffering, unsatisfactoriness (first of the Four Noble Truths, and the third mark of conditioned existence).

Hinayana 'Lesser vehicle', used as a derogatory term by Mahayana Buddhists of the early schools of which the extant one is the Theravada.

hua-yen The interpenetration of all things (Japanese term for the Mahayana development of the original Buddhist idea of conditioned co-production).

koan Riddle or question without a logical answer, used in Zen as a means of achieving insight.

magga The 'Middle Way', fourth of the Four Noble Truths.

Mahayana 'Great vehicle', the Buddhist tradition originating in India but developed particularly in The Far East and the Himalayas.

mandala A spiritual diagram or map.

mantra A chant, repeated as an aid to devotion and meditation.

maya Illusion; used of the world of the senses.

nirodha Literally: 'cessation'. Describes the exhaustion of the karmic fuel from the fires of greed, hatred and ignorance, and thus equated with nirvana.

nirvana (nibbana in Pali) The state in which the triple fire of hatred, greed and ignorance is extinguished, characterized by peace and knowledge.

paramita Perfection (used of the six qualities of an enlightened being).

prajna Wisdom.

pratitya samutpada (paticcasamuppada in Pali) The arising and ceasing of things in dependence upon conditions; translated as 'conditioned co-production', 'dependent origination' or 'interconnectedness'; the fundamental feature of the Buddha's teaching.

punabhava Re-becoming (the Buddhist equivalent of reincarnation).

rupa 'Body'; one of the five skandhas.

samadhi Meditation.

samjna 'Mental concepts'; one of the five skandhas.

samsara The world of change and re-becoming.

samskara 'Desires'; one of the five skandhas.

satya Truth (*samvrti* – conventional truth; *paramartha* – ultimate truth) also used in the sense of 'right' to designate the steps of the Noble Eightfold Path.

sila Morality.

skandhas the five elements (literally 'heaps') of which the self is made up (matter; feeling; mental concepts; desires; consciousness).

shunyata 'emptiness'; used to describe that which does have its own inherent existence, but is dependent, conditioned and liable to change.

sutra (literally 'thread') used of a teaching of the Buddha. The Buddhist scriptures are divided into 'Sutras'.

svabhava Inherent existence (things lack this).

tanha Craving, the cause of suffering.

Tathagata 'One who has gone beyond'; a title used of the Buddha.

tathata 'Suchness' - the reality of things just as they are.

Vajrayana 'Diamond vehicle' or 'Thunderbolt vehicle', used of the development of Mahayana Buddhism incorporating Tantric elements.

vedana 'Feelings'; one of the five skandhas.

vinjana 'Consciousness'; one of the five skandhas.

vipassana Form of meditation which seeks to develop insight into the nature of reality.

Confucian

ch'i Morality.

chiao 'Teachings'; the term used for systems of thought, including Confucianism and Taoism.

dao (Also tao) Used of the moral life. *See* also the Taoist use of this term.

de Inner passions and energies.

fa The principle of justice (legalist school).

hsin Trustworthiness (one of the five cardinal virtues).

jianai Respect; a term used particularly by Mo Tsu.

junzi 'Gentleman'; a person who strives to do what it right.

li The rites that determine good conduct; in Neo-Confucianism, *li* refers to the principle that governs the universe.

ming Destiny or fate.

ren (jen) The essential quality of a mature human being; also used as 'person'.

ru (ju) The scholarly class to which Confucius belonged; used also of the school of thought based on his teachings.

sheng-ren A sage; one who both embodies and teaches wisdom.

Tai Ch'i 'The supreme ultimate', representing the *li* of heaven and earth.

te Spiritual power.

T'ien 'Heaven'; a sense of order in the world.

xiao-ren 'Small man'; one who acts without reference to moral values.

yi Duty; the principle of right conduct.

Taoist

ch'ang The eternal principle governing the process of change.

ch'i The life force (literally 'breath') or energy that flows through all things.

hua Transformation.

jing Vital essence.

li 'Principle'; used by Chuang Tzu to describe the operation of the Tao.

ming State of enlightenment.

Tao (Dao) 'Way', used of the cosmic order and first principle of the universe.

te Power; the Tao operating through individual things.

wu-wei 'Non-action'; avoiding that is unnatural or forced; used positively in the sense of living naturally and harmoniously.

yin/yang female/male, passive/active; the balance of forces within nature (found within Taoism and Neo-Confucianism, probably originating as a separate philosophical tradition).

Tantra

(in addition to terms listed already under Hinduism and Buddhism)

Anuttara Tantra Highest form of Tantra, which requires no physical action, but is based entirely on visualization.

bodhicitta The impulse of the mind towards enlightenment.

mahasukha The great bliss, the spiritual equivalent of orgasm in sexual Tantra.

mandala Pattern representing spiritual or metaphysical entities, creation of and meditation upon which is part of Tantric ritual.

mudra Position of the hands in Buddha and Bodhisattva images, conveying a particular quality and adopted also by the Tantric practitioner.

vajra Tantric symbol; literally: 'diamond' or 'thunderbolt'.

Yab-Yum Literally: mother-father. Images showing male and female locked in sexual embrace.

yidam A personal deity, used in Tantric visualization.

Zen

(in addition to terms already listed under Buddhism)

Ch'an (Zen) Meditation (derived from the Sanskrit *dhyana*).

kinhin Walking meditation.

koan A recorded saying or question, designed to frustrate the application of conventional thought.

mondo Record of a question and answer session between master and disciple.

mujo Japanese term for impermanence.

satori Moment of insight (in Rinzai Zen).

zazen Sitting meditation.

Index

Abhidharma *56, 59, 91, 98*
advaita *23, 26–27*
ahankara *17*
ahimsa *35, 36, 71, 84*
Akshobya (Buddha) *187*
alaya-vignana *108*
Amida Buddha *115, 217*
Analects, The *124ff*
anatta *42*
anekantavada *74*
anicca *42*
aranyakas *8*
arhat *55, 59*
Aryans *1, 7, 28*
Asanga *104*
asramas *31f*
atisha *114*
Atman *4, 23*

Bankei *211*
Bhagavad Gita *10, 16, 31, 34f, 48*
bhakti *2, 35*
bhaktimarga *10, 35*
bodhicitta *187f*
Bodhidharma *197*
bodhisattva *92, 111*
Brahma *3*
brahmacarya *32, 34*
brahman *3f, 22f* and throughout Hinduism
brahmanas *9*
Buddha mind (in Zen) *200*
Buddhaghosa *60*

Chandogya Upanishad *4, 9*
Chu Hsi *139f*
Chuang Tzu *156, 160f, 164ff*
cosmology (Buddhist) *112f*

Dhammapada *52*
Dharma *2, 5, 6, 21, 31, 33*
dharmas *25, 56f*
digambaras *73, 86*
Dogen *206ff*
dukkha *42ff*
Dvaita Vedanta *26, 27*

Eightfold Path, The *45f*
Eisai *202*

feng shui *162f, 168*
five cardinal virtues *146*
five powers theory *142*
five vows (Jain) *84*
food, taoist balance in *168*
four levels of Tantra *178*

Gampopa *114*
Gautama (Gotama) Buddha *37ff*
govinda, Lama Anagarika *193f*
gunas *17*

Hakuin *202*
Han Fei *128f*
Heart Sutra *97f*
hinayana *58*
Honen *115*
Hsun Tzu *138, 145, 146*

Hua-Yen *113*
Hui-Neng *198*

I Ching 156
immortality, taoist view *169*
indus valley civilization *1f*
Isvara *19*

jen *125, 127*
jiva *17, 76, 78, 81*
jnanamarga *10, 23, 34*
joshu *203f*

K'ung fu-tsu *122f*
Kakuan ('The Bulls') *212*
kama *33*
Kapila *116*
karma *6, 21, 22, 52f, 59, 81, 108*
karma-vada *79*
karmamarga *10, 33f*
Kasyapa *197*
kevala *77*
koans *203*
Krishna *54*
Kukai *115*
Kundalini *180*
Kyoto School *217*

lam rim tradition *189*
Lao Tzu *152ff*
Legalist tradition *128, 134*
Li *127*
Lokayata philosophy *29, 37*
Lotus Sutra 94, 112, 115

Madhva *27*
madhyamaka philosophy *97, 184*
Magadha *72*

Mahabharata *10, 16*
Mahasanghikas *58*
Mahavira *71ff*
Mandalas *178f*
Mantras *176*
Manusmrti *33*
marks of existence (the three) *41ff*
Meng Tzu (Mencius) *132, 136f, 144f*
middle way, the (Magga) *43, 45f*
Milarepa *192*
Mimamsa *20f*
Mo Tzu (Mohism) *131, 166*
moksha *2, 6, 33, 80, 175*
monasticism *65f*
mondo *204*
mudra *179*

Nagarjuna *99f, 103f*
Neo-Confucianism *139ff*
Nichiren Buddhism *116*
nidanas *54*
Nigantha Nataputta *73*
niruguna brahman *23*
nirodha *43ff*
Nirvana *45, 54f, 175*
Nishida *214f*
Noble Truths, the four *43*
nyaya school *11, 18*

OM *4*
One Mind (in Tantra) *191f*

Paramitas *59, 92f*
political action, Taoist minimalist
  view *168*
prajna *47, 64*
Prajnaparamita Sutras 97
prakrti *226*

pratitya samutpada
  (paticcasamuppada) 40 and
  throughout Buddhist chapters
Precepts, the five 64
punabhava (Buddhist re-becoming) 53f
Pure Land Buddhism 15
purusha 16f, 181
Purusha 5, 8, 32

Ramanuja 26
Ramayana 10
rectification of names 128f
reincarnation 53
religious Taoism 169
Rig Veda 5, 7
Rinzai Zen 201f
rta 31

Saguna Brahman 23
Saicho 115
sallekhana 88
samadhi 47, 64
samatha meditation 61
samsara 6, 54, 78
sanatana dharma 5
Sankara 22f
Sankhya 16ff, 24, 81f
sannyasa 32
Sarvastavadin school 59, 100
satcitananda 23
satori 199, 203
Sautrantika school 59
sexuality, Confucian views on 146f
sexuality, in Tantric thought
  180, 182
sexuality, Taoist views on 170f
shakti 176, 179f
Shingon Buddhism 115

Shinran 115f
Shiva 3, 176f, 179f
shramana 37, 72
shramanera 65
shruti 10
shunyata 52, 99ff, 103f
siddha 80
sila 47, 64
six Confucian arts, the 145
skandhas 25, 42, 49
smriti 10
Soto Zen 110, 206
Sthaviravadin school 58
sutra 56
Suzuki 205, 213
Svetaketu 4
Svetambaras 73, 86ff

T'ai-chi-t'u 158
tai ch'i 141f, 168
Tanabe 217
tanha 43, 44
Tao 123, 153
Tao Te Ching 152f
tathagata 55
tathagatagarbha doctrine 109f, 184
Tattvartha Sutra 74, 79, 80, 84, 85, 88
Tendai 115, 206
Theravada Buddhism 58
Tibetan Buddhism 114, 188f
T'ien 123
Tirthankaras 7
trikaya doctrine 110
Tsou Yen 157

Udayana 15
Umasvati 74
Upanishads 4, 9f, 16, 22, 49

Vaisesika school *11*
vajra *184*, *190*
Vajrayana Buddhism *58*, *184*
varnas *5*, *31f*
varnashramadharma *31*
Vasubandu *108*
Vedanta *20*, *22*
Vedas *2*, *7f*, *20f*, *37*
vipassana meditation *61*, *62*
visistadvaita *26*
visualizations *177f*
Vratya philosophy *28f*

Wang Yang-Ming *142*
wu wei *161*, *163f*, *217*

Yab-Yum images *186*
yamas *34*
Yang Chu *134*
Yin-Yang theory *139*, *157*, *167f*
Yoga school *2*, *16*, *19f*
Yogacara philosophy *104*

Zazen Wasan (by Hakuin) *203*
zazen *206*, *208f*

Index of Western thinkers, schools and concepts referred to in the text:

Anselm (ontological argument) 19
Aquinas 14, 19, 25, 67, 124
Aristotle 124, 154, 215
Atomists 12, 77
Augustine 211

Bergson 67, 77, 208, 215
Berkeley 60, 106
Calvin (predestination) 28

Democritus 12, 77
Descartes (cogito ergo sum) 54, 67, 77, 162

Epicurean philosophy 30, 37
epiphenomenalism 30

Freud 109

gnosticism 77, 160

Hegel 214
Heidegger 208, 217
Heraclitus xiv, 67, 143, 208
Hobbes, Thomas 136, 137
Hume 49, 133

James, W. 21
Jesus 65, 112, 133

Kant (Copernican Revolution) 106
Kant (noumena/phenomena) 18, 24, 60, 215

Logical Positivism 12, 15, 30

mysticism 113, 161, 162, 199f, 205

Natural Law approach to ethics 124, 143, 182, 183

Paley, William 25
panentheism 155, 216
Plato (Theory of Forms) 7, 13, 160
Plato The Republic 32, 144, 192
postmodernism 69
prescriptivism 21
process philosophy 208
Proudhon 169
Pythagoras 143

Rawls A Theory of Justice 136
relativity, theory of 208
Ryle, Gilbert (The Concept of Mind) 50, 101

Schleiermacher 193
Socrates 100
Sociology 120

Teilhard de Chardin 77, 208
Tillich 217
Tolstoy 169
Trinity (Christian doctrine of) 111

utilitarianism 30, 132, 133

Van Buren 217

Whitehead 67, 208
Wittgenstein 12, 161